TROUT
FISHING
and
TROUT
FLIES

"THERE IS CERTAINLY SOMETHING IN ANGLING THAT TENDS TO PRODUCE A GENTLENESS OF SPIRIT AND A PURE SERENITY OF MIND."

—*Washington Irving*

TROUT FISHING
and
TROUT FLIES

by Jim Quick

Illustrations by the Author

South Brunswick
New York: A. S. Barnes and Co.

YOU CAN FOOL SOME OF THE TROUT
ALL OF THE TIME, AND ALL OF THE
TROUT SOME OF THE TIME BUT, ALTHOUGH
ENTIRELY POSSIBLE, IT TAKES A
REMARKABLY STUDIOUS AND SKILLFUL
ANGLER TO FOOL ALL OF THE TROUT
ALL OF THE TIME.

Variation of an old truism

Foreword

IN FORTY years of pursuing the trouts and the chars I've suffered and exhilarated through a number of stages. First, as is everyone at the beginning, I was a pure innocent knowing nothing of the art of fishing. As time went by I collected a modicum of skill in enticing run of the mill fish to my lure. Then I accomplished the next stage of fishing for certain individual working fish and many times taking them. This made me an authority to my friends. The next step was when I began to believe it myself. Then later the sub-climactic range when I was considered a fly fishing expert by others and I felt they were right. Boy, what an egoist I turned out to be! Then, thankfully, I zoomed through the barrier. I am now at, or near, the top bracket, I am sure. This is the point at which, regardless of the opinions of anyone else, I discover in my own secret self that I actually know very little of what there is for us to know. In fact, if I work and study harder and if I am very fortunate, I may be allowed to enter the first grade in a year or so.

I became extremely observant not through any particular will power or ambitious zeal to excel but because I was inherently lazy. I believed that the more I know about what goes on under the water surface the easier my fishing labors would be to accomplish the desired ends.

I experimented with all types of tackle and lures which

appealed to me and nearly everything did. I ran the gauntlet with seriously expounded theories and found many that, to me, were just idle and silly. I tried silly theories and silly ideas and found many that, in spite of my personal logic, worked surprisingly well.

Liking fly fishing best and proving to myself that it was the more efficient in attaining results, I found out everything I could about aquatic "bugs." I learned to tie my own flies. That sounds like a simple procedure but it took me a number of years. One doesn't just learn to tie flies overnight any more than one learns to be a surgeon by watching someone remove a sliver from his finger. After thirty years of tying flies, many of them professionally, I still learn something every day.

In learning to cast and fish trout successfully you will be accosted by well meaning friends and others who will take it upon themselves to instruct you in the way THEY do it. Tactfully listen to their instruction, and if they're observing you do it the way they outline with a smile and a thanks. That's part of the cost you must suffer. *When they have gone, go back to doing it the right way!* The exception to the above is in casting. If you're fortunate enough to live in a vicinity where there is a regular tournament casting club, visit it or even join it. You'll find, usually, one or two good fly casters in the group. Watch and study their casting procedure carefully. If you question them they'll be pleased to help you (that's one of the nice things about these clubs), but you'll find they'll be telling you what you'll read in Chapter Four.

Generally good "Tournament" casters handle their rods and tackle with much greater agility and skill than does the "just" fisherman. I have observed the finest of this country's tournament fly men in action, however the two most efficient and competent fly casters I have ever seen perform have never faced the rings in a casting pool. So if you do not have the opportunity of visiting a club and seeing some of the better tournament casters work it is unlucky but not calamitous.

In the desire to present you with information that you may use constructively in your fishing ventures I will make a few flat statements for which I have no apology. Those I will stick with and may the devil take the learned professors and the self-styled experts who try to marshall me into a corner. I won't swear that anything I expound is completely true. I have revealed an honest belief and I will attest and vow that it is sincere.

In my expression of opinions, please do not take them to mean that it's the final word and there is no other. I may believe that but you must not until you've exhausted every other reasonable theory that comes to your attention. Try everything that's within reason. Learn for yourself, then you'll have convictions and convictions breed confidence and confidence brings skill and success. You may be the one to hit on an entirely new method or an entirely new approach. Somebody has to—that's progress!

The fact that you are reading this discourse is partial proof that you either wish to learn what this writer can tell you or you are searching for concurrence with your own ideas or findings. In perusing this or any other expression of experience I suggest that you be open minded. Do you have theories on tackle, or on fishing methods that are the reverse of others? Do you have doubts about manners, systems, solutions or radical recipes of procedure on the taking of fish? Won't you, if only temporarily, put aside those theories or doubts and give the "other" thought a fair trial? It's a cinch one of them is the better, at least equal, it may be that "other" one. The whole process is experience and you might learn something different that will improve your own skill. If you are the type of fisherman who is desirous of saving face you don't have to broadcast the fact that you did try something new.

In my equipment recommendations, although at this writing I have definite views and would enjoy naming the manufacturer or naming the article, there are constant changes and new products originating, literally, every month that could make those I would name obsolete or dated, for all practical purposes.

This book covers a wide assemblage of pertinent material that will, I am sure, assist you in achieving the success in trout fishing that may have been avoiding you on most occasions during your fishing expeditions in the past. Employing the suggested measures, which are disclosed, to as great an extent as you choose, will help you overcome mediocre or just average fishing results to the length in which the tested procedures are accepted and used.

Because of the tremendously wide scope of the subjects treated, single subjects alone upon which books, and excellent books in a few cases, have been published, I have deliberately reduced much of the substance to a digest form. This was done in my effort to hold the train to the track and give you the relevant meat, promised you in this book's title, in the most convenient manner. I've emphasized, I've repeated and I've ranted, perhaps beyond the limit of good form, for the sole purpose of impressing some particular detail upon you. I've approached many theories and factual ideas from a negative angle so that you could better see the right and wrong picture more clearly. In a rough way I have tried to make the treatise interesting reading because in that way there is more likelihood of the essentials being remembered, thus used to accomplish the results you covet.

If I may seem to, at any time, inject my own personal experience it is done to bring out a point I am trying to explain and not for the purpose of padding this discourse with wordage or to elaborate on my own ego. I sincerely doubt the possibility of anyone gathering usable information from pages of my own exploits or of others whom I may have observed. True, these tales might make interesting reading but your chances of duplicating the action is practically nil. Were you to be fishing in exactly the same location, at exactly the same time of day and same time of the season, with all other conditions of tackle, weather, stream, fish movements and with the same temperament I might have been obsessed with at the moment, perhaps the telling of the incidents, if you remembered and recognized the situation, might be of help to you, but don't place a wager on it. I am not making an attempt to impress you with whatever skill I may possess in taking trout, I am merely doing my darndest to set you up so that you may be able to experience and to relate *your own* successful exploits. Good luck!

                                                                    Jim Quick

Preface

MY FIRST recollection of fishing was with Dad on Lake Maceday, near Pontiac, Michigan, a lake containing the usual panfish species of bass, pike, bluegills, sunfish and perch, among others perhaps less desirable. I remember being tied with a short length of clothesline to the rear seat, (no, we had an anchor, even tho' rarely used) and I had my own tackle which was far from just a makeshift assembly. I was progressing then through the schooling of the dunked worm while enviously, I guess, watching him toss his little flies around. It was some time before I was judged mature enough to try fly casting myself under his tutelage. This was about the time I entered kindergarten and only after a brief and quite unexciting series of lessons on the side lawn.

To me, then, Dad was an avid angler and always seemed to be able to catch fish when he wished, but I thought all fathers were like that. A few years later, trout fishing on the Pigeon and the Sturgeon, near Vanderbilt, Michigan, the realization began to form that my pop confidently knew what he was doing. He was taking fish consistently when other fishermen were disgustedly leaving the stream with unsoiled creels. Then I noticed anglers talking to him, doing what he suggested or accepting flies from his supply and thanking him later because their luck seemed to change for the better.

Throughout the years, until I was graduated from Redford

High School, in Detroit, we never missed our two weeks together on some cherished trout stream. I learned much trout lore under his guidance and example. I often wondered if I would ever reach the pinnacle of confidence he possessed. As a Marine, World War II took me to the other side of the globe for a long time, then another year in Korea, plus my race to catch up on schooling and our annual sojourns, in the avocation we both love, regretfully for both of us, I know, came to a pause.

Dad was not of a mind to even vaguely try to impress others with his trout knowledge and skill but should a friend request assistance he would go all out in his eagerness to help. When I heard of this book I was immensely pleased that he had decided or had been persuaded to expose those things he knows.

Dad has a fine philosophy as it pertains to trout fishermen and which I think describes him best. He has said, "Son, I've fished for the trouts all my life and in so doing I've met thousands of anglers on the streams and lakes, at campfires and in fishing lodges and in all those years I've never yet encountered a stranger."

J. Larry Quick
San Jose, California

Acknowledgment

IT IS customary, and a pleasant duty, I believe, for a writer of a tome, such as this, to express appreciation to those from whom he has quoted, or from whom he has garnered helpful assistance.

I can only say that I must render thanks, in an encompassing way, to every writer, of every book published in the English language, on the subject of fish and fishing, since the advent of Izaak Walton . . . that is, every book I could get my hands on to read and absorb. From the galaxy of material, I'm sure, came many of the basic theories with which I experimented and which became a part of my fishing life.

Also, I am indebted to many, many fishermen, guides and conversationalists from whom I, consciously or unconsciously, gathered "try out" ideas over a period of two score years.

Directly, I wish to express my gratitude to Mr. Leo Shapovalov and Mr. Scott Soule, of the Department of Fish and Game, of the state of California, for vital information on source material, and data itself, for the "Hatchery Procedure" section of Chapter Five.

Lastly, and earnestly, I want to thank my loyal and sincere friend, Cliff Wyatt, the finest tournament caster of the fly it has been my fortune to know, or know of, and a fishing sportsman of the old school, for his able, constructive and authoritative assistance in the development of "Basic Casting" methods in Chapter Five, and for just being around when I wanted to talk fishing.

The Author

Table of Contents

SECTION ONE

TAKING TROUT AND HOW

SECTION TWO

Modern Fly Tying

List of Illustrations

SECTION ONE

SECTION TWO

Why This Book

THERE ARE few books written on the subject of trout and trout fishing that the writer has not studied earnestly—many of the better ones numerous times. I have sincerely tried to follow the theories outlined in these books. As in other subjects, a great number of theories that were truisms a few years ago, have gone through the mill and were replaced by others without quite so many knot holes.

Through the course of over four-tenths of a century of trout fishing I have observed many things that were not outlined in books; I have also noted many published theories and expositions that were not as accurate as they might have been. In all justice to the writers, the facts expounded by them could have been correct at the time and in the place of which they wrote.

It was not so many years ago, when many of the better "Fishing" books were published, that successful results were much less difficult to attain. The just moderately successful fly fisherman of today would have been an outstanding expert thirty or forty years ago on any water. I often think of Halford, Skues, Gordon and LaBranche, honored, respected and highly skilled pioneers of an earlier period and how they would fare today on the Beaverkill in the Catskills, the Au Sable in Michigan, the Brule in Wisconsin, the Firehole in Yellowstone, the Rogue or Klamath in Oregon or the Owens in California.

The chances are that because these sportsmen were exceptionally observant and exceptionally skillful that they would adapt themselves to present day conditions, but for a long while they'd be just ordinary run of the mill fishermen as are you and I.

For too many years we have been regulated by custom, habit and a dutiful faithfulness to the old country. We have trod the road right down the "rut" looking forward blindly and back to the rear with keen discernment following only the old traditional modes of tackle and its uses as outlined and taught by the masters of previous generations. We stuck to the old Scotch, Irish and English fly patterns regardless of the form, size and color of the naturals in and on our waters over here.

I discovered, in my study of books on the subject of which I write, that so many authors took for granted an ability presumed to be possessed by the reader. They advanced their ideas and suggestions on the premise that all the reader had to do was follow in their footsteps and do likewise. Those are the books that will never become dog-eared from earnest study. The troublesome fact is that, despite the acknowledged skill at the command of some of the writer-fishermen, they failed to recognize that the neophyte, like the child who must learn to walk before he can run, must have a grasp of basic fundamentals, and a smattering of knowledge of the game itself, before he can do those things directed by the true expert. The fisherman-reader is most unlikely to admit weaknesses in skill to anyone but himself. It is very possible he doesn't know that the failings are there and blames every kind of cause except the real one which is not "luck" or "poor fishing" or "phases of the moon and movements of the tide," but right inside his own hatband.

Because I believe that I have a message for the present day trout fishermen that will help them add to their skill or that will take an embryo student of fishing and give him the facts he needs to secure satisfying fishing results, I present my findings, sincere beliefs, personal opinions and my best wishes.

Jim Quick

Section One

TAKING TROUT AND HOW

Chapter 1

The Trout Fisherman's Equipment

"HEY, CHARLIE, cut me another willow, will you? Ol' Scarface just took my hook, line, and the top three feet of my pole."

I won't say those days are all gone but they're gasping feebly. Today there are few fishermen who do not have the semblance of an outfit. Rods, reels, lines and terminal tackle are more or less standardized even though the range between good and indifferent equipment is on the increase.

There are many die-hards who cling to tradition and refuse to acknowledge progress. I have no doubt but that old Izaak Walton would have cast a fishy eye on an upstart who might have tried to convince him that this new bamboo stuff makes a mighty fine stick.

FLY RODS

And today there still are a number of followers of Izaak who cast a gloomy eye on the upstarts shouting about the superiority of the Fiberglas rods over the bamboo. It was ever thus!

Sure we love our split bamboo rods. They are a delight to look at and feel and they are a pleasure to use. It actually hurt me when I found that a new glass rod, which I was testing, was lighter, stronger, had an apparent superior dry fly

3

action, was definitely more accurate, was able to deliver longer casts when required and all this with much less effort on my part when I finally discovered the casting tempo of the glass which was speedier than the bamboo. I tried vainly to match these abilities with my favorite custom-built bamboo rod but the bamboo just didn't have it in as marked a degree. So now this beautiful rod, which in my personal opinion is the finest rod this unexcelled rod builder ever turned out, has been retired. In spite of its having to take second place I love it and wouldn't consider selling it for all the Andalusian capes in existence.

In the top quality rods the features are close to a toss-up, but in the ordinary market productions the glass, ounce for ounce and dollar for dollar, is much superior. For myself I am using custom-built glass rods which I have found to be much better than any mass-produced rod now offered for sale and the custom-built rods are less expensive than some of the others. Don't take my word completely, try both. There is a marked difference in the way each type of rod is manipulated to bring out its finest action. The quality glass dry fly rods have a much speedier action, and less effort on the part of the caster is necessary. The rod does much for you that you are required to do yourself with the bamboo rod. A confirmed bamboo rod user applying the same casting stroke with a comparable glass rod will perform like a rank amateur and give up in disgust. Timing is an important attribute to good casting but the timing is different between bamboo rod casting and glass rod casting.

A few years ago there were dozens of rod builders who could turn out a top quality bamboo rod. Those dozens have dwindled down, at this writing to two or three, in fact I know of but two that I could, without reservation, recommend.

The size of the rod or rods in length and power depends upon the types of fishing you do. Many fishermen have "compromise" rods with which they do bait fishing, fly fishing, spinner fishing and bug casting. If they enjoy their fishing, more power to them, but to fish a certain way with a rod designed to do that particular job best, is the ultimate in enjoyment. One certainly would not expect to fish for steelhead with a dainty dry fly rod. The reverse is almost as quaint an idea.

Wouldn't it be pleasant, once anyway, to go out on your favorite stream accompanied by your caddy carrying the rod bag with rods for every purpose all set up for you? You study the lie (of the fish, not the ball) and you call for the "35-Footer" or the wind being strong in your face you ask for the "Number three power rod." You do or you don't succeed with that fish and you move a few feet to the next lie or pocket. A bit impractical isn't it? But you know it's done almost that way in some other countries. Inasmuch as our personal frugality and our aversion to inconvenience prohibits a dozen or so rods with us on the stream at one time we are compelled, therefore, to choose one that fits us or fits the water we're fishing.

Choose the rod for your kind of activity whether it be a nine-foot power rod or a seven-foot wand for delicate fly casting. With the exception of fishermen who wade waist deep and who must use a somewhat longer rod to get their line out and keep it up, the tendency is for shorter and lighter rods. The average at this writing is the 7½- and 8-foot rods being the most popular. In glass rods the weight, within reason, has no bearing on its quality or efficiency, neither is it a criterion of what the rod can do. "Action" is the important factor to look for. A glass rod weighing 4 or 4½ ounces, correctly balanced with reel and line, may feel lighter than a 3-ounce soft rod incorrectly balanced.

So we pick a 7- or 7½-foot light dry fly rod or an 8-foot medium dry fly action rod or a 9-foot power rod according to our waters, our ability or our choice of rods regardless. We may even indulge our ego by selecting a 6-foot 2-ounce or a smaller and lighter wand to fish and play with.

REELS

The reel is a necessary tool on which to store our excess line while using the rod. The quality of the reel is of much less importance than the quality of the rod. The exception is the incongruity of a top-line dry fly rod being fitted with a "Five and ten" quality reel. It may work all right and then again—and the "then again" always happens at most inconvenient times.

The single action reel is by far the most popular reel for fly rods. It balances the finer rods more efficiently than the automatic reel which is much too heavy for the small part they play in fishing. However, there is still a contingent of good fishermen who cling to the automatic reel and I have no argument with them.

LINES

FIT THE LINE TO THE ROD!

The line is an important aid for two reasons. First it is a part of the connection from you to the terminal fly or lure. Secondly, the line, in case of fly casting, is the part you cast—not the fly which merely follows along.

It's somewhat of an amateurish gesture to attempt to "guess" the size line that will work with a rod where only the descriptions of weight and length of the rod are given. I have handled rods of, for example, four ounces and nine feet in length where one might have the English softness and another be as stiff in the tip as the proverbial poker. Those two rods would require lines quite different in weight. I have perused charts in books wherein the writers have done this guessing. From there on in their books I'm just a bit leary of any statements that a writer might make, and I cast a querulous eye on pronouncements of that writer's experience or his qualifications to advance serious advice. Just for an example, an HDH line whether silk, nylon or any other material is merely a designation of its diameter, not its weight or casting quality. Neither does it tell you what the length of taper is from tip to belly. It seems that every line manufacturer has his own interpretation of what a line is and should do. Then there is the casting characteristics of the individual that must be taken into account. I've observed top tournament casters' lines. Rarely do they ever use a "market" line for their rod and their own peculiarities of casting. Usually they splice their own lines and this is done again and again until they produce the one that seems to work best for them on their rod.

Dry fly casting (and most other normal fly fishing methods) is done with a 90-foot double-tapered line. This means a fine line at each end tapering within a few feet to the belly of the line which is the part with the greatest diameter and greatest weight. You select lines by tapers such as HEH, HDH, HCH, GBG, etc. The letters identify the diameters of the tip end and the belly in thousandths of an inch. (Sometimes some enterprising progressive line maker will devise an identifying symbol which will indicate the line's weight and we all will be pleased to drop the alphabet.)

As noted in Fig. 1, an HDH line diameter starts with .025 and tapers in a few feet to .045 at each end of the line proper. The only purpose in the double taper is to permit changing ends occasionally, giving us double the wear time. Nylon lines, in weight, are about one step lighter than silk in the same diameter. The rod casts "weight," not diameters, and in selecting your line pick one, not because you like the letter combination or someone guessed a diameter to possibly suit the length and weight of your rod, but because it works best for you on the rod. Every rod requires one definite weight line to bring out its finest action, although many rods will also handle two or three sizes fairly well.

Most dry fly lines now are nylon, primarily because they generally are better floaters and less attention is required in dressing them to stay on the surface of the water. Nylon, itself, is not affected by moisture, heat or cold. Silk, if not cared for religiously, and pampered, will deteriorate rapidly. The finish of lines is as good or as bad on one type as on the other— that's up to the manufacturer. Plastic finishes, on many nylon lines, give us a line that requires a minimum of dressing to float excellently.

The "big head" or "torpedo" or "bug" taper is designed for more distance casting and the handling of flies that have considerable resistance features such as fluffy flies, hair bugs, etc. This line is woven with a comparatively short taper from the fine end to the belly. The belly of the line, too, is shorter, terminating directly into another taper, then to a long running line. This running line is usually supplemented with additional backing on the reel. This backing not only assists in filling the

NYLON AVERAGES APPROXIMATELY ONE GRADE LIGHTER PER DIAMETER

LINE DIAMETERS (IN THOUSANDTHS OF AN INCH)

I	.0225
H	.025
G	.030
F	.035
E	.040
D	.045
C	.050
B	.055
A	.060
AA	.065

FIG. 1 — TAPERED FLY CASTING LINES ~ SILK OR NYLON

DOUBLE TAPERED LINES ~ "AMERICAN" TAPER ~ AVERAGE LENGTH 90 FEET

LINE	TIP	TAPER	RUNNING BELLY	
IFI	36"-I	24"-H 48"-G	72 FT. F	EXTRA LIGHT
HEH	36"-H	36"-G 48"-F	70 FT. E	LIGHT
HDH	36"-H	18"-G 30"-F 48"-E	68 FT. D	MED. LIGHT
HCH	36"-H	12"-G 24"-F 36"-E 48"-D	64 FT. C	MED. HEAVY
GBG	36"-G	18"-F 24"-E 40"-D 60"-C	60 FT. B	HEAVY
FAF	36"-F	18"-E 24"-D 40"-C 60"-B	60 FT. A	EXTRA HEAVY

(TAPER AND TIP — SAME EACH END OF LINE)

"BIG HEAD" or "TORPEDO" TAPERS — AVERAGE LENGTH 100 TO 115 FEET

LINE	TIP	LEAD TAPER	BELLY	REAR TAPER	RUNNING LINE
HEG	36"-H	24"-G 30"-F	20 FT. E	96"-F	70 FT. G
HDG	36"-H	14"-G 18"-F 24"-E	20 FT. D	60"-E 36"-F	70 FT. G
HCG	36"-H	8"-G 12"-F 18"-E 24"-D	20 FT. C	48"-D 30"-E 18"-F	70 FT. G
HCF	36"-H	8"-G 12"-F 18"-E 24"-D	20 FT. C	60"-D 36"-E	70 FT. F
HBF	40"-H	6"-G 12"-F 14"-E 16"-D 20"-C	22 FT. B	48"-C 30"-D 18"-E	70 FT. F
GBF	42"-G	8"-F 14"-E 18"-D 24"-C	24 FT. B	54"-C 42"-D 24"-E	70 FT. F
GAF	48"-G	6"-F 10"-E 12"-D 18"-C 24"-B	24 FT. A	48"-B 36"-C 24"-D 12"-E	70 FT. F

ADDITIONAL BACKING, IF DESIRED, SPLICED ON AT THIS POINT

IN GRADING LINE DIAMETERS, AN ALLOWANCE IS GRANTED OF .0025 EITHER WAY ~ THUS WITH TWO SIMILARLY GRADED LINES OF SAME MANUFACTURER, ONE COULD BE HEAVIER THAN THE OTHER.

line area of the reel but is of greater assistance in retaining the connection to a sizable fish that has ideas of travel beyond the limit of your regular tapered line.

As far as actually affecting your fishing, the color of the line means not one thing. Choose the color you prefer whether it be light gray, dark green, amber, brown, mahogany or red, white and blue.

Until recent years it was considered correct to use tapers for dry fly fishing and level lines for wet fly work. Now the taper is generally used for both in ordinary fishing.

LEADERS

This junction between line and lure is the weakest part of your tackle. For that reason alone you should not attempt to economize on this comparatively inexpensive but extremely important section of your fishing equipment.

Whether your choice is for the traditional "gut" or leaders of nylon is not a critical matter. Wet nylon is approximately the same strength as dry. Wet silk gut, and that means well soaked, is considerably stronger than the dry. Gut leaders must be judged and tested in the dry stage to determine if its age has resulted in its becoming brittle and unsafe to trust. Gut leaders are built of a series of sections of various diameters to construct the taper. Fourteen or fifteen inches is the approximate maximum length of these sections, before tying, and lengths up to eighteen inches are occasionally available. Nylon leaders are either tied in sections or tapers are built from the butt directly to the tip without knots. This latter type is the leader I use for both dry and wet fly fishing. I do however add tippets of a slightly smaller diameter to extend the length of the leader. I rarely use shorter than nine feet and later I'll outline my reasons. For those of you who like to tie your own, Fig. 2 outlines some formulas.

CREEL

Whether it be the old tried and true willow or rattan woven creel, or the flat or semi-flat fabric creel, is entirely a personal choice. The latter type is less troublesome and much easier to wear. I do use the willow or rattan regular creel, not because I believe it superior, but because I need the space to carry "stuff" my jacket and my pockets have no further room to handle. I am firmly convinced that the items a fisherman carry with him on the stream should be limited but I don't live up

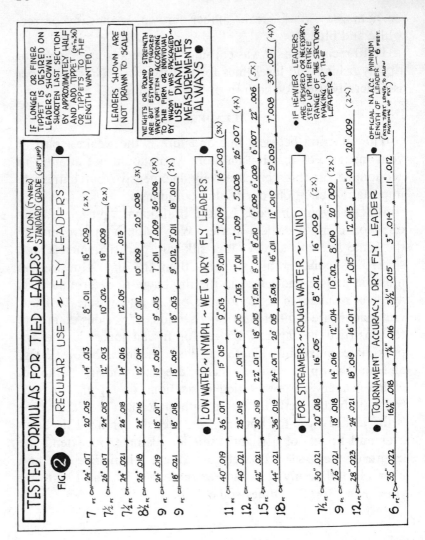

to that belief. I have boxes of dry flies in regular patterns, boxes of larger dry flies and bugs, boxes for nymphs and wet flies, fly and line dressing, an extra reel and line, leader packs and leader soak boxes, tools, bottles for aquatic fly and nymph samples, a small fly-tying kit with both tools and materials, snake bite kit, hook sharpening stone, adhesive bandages, a canteen for water, smoking equipment, patching kit for boots or waders, flashlight, sun glasses, thermometer, fish weighting scales, a supply of waxed paper and Kleenex, small bar of soap, hand warmers (in season), aspirin to alleviate head= aches occasioned by frustrations, perhaps a sandwich or two, and if in leaving the car or cabin I see a piece of string on the ground I grab that too. One can never tell but that it might come in handy for something. I never carry a portable toilet or a kitchen sink with me, not because of lack of space but because there is a limit, even in my case, to silly excesses. I know it's wrong to a degree to go out overloaded like this. I gather some consolation, however, in practicing this failing in the knowledge that I am not alone. It seems there are others who do the same thing. One must have a couple of acknowl- edgeable vices at least or he becomes a bore, much quicker, to his associates.

TROUT NET

I believe the net is a necessary item of equipment. How it is carried or slung on you is of little matter providing you can reach it and use it when occasion demands it. Some carry the net with the elastic over their left shoulder and the net under the right arm. Some carry it under the creel, some carry it clipped to a ring on their back immediately below the collar. Some clip it to their belt and some use the folding or collapsi- ble type secured to the creel harness or belt. There are numer- ous other ways and each fisherman to his own method.

The primary purpose of the net is to assist the troutsman in landing the fish after the battle when the fish has decided there's no further use to fight you or perhaps he just tires.

I release most of my fish and the net makes it much easier on the fish and on myself. By grasping him from the outside of the net I can hold him without squeezing to remove the fly then let him slide out of the net not too much the worse for the incident.

Personally, I like the wood frame type net; however the other types, metal frame, or the collapsible kind have their adherents. I use one that has a spring set into the frame with a heavy nylon cord running through the handle. The spring holds the weight of the net easily and when in use the fisherman can grasp the handle, reach out as far as necessary, and the cord stays taut. The net then is pulled by the spring back to its original position. I carry the net on my back clipped just below the collar and it is reached with either hand when needed.

FISHING JACKET OR VEST

I am firmly convinced that the fishing jacket or vest that would suit, completely, over one per cent of the fishermen has not yet been devised. The happy creation may come sometime but I doubt it. So, if we use this garment and we should, we get the one most closely fashioned to the one we would like. We put it to use even though handicapped because of lack or location of pet pockets, of pockets too small or too large, too shallow or too deep for our fly containers, utility items, etc.

Were it convenient to secure the fishing jacket custom made for our own desired pocket size and pocket arrangement, plus being economically practical, it would be fine providing the lapse of time from measurement and detailed description to completion and acceptance was only a couple of hours. Longer than that and we'd have another idea.

WADERS AND HIP BOOTS

Every fisherman to his choice on this part of his equipment. Much depends upon the waters you fish whether you use chest-high or waist-length waders or hip boots. Whether you use rubber fabric, rubber or plastic is up to you and your budget allowance or choice of material. Whether you use the boot foot wader or hip boots or the stocking foot type, with wading shoes, again is up to you. This latter, if well fitted, is a bit more comfortable in use and they are much less difficult to dry out. The brogue or designed wading shoe is, of course, the ideal footwear for the stocking foot kind but many who use the more economical plastic "form-foot" boots or waders, use an inexpensive or old pair of tennis shoes. If you're going that way be sure the tennis shoes are the type that cover the ankles. The oxford or low style do not protect that ankle knob and you don't realize how prominent it is until you rap it a few times on underwater objects.

I would suggest you discuss this apparel with fishermen friends or a fisherman dealer you can trust to give you the right advice. Get the best you can afford when you buy. The better they are the less expensive they will be, in the long run, to you. AND DO NOT BUY WITHOUT FIRST TRYING ON! This is important. If they do not fit now they never will.

HEAD NETS

I was going to pass this one up as being too lacking in importance. I knew a fisherman once who had one, and he did wear it on occasion, until in exasperation he tossed it in a trash barrel. If I must protect myself I like the use of mosquito dope better.

MISCELLANEOUS ITEMS

Part of the fun of preparing a fishing jaunt is the selection and rejection of those items that we believe either essential or unnecessary. I hesitate to make any recommendations along this line inasmuch as I am a confirmed "junk carrier" and I know it. I do believe sincerely, however, that the following miscellaneous articles should be with you:

> A good fisherman's knife
> A hook hone or hook sharpener
> A leader clipper or small scissors
> Dry fly floatant
> Line dressing
> Stream thermometer
> Small wire cutting pliers
> Small first-aid kit
> Cellulose or adhesive tape
> Ferrule cement
> Extra matches
> Box of split shot, fine lead wire or equivalent

Chapter 2

Care of Equipment —
Supplementary Information

IN ASSEMBLING fly rods, many anglers rub the male ferrule in their hair or along side of their nose in the hope that it will coat the metal with a semblance of oily surface. A better and surer way is to carry a small pellet of paraffin wax and rub this on the ferrule. Never actually use oil—it will tend to create a vacuum and make separation of ferrules difficult.

When taking good rods apart at the ferrules after a day's use (and they should be taken apart), never, never try to pull them away from each other in your hands, across your chest or by twisting. The best method is to place the rod butt under your right arm (presuming you are right-handed), grasping the rod just above the ferrule with your right hand and with the rod tip end slanting toward the ground or floor. In gripping the rod with the hands do it between guides, never include them in or against your grip. Grasp the rod tip or next section just below the ferrule with your left hand. Raise your left knee up to the rod so that your left hand is on the outside of your leg or knee. Holding tightly with both hands use your knee to push your left hand outwardly or toward the tip end of the rod. (See Fig. 3.) This will usually separate the most normally stubborn stuck ferrules without danger of damaging the rod in any way.

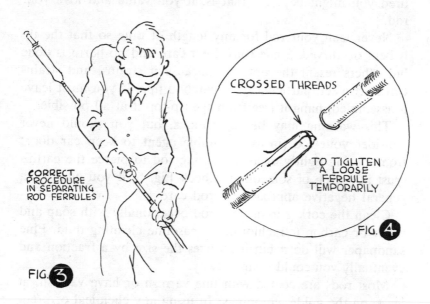

CROSSED THREADS

TO TIGHTEN A LOOSE FERRULE TEMPORARILY

FIG. 4

CORRECT PROCEDURE IN SEPARATING ROD FERRULES

FIG. 3

If the ferrule is stuck so firmly that reasonable measures will not separate, try putting a drop or two of carbon tetrachloride, kerosene or baby oil where it can seep into the aperture where both parts join. If after soaking for a time and separation is still no go, use it as is until it can be taken to a tackle repair shop to have it done right. If you value your rod do not use pliers and I repeat, do not twist. If care is taken to not overheat, hold the ferrule in flame of a match for a couple or three seconds and expansion may release its hold. If the ferrule becomes loose during a fishing trip and there is no opportunity to get it swaged back into size, a temporary and safe method of tightening the fit is to cross a couple of threads over the end of the male ferrule before putting together. (See Fig. 4.)

All rods, regardless of the material of which they are made, should be wiped dry or if dirtied from fish slime, salmon egg slime or worm juice they should be washed with warm mild soapy water and rinsed clean, then thoroughly dried before putting away. This is to be done every day during your fishing trip when you're finished fishing for the day no matter how tired you might be . . . that is, if you value and love your rod.

Never lean your rod for any length of time so that the tip is bent or curved. Some rods don't care and no harm is done but others resent the practice because it strains, and strains can start a set, particularly in bamboo tips. If you must leave it assembled, hang it free from the tip-top if at all possible.

This warning may be superfluous, but you should never consider your rod tip as a suitable agent to keep car doors from closing tightly or as a divining rod to pierce the earth's crust in search of something. Check Fig. 5, if you will, for a general negative approach on rod care.

Clean the cork grip of your rod occasionally with soap and water or carbon tetrachloride or gasoline cleaning fluid. Fine sandpaper will do it but it reduces the size by a fraction and eventually you could wear it away.

Most rods are coated with fine varnish or have varnish, at least, on the guide wrappings. In using any chemical or preparation such as mosquito dope, fly floatant, leader sink, suntan oil, etc., care should be taken to keep it away from the varnished surfaces. It may do no harm but there's no necessity of taking chances.

All types of creels should be carefully washed with common soda in the water at least weekly if in use and oftener is better.

Reels should never be allowed to operate if they contain dirt or grit. Clean them thoroughly with a solvent such as kerosene, gasoline cleaning fluid, carbon tetrachloride or white gasoline. Dry and re-oil or grease. Good reels, too, even if clean must be oiled daily if in constant use and oftener won't hurt. Just a drop is customarily sufficient at the locations where it is called for.

If your reel has a drag, as a working part, and is used, be sure and release it completely at day's end. When not in use reels should be kept in a comparatively dust-free cloth or leather sack or container—never tightly closed in a plastic bag —they will sweat.

Fly lines should be dressed carefully as often as needed to keep them afloat, if you want them to float. Never dress your

-WALK ON ROD

-DEMONSTRATE A ROD'S QUALITY THUS

-USE ROD TIP AS A CAR DOOR JAMB

-TWIST FERRULE

-PROBE THE EARTH OR FLOOR WITH ROD TIP EVEN BY ACCIDENT

-PUT ROD AWAY IN A WET SACK

-LEAN ROD AGAINST ANYTHING AND LEAVE IT

-SEPARATE FERRULE ACROSS YOUR CHEST

DON'T EVER ~ FIG 5

JIM Q.

line with a greasy or waxy dressing if the line is wet. You'll waterlog it, then you'll have a heck of a time getting it dry. Be sure the fabric surface of the line itself is free of moisture before dressing it. Drops of water on the surface is not an indication, they can be wiped off easily. To be done right, it's going to take quite a few minutes to clean and dress a line as it should be done.

Stretch the line above the ground its whole length if possible, at least the length from reel to tip end that will be your customary maximum working distance. Rub line dressing, not too sparingly onto the line, covering every bit of its surface. Let rest for a few moments then work again from the starting point and rub briskly with the fingers. The next step is to wipe surplus dressing from the line with chamois or soft absorbent paper and polish with chamois or kid. This means vigorous rubbing until friction develops some heat. When finished there will be no discernible oily surface when touched with dry fingers but it's there and your line will float perfectly for a varied length of time, according to its type. One caution: In dressing nylon lines do not stretch excessively. The finish coat on the elastic nylon could be separated and broken if pulled too tightly.

I know of a manufactured silk line which is regarded highly by many anglers, but in constant use must be dressed every four or five hours. I know, too, of an uncoated woven nylon line that, if dressed properly, has been known to be still jauntily bobbing on top the water after thirty hours of use. I can attest to that because it is one of my own fly lines. I know of other owners of a like line who, using it every day, dress it once a week, as they say, "Whether it needs it or not." The only feature of this line that can be criticized is that it is noisy. Its coarser weave causes the line to sing as it slides through the guides. This rasp sounds like wear but it is completely harmless as any line. Recently a new type line, with a somewhat elastic plastic coating has been offered the trade. These lines have, reportedly, become quite popular because of their floating attributes. The coating of plastic has a specific gravity that permits their staying on the water surface without floatant. Because fishermen feel that thoroughly dressing lines is a tedious job they welcome a product which eliminates that detail. The truth is that the plastic has a tendency toward "hold-back" as it goes through the guides. The only procedure that prevents that friction delay is a light coating of line dressing. The combination of a "floater" line and the minimum lubrication gives us a line hard to beat. The diameter of these lines, for the required weight is, in most cases, larger than usual.

Fly lines should have spliced loops or natural woven loops on the line instead of tying an unsightly knot to attach the leader. (See Fig. 6 on splicing directions.) Even the best knots will catch in the tiny tip-top or guides, at times, loops rarely or never. Generally, lines do not come with this added feature because the manufacturer knows that no doubt you'll wish to cut off some of the excess tip end to suit your fancy, and to better fit your method of fishing or style of casting. Most tip ends of new lines are far too long, being patterned after the old English chalk stream lines, which for American waters are up to six and eight feet longer than is necessary.

When determining the length taper you wish from belly of line to leader and you are not familiar with the particular line you are to work with, cut off one foot and try it. Keep at this cutting foot lengths or less until you are satisfied that the line is right for your rod, then splice a loop in the end. You have the correct measurement now for the reverse end should you wish to cut it also.

If a line is not in use or is not used oftener than every fifteen days or so, the line should be removed from the reel and stored in a cool dark spot in large coils at least a foot in diameter. A cardboard shoe box is a good storage vehicle for the line. It should be placed in the box as loosely as possible and nothing else placed with it. This caution has relation to both silk and nylon lines, particularly the silk. Hanging the coils from a wood peg or protected nail is O.K. if not left too long. Placed on a line dryer or wrapped around a circular cardboard drum is all right if the arrangement is protected.

Should you notice that your silk line is at all tacky or sticky, give it a bath immediately. A large enamel dish is best for this procedure. Place line, loose coils preferably, in dish and cover with a lime solution.

Lime solution:

To one gallon of distilled or soft water add one eleven-gram package of Lilly's Lime (slaked) or proportionate measure. (Lilly's Lime can be secured at any drug store.)

THE LINE SHOULD NEVER BE LEFT IN THE SOLU-
TION LONGER THAN FIFTEEN MINUTES. Take from
liquid and string out full length and permit it to dry. When
dry wipe carefully with a soft cloth. If line is still tacky, repeat
the operation exactly as before. Re-using the same lime solution is O.K. If, after a third soaking and drying, the line is
still sticky it has passed beyond the restoration stage and is of
no further value as a fly fishing line. If line comes out smooth
after drying with cloth, let it air dry for at least twenty-four
hours before dressing.

Examine your leaders often during fishing. Look for cast
knots in the tippet end and remove them. Inspect for abraded
areas. If bad, replace the section or change leaders.

Keep leader free from fly floatant or line dressing. It will
prevent it from sinking, as it should do. Floating leaders are
an abomination. There has been a parade of leader sinking
agents on the market, some worthless and some that worked
for varying periods of time (until the preparation washed off
or out of the leader). For two or three years I made a concoction consisting of distilled water, a few drops of glycerin, a
small piece of yellow naphtha soap, well dissolved, and a few
drops of photographic wetting agent. I kept my leaders, nylon
and gut both, between wet pads of this liquid. My theory was
that inasmuch as both gut and nylon absorbed some moisture
why not supply that moisture, mixed with sinking materials,
before use. This mixture worked for from periods of an hour
or two up to as much as four hours. When the leader displayed
signs of floating I changed it to another leader from the
"soak." The replaced leader I permitted to dry thoroughly
before I put it back in the leader box. We may be on the edge
of being able to overcome this floating leader problem. A new
preparation called "600," made in Reading, Pennsylvania, can
be procured and in all my experiments with it I have had no
failure in keeping leaders under water all day without further
treatment. It appears that by filming the leader with this
liquid the surface tension is eliminated, letting the leader sink
without trouble. I mention this product solely because it's the
only preparation I've ever heard of that really does work

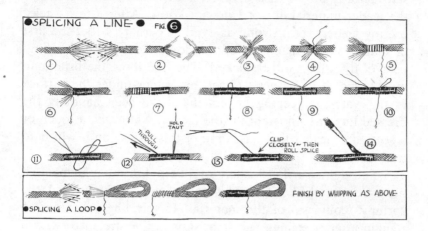

SECURING ONE END OF LINE BEING SPLICED, ABOUT A FOOT OR
SO FROM THE PART TO BE WORKED, MAKES SPLICING EASIER BY
SUPPLYING A STEADYING POINT TO PULL AGAINST. IF LINE SEC-
TIONS BEING SPLICED ARE NOT OF THE SAME DIAMETER, IT IS
SUGGESTED THAT THE SMALLER OF THE TWO BE THE ONE TO
THE RIGHT AND THE ONE TO BE SECURED.

1. After finish or plastic covering has been removed from about
½ inch of line ends, tease or pick out strands of line fabric.
Stroking it with back of knife blade helps. Clip to an approximate diamond shape.   2. Dip ends in varnish, remove excess.
Split fiber segments into two spread sections.   3. Join together
closely.   4. Using well waxed thread or floss (preferably silk
in either case), take two or three wraps at center junction as
tightly as possible. THIS IS IMPORTANT.   5. Wrap thread
in ribbing move, tightly to cover end of fibers of one section.
6. Return wrapping closely to center.   7. Repeat second half
ribbing move.   8. Return close wraps to center.   9. Extend a
few wraps beyond center and prepare to whip by inserting loop
of thread under wraps.   10. After six or seven turns of thread
over looped thread—11. Put end of wrapping thread through
loop. Hold.   12. Pull loose ends of loop threads through.
Tighten.   13. Clip closely. At this point rolling the splice between two flat surfaces will smooth out any minor thread bumps.
14. Varnish lightly with *good* varnish. Varnish again when completely dry.

satisfactorily for me. It is claimed not to, but whether it harms the leader material or not I do not know. After a few weeks' use my leaders seem strong as ever. It perhaps is but the first of many "sinks" that will follow along shortly and this bugbear of fly fishing will be licked. The one thing the fisherman must avoid, if he wishes to keep his leader under the surface of the water, is keeping fingers that have been handling the dressed line or fly floatant off the leader. Naturally, a touch or a section of leader that has some of this grease on it will hold to the surface.

To straighten nylon leaders or just nylon monofilament, it must be stretched a bit. This takes out the kinks and the springy "coiliness" of the material. If spiraling still tends to remain after stretching rub it briskly, while stretched, with a piece of chamois or draw it through a piece of rubber. This supplies a bit of heat, which you would discover if you attempted to use your hand or fingers alone, and will always straighten the normal nylon and the synthetic monofilaments.

After tying a leader knot of nylon some anglers, instead of cutting or clipping the waste ends, will touch them with the coal of a cigarette. They claim it leaves a small bulb of melted nylon which resists the possibility of the material pulling through and untying itself.

There are a few fishermen left who still insist upon and use silk gut in their leaders. Even though I use the nylon or the synthetics, altogether, I have no argument with them. A gut leader carefully tied of fresh strands is not as strong as comparative diameters in nylon or the other synthetics. The gut leader will sink much more readily than nylon under equal conditions and it casts as well, sometimes better, than the synthetic leaders. I, personally, just don't like all the knots that are required in making a gut leader. Every one is a weaker point and there's always the possibility of one of the knots being faulty. I like the elasticity in nylon leaders which assists greatly in taking up the shock of a striking fish. Gut leaders do not have that feature in as great a measure.

It is well, at all times, to keep your flies in storage containers. Many fishermen like the large transparent plastic boxes for this purpose. A warning at this point: Do not place paradichlorobenzene crystals in lucite plastic boxes and some others. The vapors will attack the plastic, turning it a milky frosted color if not actually eating right into the material. Flies, recently dunked or treated with silicone floatants, should be allowed to dry thoroughly before placing them in these boxes. Apparently, many of the volatile chemicals or liquids used as a base for these preparations contain ingredients that will also fog up the plastic.

I mentioned paradichlorobenzene crystals as a moth killer and preventative in the paragraph above. It is by far the best I've ever found, even though its evaporation rate is exceedingly fast unless completely air sealed. There are liquid preparations in which flies or materials of which flies are made, may be dipped or treated. I see no reason why it should not be effective, however I cannot speak one way or the other from personal experience, because those materials that I am testing have not been exposed long enough to render a positive verdict. Thus far, after about five months, it seems to be working.

Flies, having been used on the stream and replaced with another, should not be returned to a closed container. Stick them in your hat or someplace temporarily, allowing them to dry out thoroughly. Most fishermen have a patch of clipped sheep or lamb's wool on their person for just this purpose or they have a supplementary hatband of the same material. At the end of the day remove the dried flies, check the eyes of the hooks for knots or pieces of leader, and remove. If possible pass the flies through a jet of steam from a tea kettle or similar container. This renews and raises the hackle to its original spread. Be sure fly is dry, then replace in your storage or stream fly container.

Inspect your fly occasionally on the stream and always before replacing in your fly box at night for broken or blunted points and barbs or expanded bends. Every angler of long experience can relate numerous instances in which fish escaped because of dull hooks or hooks broken at the barb or hooks that straightened out on him. This latter could have been caused by an expanded bend in the hook or by the fisherman horsing his fish beyond the limit of the hook's capacity or the hook could have been trying to pierce a bony part of the fish's mouth at an extreme angle and the pulling strain was against the bend at that angle instead of pulling direct in line with the shank of the hook.

Carry a hook sharpening stone with you on the stream. In examining the hook, if there's the slightest doubt about the hook having or not having a needle sharp point give it a few licks with the stone to be sure. This seemingly unimportant detail has been known to be the difference between hooking and failing to hook good fish.

The smart angler who owns a pair of good rubber waders or boots, not the fabric type, should treat them to a glycerin-alcohol application a few times during the season. Apply with a saturated ball of cloth or a soft brush—let stand for ten minutes or so then wipe dry if any of the solution is not absorbed or evaporated. The solution consists of half glycerin and half grain alcohol. This treatment will add greatly to the life of the rubber.

Carry a roll of fresh adhesive tape with you for emergency repair of boots or waders when on the stream. If a leak is discovered and the opening is found remove the waders or boot, dry the surface both inside and outside around the hole and apply warmed adhesive tape on both sides. Press down firmly. It will usually hold until you have an opportunity to have the leak repaired permanently.

Along with the adhesive tape, a roll of scotch tape may be of extreme value to you, if a guide is somehow torn loose. Even a broken tip can be lapped and secured with this tape, permitting you to continue the fishing. You will, without question, discover many other uses for this addition to your "miscellaneous" items. Some of these uses, besides emergency repairs to tackle or sealing leaks, repairing waders or clothing temporarily, are: Repairing broken glasses, sealing canned milk punched holes, as a protective cushion on blisters, fashioning hinges on small boxes, securing the paper wrapped about the fish you are going to transport, as a binding on bandages, securing the reel more tightly to its seat if it does not fit properly—its uses around camp are too numerous to mention.

Chapter 3

Leader Material—Leader Knots

NOT TOO long ago I was enjoined by an angling club and a group of fishermen, because I had access to stocks of nylon, silkworm gut and other synthetic monofilaments, to determine by consultation and test just what the answer was to the controversial subject of knots and their comparative strength. This was to find out also what material was best and to what degree, and which type of leader I would recommend, based upon my findings.

This was going to be easy thought the "freshman"—in a few days I'd have the answer. It took months.

First, to eliminate what might be personal prejudice in favor of certain material and certain connections of the material, I made up a questionnaire and sent it along, with an explanation, to a number of friends who are ardent fishermen —those whom I knew would be honestly blunt in their opinions and I solicited their cooperation. Then I wrote to, in my humble judgment, the three top angling writers of this country explaining the survey and the tests I was about to make and wondered if I could ask their help and valuable advice. To their credit and their honesty I must genuflect and bow because each one stated frankly that they too had opinions but weren't sure what the true answer was in all cases. They would, they said, lend every assistance in helping secure definite determinations. And they did.

I concocted a revolving drum arrangement over which I could secure the monofilament or gut which extended down to a section of size D splice-looped fly line. This line was secured to a spring scale which would give me a check on the poundage pulled for purposes of comparison.

Each knot was carefully tied and each type of knot was tested from eight to twelve times on both well soaked, unused silkworm gut and the synthetic monofilaments which included nylon. Each test was with fresh new material and in testing the knots I used not one diameter of the material but several sizes. Only in this way could I be sure of my ground.

The consensus of findings were:

The manufacturer or packager, in the majority of cases, had stated the pound test of the materials approximately the same as my conclusions, only slightly in our favor. A few, unfortunately, were considerably off in both directions. It seems that in tinting or dyeing the material some were possibly not as careful as others and apparently the dye or the process of dyeing had something to do with the material being weakened over the original natural white or transparent type. Some of the synthetics, I found, had definable flat spots which could hardly stand half the pull with which they were credited. (This fault was quite evident in one well-known brand of knotless tapered leaders.)

Silkworm gut, in its natural undrawn state is as strong or stronger than nylon and other synthetics in the same diameter but the size of most natural gut strands varies from two to five thousandths, at times, in their short length. Diamond drawn gut is weaker than nylon in the same diameter. Gut, too, has much less stretch and hardly any elasticity by comparison, but holds up better under quick shock jerks than does nylon and other synthetics. SIMPLE knots in silkworm gut hold better than SIMPLE knots in nylon.

Contrary to many opinions, we found that the materials tested, insofar as strength and knots were concerned, were not affected by any heat or cold to which they might be subjected in normal fishing use under extreme conditions. The synthetic materials did seem to stiffen somewhat in the cold but that was the only condition noted.

When a knot, any kind, is tied in either gut or monofilament the strength of that section is reduced up to 80%. The best that can be expected is that the strength will not be reduced more than a third to a half. A simple overhand knot, the kind that appears at times in leader tippets when casting in a wind, will reduce the strength of the section more than two thirds. (See Fig. 7.) If your tippet is 3X, for example, and contains even one of these knots, you are fishing actually with much less than a pound pulling strength.

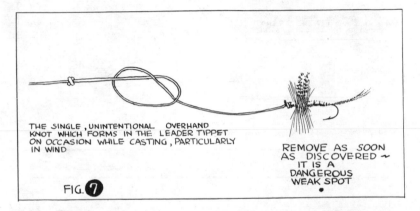

THE SINGLE, UNINTENTIONAL OVERHAND KNOT WHICH FORMS IN THE LEADER TIPPET ON OCCASION WHILE CASTING, PARTICULARLY IN WIND

REMOVE AS *SOON* AS DISCOVERED — IT IS A DANGEROUS WEAK SPOT

FIG. 7

The most secure and satisfying connection knot for either nylon or gut is the Blood Knot, which isn't too easy to tie. The Barrel Knot is so similar that most users cannot distinguish the difference. It is merely that in the Blood Knot the turns of the material around the main line are both the same, in other words, either clockwise or counterclockwise but both the same. In the Barrel Knot the first half turns are completed in one direction and the second half in the opposite direction. Both methods are good and are approximately the same quality in strength with a nod in favor of the Blood Knot. (See Fig. 8.)

Actually the strongest connection is the Double Surgeon's Knot (Fig. 9). It is by far the easiest to tie but it usually results in a slight dog-leg angle at the knot. (Standing in fast water up to one's hips, with rod under arm, with cold fingers trying to bend on a new tippet to the leader and with tobacco smoke channeling direct to watering eyes, one will forego

niceties to get the job done. This means that the Double Surgeon's Knot would be the one selected by most anglers.)

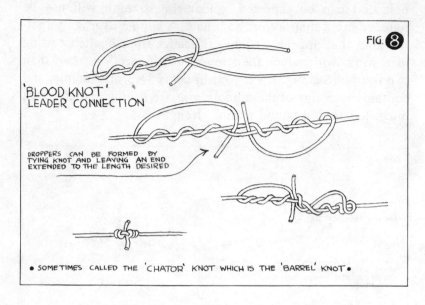

'BLOOD KNOT'
LEADER CONNECTION

DROPPERS CAN BE FORMED BY
TYING KNOT AND LEAVING AN END
EXTENDED TO THE LENGTH DESIRED

FIG. 8

● SOMETIMES CALLED THE 'CHATOR' KNOT WHICH IS THE 'BARREL' KNOT ●

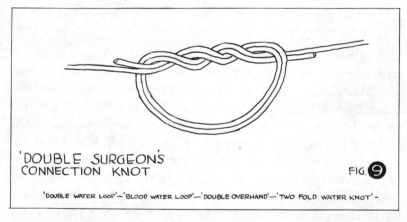

'DOUBLE SURGEON'S
CONNECTION KNOT

FIG. 9

'DOUBLE WATER LOOP'—'BLOOD WATER LOOP'—'DOUBLE OVERHAND'—'TWO FOLD WATER KNOT'—

The connection knot called the Double Water Loop (Fig.
10) is good but doesn't come up to those two mentioned
above. The Wolf Splice (Fig. 11) is about equal to the Double
Water Loop.

The strongest end loop is the Double Surgeon Loop (Fig.
12) but because of the resulting angle at the knot, most times

when tied, the Perfection Loop (Fig. 13) is the most satisfactory because it lies straight, is not a difficult tie and if formed correctly will be stronger than the other connections, of a finer diameter, down the leader. The Flemish End Loop (Fig. 14) unless tied double at each knot is not too secure with nylon. If tied double the resulting knot is quite large by comparison. The Single Overhand Loop (Fig. 15) is speedily tied but results in that dog-leg angle at the knot.

'DOUBLE WATER LOOP'
LEADER CONNECTION

'DOUBLE FISHERMANS KNOT'-

FIG 10

'WOLF SPLICE'
LEADER CONNECTION
• A VARIATION OF THE WATER LOOP •

FIG 11

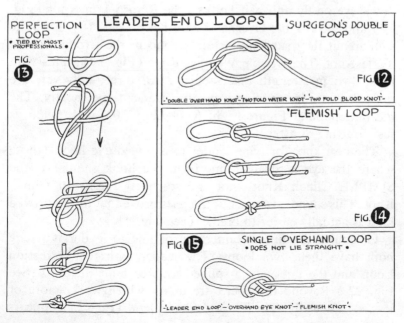

PERFECTION
LOOP
• TIED BY MOST
PROFESSIONALS •
FIG.
13

LEADER END LOOPS

'SURGEON'S DOUBLE
LOOP

FIG 12

-'DOUBLE 'OVER HAND KNOT'-'TWO FOLD WATER KNOT'-'TWO FOLD BLOOD KNOT'-

'FLEMISH' LOOP

FIG. 14

FIG 15
SINGLE OVERHAND LOOP
• DOES NOT LIE STRAIGHT •

-'LEADER END LOOP'-'OVERHAND EYE KNOT'-'FLEMISH KNOT'-

In securing the hook to the leader, there are several meth-ods. The outstanding knot is the Turle Knot for gut and the Double Turle Knot for nylon or other synthetics. (See Fig. 16.) This knot applies, of course, to the turned up or turned

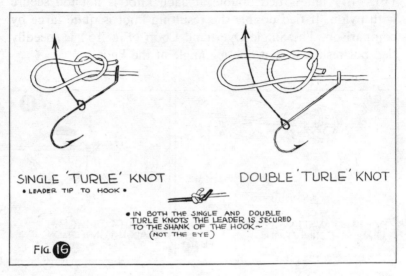

SINGLE 'TURLE' KNOT
• LEADER TIP TO HOOK •

DOUBLE 'TURLE' KNOT

• IN BOTH THE SINGLE AND DOUBLE TURLE KNOTS THE LEADER IS SECURED TO THE SHANK OF THE HOOK~ (NOT THE EYE)

FIG. 16

down eye on fly and bait hooks. The Return Jam Knot (Fig. 17) and the Double Overhand Jam Knot (Fig. 18) are quite similar but they run only a fair second to the strong Double Turle Knot. The Double Wemyss Knot (Fig. 19) ranks with those two in strength and security. All three, however, are difficult to tie in securing a fly to a leader tippet neatly. The old time popular Figure Eight Knot (Fig. 20), with nylon, is just courting disaster.

The best knot for tying leader to a ringed eye hook (those where the eye is straight out from the hook shank) is the SIMPLE Clinch Knot—not the so-called Improved Clinch Knot. This sounds strange but the tests prove that the Improved knot is actually easier to break. (See Fig. 21.)

Of course the finest connection of line to leader is where both have their own loops. The leader with the Perfection Loop and the line with a spliced loop or built in loop. (See Fig. 22.) Beyond this there are a few which work, more or less, satisfactorily. The Tucked Sheet Bend (Fig. 23) appears

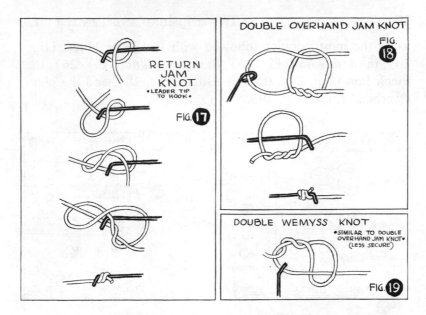

RETURN
JAM
KNOT
•LEADER TIP
TO HOOK•

FIG. 17

DOUBLE OVERHAND JAM KNOT

FIG. 18

DOUBLE WEMYSS KNOT

•SIMILAR TO DOUBLE
OVERHAND JAM KNOT•
(LESS SECURE)

FIG. 19

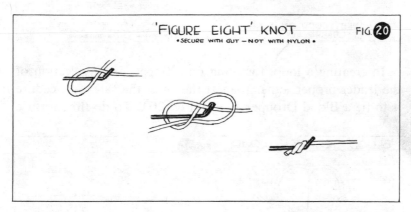

'FIGURE EIGHT' KNOT   FIG. 20
•SECURE WITH GUT — NOT WITH NYLON•

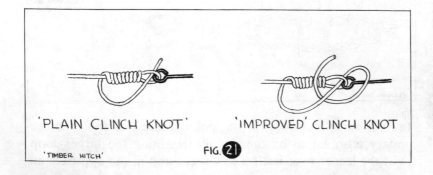

'PLAIN CLINCH KNOT'   'IMPROVED' CLINCH KNOT

'TIMBER HITCH'   FIG. 21

to be the most popular followed with the Tiller Hitch (Fig. 24), the Jam Knot (Fig. 25), the Clinch Knot (Fig. 26), the Pinch Jam (Fig. 27), the Jam Hitch (Fig. 28), and the plain Overhand Knot (Fig. 29).

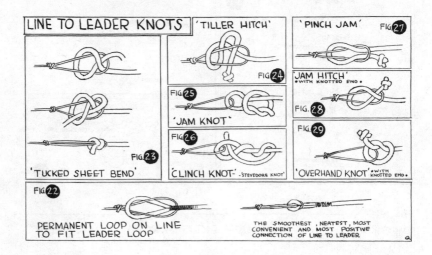

In creating a loop, for tying on a tippet, on any section of the leader proper, other than at the ends, the safest procedure is to tie a Blood Dropper Loop (Fig. 30). To do this, form a

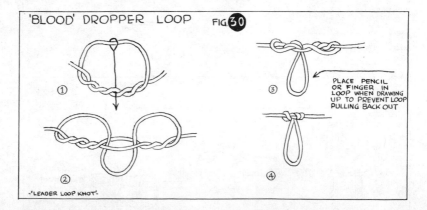

two- or three-inch loop at the point where you wish the secondary terminal to be then, while retaining the larger loop, twist the leader over itself a few times and in the approximate center of the twisted section open it up and pull the large loop through and tighten. As it is drawn up insert a pencil or small stick or your finger in the loop until the knot is secure. This loop wants to get back where it came from as you will discover unless you prevent it.

In learning to tie these knots, if one does not already have that knowledge, the best procedure is to start with a piece of clothesline type rope. When the operation of tying the knot has been learned then graduate to a comparatively heavy nylon or gut (well soaked) then down to the size which will customarily be used. In tying gut knots gently jerk the union together but with nylon or synthetic monofilament pull the knot up slowly, steadily and tightly.

Tests of the nylon type material were made with both the standard type and the limp or soft type. Until something new is discovered the standard type nylon is far superior, for leaders and leader material, to the limp nylon which was developed for spinning line and casting line. The limp nylon is just too soft for leaders to be used in average fly casting. Its "turn-over" is poor by comparison and many times the fine tippet, unless very skillfully handled, will actually fall back on itself which is anything but desirable.

The leaders I had been using for fly fishing and will continue to use, inasmuch as the tests made indicated that no change was needed, are the tapered knotless nylon leaders in the better quality bracket. I usually use nine- and twelve-foot tapered leaders in their regular state and with tippets added to increase the length when I feel that extra length is called for. In mentioning above that the leaders I want come in the better quality bracket doesn't mean that I'm putting on the dog or becoming extravagant. The difference in cost is so little compared with the price of losing a battle with a fish because of inferior terminal tackle that I just cannot take the chance.

I have no gripe against the tied tapered leaders. They really have a better "turn-over" in casting than do the knotless tapered leaders. Why this is so is problematical but the connecting knots have something to do with it. Tournament dry fly casters, generally, use the tied leaders and they are noted for finding and using those items and materials that tend to give them greater accuracy and better scores. I have known throughout most of my fishing years that, in a leader, the knots are the weakest links, so for my own use I have tried to produce leaders that would do the required job with the least number of connections. Thus when the knotless leader reached the market I was an apt prospect and have been using them since for all my fly fishing ventures. In my tournament casting I still use the tied leaders because they perform more to my liking, particularly in dry fly work but, of course, in this activity I do not have the fear of a knot weakening or pulling loose or breaking—I have no fish to net. All I lose is a minute or two for retying or replacement if it parts for any reason.

It may be interesting to note, while on this subject, that in all our tests, which included the limp monofilaments, the limp type manufactured in this country was superior to the imported brands, regardless of claims. That fact may change tomorrow but at this writing that is the condition according to our findings. This same determination applied also to the standard types of monofilament, the kind most used for trout leaders.

We have developed a CONSENSUS OF RATINGS chart (Fig. 31) which was based on this study, plus the published size and strength determinations of both silkworm gut, the nylons and other monofilaments.

I have reason to believe that within a short time we will be given new improved monofilaments that will be superior to those now in use. Finer diameters with equal or a better strength test will be a welcome refinement to our terminal tackle.

A CONSENSUS OF RATINGS
AS TO SIZE, DESIGNATIONS AND
STRENGTH OF NYLON AND SILKWORM GUT

BASED ON PUBLISHED FIGURES CONSISTING OF DETERMINATIONS OF 16 SUPPLIERS, AUTHORITATIVE WRITERS AND OUR OWN TESTS

SIZE OF MONOFILAMENT OR GUT IN THOUSANDTHS	DESIGNATION			APPROXIMATE STRENGTH IN POUNDS		
	NYLON (TYNEX) STANDARD	SPANISH SILKWORM GUT	LIMP MONO-FILAMENT	NYLON ETC.	GUT	LIMP MONO-FILAMENT
.003	8X			¼ – ⅜	⅛ – 3/16	¼
.004	7X	8X		½	3/16	⅜
.0045		7X			¼	
.005	6X	6X		¾	⅜	⅝
.0055		5X			½	
.006	5X	4X		1 ¼	⅝	1
.007	4X	3X		1 ¾	¾	1 ¼
.008	3X	2X	SAME AS STANDARD NYLON	2 ¼	1 .	1 ¾
.009	2X	1X		3	1 ½	2 ½
.010	1X	REFINUCIA		3 ½	2	3 ¼
.011	OX	REFINA II		4 ¼	2 ½	4
.012	9/5	REFINA I		5	3	4 ¾
.013	8/5	FINA II		6	3 ½	5 ¾
.014	7/5	FINA I		7	4	7
.015	6/5	PADRON II		8	4 ¾	8 ½
.016	5/5	PADRON I		9	5 ½	9 ¼
.017	4/5	MARINA II		10 ¼	6 ¼	11
.018	3/5	MARINA I		11 ½	7 ½	12 ½
.019	2/5	IMPERIAL II		12 ¾	8 ¾	14
.020		IMPERIAL I		14 ¼	10	15 ½
.021	1/5	HEBRA ②		15 ½	12 ¼	17
.022		HEBRA ①		17 ½	13 ¾	18 ¼
.023	0/5	EX. HEBRA		20	15	20
.024						22
.024				24		24
.026						26
.027						28
.028	0/4			30		30
.029						33 ½
.030						37
.032	0/3			40		40
.034						45
.038	0/2					51
.040				50		62
.045	0/1			60		79
.050	0/0					98

FIG. 31

Chapter 4

"Basic Casting"

PARADOXICALLY, so difficult yet so simple.

The procedure of fly casting has been outlined so often in articles, books and pamphlets that the very multiplicity of the instructions may have caused confusion. Many varying methods of describing the "DO'S" and "DON'TS" by each individual writer, each trying to tell it differently, makes it seem as if there were a number of correct ways to perform. There is however exactly one, and only one *right* method.

If the reader has done considerable casting or if he has done none to speak of, I am going to request that we enter into this dissertation as if we're just starting to learn the process.

As you work, THINK every cast through. Do not be haphazard and do not presume that good results might accidentally come to you without too much work. They won't! And casting is a two-handed job (you'll wish sometimes you had a couple of extra hands but two is enough if manipulated correctly). If you're right-handed you'll find your left one is of equal importance in working with the other. The rule of successful fly rod casting is easily stated, and easily imagined, but it may take a bit of practice to have it become more or less automatic.

NEVER, NEVER, NEVER PERMIT THE ROD, ON THE
BACK CAST, TO GO BEYOND A PERFECT VERTICAL!
(This has been described as 12 o'clock if you can
imagine the clockface facing you as you cast.)

WHEN MAKING THE BACK CAST TOSS OR CAST THE
LINE, NOT BEHIND YOU, BUT STRAIGHT UP IN THE
AIR!

(Now here's where imagination will play a strong
part. The line will not go straight up but it will go
high enough so that there is no danger of low bushes
being lassoed and the formation of a controlled loop
in your line will follow as a matter of course.)

If you are using a soft action rod, as are most bamboo rods
and many of glass, too, the rod will necessarily have to come
back slightly further on the back cast than the "vertical"
restriction. Do not permit the rod to go back, however, more
than one hour on the clock if you desire a real good cast. In
the following instructions, we will suppose that your rod is
one of the better grades of the modern tip action variety,
where the power is generated comparatively slowly at the butt,
racing faster and faster up its length to the tip where it literally
sprints with speed and power.

Many good casters permit even the best rods to drift backward beyond the vertical, particularly on casts where the line
is extended beyond the 35-foot and 40-foot distances. It seems
a natural thing to do, but certainly is not necessary, and those
same casters would improve their score if they would restrain
themselves and hold the rod more nearly vertical. The tip is
going to go back with the line anyway to some degree, why the
whole rod? If a cast is better with the rod tilted backward
even to a minor degree why wouldn't it be increasingly better
if the rod went back to the horizontal or 3 o'clock position?
It just isn't logical. Some say they let the rod drift backward
to avoid a bump. If the timing is accurate, no bump will occur
in any instance.

Please read and reread those capitalized sentences until
they become a part of you. Regardless of any other instruction,
those are the two most important practices that you can do.
Without them your cast will fail. With them and only them,
plus just a natural sense of timing, and you are bound to
succeed. (Note Fig. 32.)

I have observed beginning students of casting working the

naked rod only to get the movement and feel in mind. Of course the total feel will not be there, however this might be a good beginning. Start with the rod exactly vertical, your thumb on the grip, your aim at an approximate 90-degree angle, *and relaxed*. Push the rod forward with the thumb, wrist and forearm. This is done, not jerkily, but with an increasing

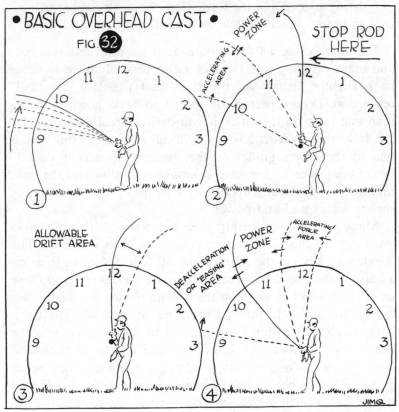

1—Take up slack—start back cast. 2—Sweep line up high —stop abruptly at 12 o'clock. 3—Hold while line is straightening behind you in the air. 4—At exact moment, when backcast line has about completed its "turnover", (too soon will cause a lashing snap—too late will permit line to fall downward) forcefully push it forward until rod has reached the 10:30 o'clock position—hold until 'turnover' of line is about complete—* then ease rod downward permitting fly to drop lightly to water surface.

    * If false casting, the next backcast will start at this point.

force that might be called a "kick" as it terminates. As you perform this accelerated movement, pierce or spear the air with the tip, which will naturally raise the whole rod somewhat. Remember, start easily but forcefully and finish strongly. Imagine the clock facing you again on your right. Stop the rod immediately at 10 o'clock. Hold, while your imaginary line is rolling out in front of you. When it has reached its length, then you can gently lower the rod tip rather than permit the imaginary fly to jerk and flick backward or sideways. Now raise the rod gently to about the 10 o'clock position. This will tend to straighten out any slack which may have formed in the line. Without pausing, bring the rod up sharply to the 12 o'clock vertical position, throwing the line straight up. As this movement is entered into, raise the whole rod to a minor extent rather than operating it as on a hinge. This is an air piercing action also. Pause for line to ALMOST complete its loop formation at your rear, then repeat the procedure.

Now you have the feel of the rod itself, let's take each necessary step in turn for a real practice session. If at all possible, practice over water. If not, the second best is a grass lawn, large enough to permit both backward and forward casts without obstructions. I had a friend say this, "Gosh, Jim, I'd like to practice on the lawn but the neighbors look at me as if I'm nuts. It's quite embarrassing!" I asked him if it was more embarrassing than playing catch when there is no batter or playing solitaire croquet or tunking a little white ball, with a putter, around the yard.

We have our rod assembled with the correct line for the rod. We tie on a six- or seven-foot tapered leader with a butt heavy enough to match your line so that you will get good turn over. If your line is an HDH the leader butt should measure at least .015; if a GBG, the butt should measure at least .017 or .018, and .020 might be better. A leader fits the line and turns over more efficiently if the butt, within reasonable limits, is heavy. Dry fly tournament accuracy leaders usually measure from .022 to .024 at the butt end. Fasten a medium-sized fly, with full visible hackle, on the leader. The fly, of course, should have bend clipped off so that the whole

structure is on a straight shank—it's safer that way. Even
experienced casters sometimes pick up their shirt or their hat
or their ear with the fly on a forward cast, if there is a bit of
breeze flitting around. I've fished in gusty winds when I wished
that some inventive genius had produced or devised a protective shield for the head to cover just such occasions.

Strip enough line from the reel so that it will measure
approximately four or five feet longer than the rod from the
tip out. If you have an eight-foot rod, for example, and a
seven-foot leader there will be nineteen feet from the tip of
the rod to the fly. Clasp the line against the cork grip with a
finger to hold it in place and bring the rod up sharply, tossing
the line straight up. (As mentioned previously, do not be
discouraged if your line doesn't go "straight up"—they never
do unless there's an extreme tail wind and in that case you
have only limited control of your line anyway, at this stage.
I keep repeating "straight up" because that's what you're
attempting to do.) Only long experience in casting will permit
one to feel a pull on a line as short as that you are using, so
forget that angle for now. If you can perform this movement
and roll your head sideways far enough to glimpse your line,
do so for a few casts at least. When the line has reached a
spot where your leader is almost ready to straighten out—it
might be termed a "J"—bring the rod forward with an accelerating tempo (kick) to the 10 o'clock position. As the line
extends ahead of you gently lower the rod tip slightly, permitting the fly to drop lightly to the surface. If the forward
cast is started too quickly, it might create a snap like a whip
crack and possibly sever the fly from the leader. If the forward
cast is started late your line will strike the ground behind you
and may not even get out to the front of you. If it does it will
probably pile up, literally, at your feet.

I feel compelled to bring up one other minor movement
in the casting procedure. You may have developed the gesture
unconsciously, many do. That is, as your rod tip travels
backward and forward it should not be in a straight line. If
it travels in a straight line, the line or leader will have the
tendency many times to strike and tangle with the rod tip on

too many casts. It is not difficult to make your forward cast slightly to the right and the back cast to the left, forming a sharp ellipse of the rod tip, with the sweeps of the rod only a few inches apart at the greatest width of the ellipse. This is an easily developed habit if it did not form itself with you naturally. You can feel this action without looking. Some say this is necessary only when combatting wind. That may be true, however the action does not detract from accuracy in any event and it's a good habit to form so you won't have to think about it.

Now go through the procedure except that the steps be continuous. Do not permit the fly to touch the water or ground surface but start it on the back cast just before the loop straightens. This is termed "False Casting" and is used constantly in dry fly fishing. The purpose, primarily, is to dry the fly after previous contact with the water and to get direction and distance required, preparatory to presentation of the fly to the trout. Extending or lengthening the distance is done on the forward cast. Line is stripped from the reel, held in the left hand during the back cast and is released on a forward false cast or immediately before dropping the fly.

In your practice sessions I would suggest that you forget distance or long casts until you have attained a measurable rhythm and a semblance of accuracy on casts up to not more than 30 or 35 feet. "Accuracy" isn't putting your fly in a teacup each time you try but you should be able to drop it on a spread handkerchief, more times than not, in continuous casting.

If you are a beginning fly caster I would hope that you would or could refrain from fishing until you had put in several hours cast practicing over a week or ten-day period. By that time, if you have worked with intent to improve and have imbued yourself with the two basic laws so that you do not even have to think about them or your timing, you will have reached a stage of skill attained by too few anglers. A bit of practice every day will result in greater benefits and more accuracy-skill than if the work is packed into one or two long sessions.

If you have followed.this instruction with the short line and have been able to make the casts behave more times than not, start extending the length of line up to 35 or 40 feet. Notice how much easier it is? You have a bit of additional weight of line to cast now which, you will observe, seems to make your casts smoother. Be sure to hold an angle of line with your left hand, if casting with your right, from a few inches up to the extent of your normal reach, whichever is natural to you. This grip on the line allows you to feed line out when needed; it permits a hasty single or double haul, also when needed (this movement is described later); it gives you better control of your line. Now you begin to feel confidence in your ability and that feeling alone is going to raise your skill several notches. You wonder how you could have been so awkward at first when this is so easily done—then—

> When your line falls and wraps itself around your neck, reel it in to the original short cast and work out from there. You're just a bit dumbfounded. What happened? I cannot tell you from here—that's something you'll have to dope out for yourself. However, as practice continues, those interludes of miscalculation will become more and more infrequent. (As you become increasingly skillful and the term "Good Caster" may be applied to you, then watch carefully because little gremlins will start taking rides on your fly and will force it to execute very unexpected reverses.)

I have purposely delayed mentioning an old rule that still is law to many fly casters. The reason it was not brought up is that I do not believe it. This law is, that your elbow must be kept rigidly at your side and close to the body, if the cast is to be any good. I remember how my dad put a handkerchief under my arm when first instructing me in the rudiments of casting a fly rod. I was told that, under no circumstances, must the handkerchief fall to the ground. I learned that way and it became a habit I had much difficulty in breaking. Some say to keep a stiff wrist and suggest tying the butt of the rod, below the reel, to the forearm to learn how it should be handled. Bologna and Salami! There is no relaxed movement evident at all when either or both of those restrictions are followed. The purpose of casting is to place your fly at a designated spot, smoothly and with a minimum of effort, with a high percentage of hits. How you do it physically is of little matter. Whether your arm is extended over your head, across your body or rippling like a hula dancer's, has no bearing on your cast, providing the rod does not go beyond the vertical on your back cast, as the line is thrown straight up in the air. Find the way, yourself, how you cast best and easiest by trying different movements of your arm and wrist in a natural manner. Adopt the arm and wrist action that handles your rod correctly, is the least tiring to you, and forget any others.

At this point you should have a rhythmic cast and can place your fly approximately where you are aiming. The next step is one of imagination. It may sound a bit absurd, but it isn't and it is quite important. In your practice sessions you have been seeing the water surface, or the grass surface, stimulating water. I'm going to ask that you raise the level of that surface two or three feet, in your mind's eye. If that doesn't picture itself on your mind, imagine a carpenter's sawhorse out there, the distance you are casting. It is your problem to cast your fly over that sawhorse before it drops to the surface. By drilling your imagination in this exercise every time you cast it will become semi-automatic, but notice how lightly your fly lands every time. If you have difficulty in the fly dropping too hard, release a foot or so of line as the cast reaches its extreme distance. That takes the shock out of the cast and the fly drops as it should.

You will have observed now that the power which propels or drives the line in the direction which the caster wishes, occurs at the butt of the rod, traveling up to the tip, is applied by a degree of pressure in the form of a forward "kick" or push rather than by an extended sweep of the rod, which either terminates in a definite whip cracking snap or the line falls weakly in front of the caster without any determined direction. A good forward cast depends entirely upon the quality of the back cast. Remember again, the perpendicular halt of the rod and the "straight up" back cast.

Practice this regular or normal cast every time you have the opportunity until it becomes a part of you. Well over 90 per cent of your fishing casts will be this one. Many fishermen know no other method of casting. As you become adept at the normal "overhead" cast, using the same movements, the same procedure, drop your rod tip to the right two or three feet and cast at this angle. Then drop the rod to a horizontal position or nearly so and work that angle. This latter cast is more difficult because timing must be perfect to keep your line off the ground or the water. The horizontal cast is somewhat important if you intend learning the "curve" or "hook" cast, which will be described later. Now try a 90-degree or right angle cast from your left side, working the rod with the arm across the body. These angle casts will be required many times when you are compelled to fight a wind or other obstacles in your actual fishing or in your casting practice. When you have these casts down pat, and not until then, go on to the trick or "craft" casts.

At this point, after a few conscientious practice hours, and the rod, line, leader and fly are not performing as you would wish, that they are not executing the maneuver as you have directed, let's take a glance at the "Delinquent Ten" of good fly rod casting. Should you be employing any of the following —that's probably your answer.

1. Are you gripping the rod too tightly, with no relaxed periods, during the cast or are you grasping the rod grip in the wrong manner?
2. Are you failing to employ force, at the 10 o'clock point, at the beginning of the back cast?
3. Are you negligent in halting the upward power stroke at the vertical point or applying enough power on the upward thrust to get a high line?
4. Are you permitting the rod to drift backward too far after the vertical power halt?
5. Are you starting your forward cast too quickly, before the line completes its roll out on the back cast?

6. Are you applying the power too gently at the start of the forward cast, then have to rush it with a too vigorous "kick?"

7. Are you employing too much force throughout the forward cast, or extending the power too far, or beyond the 10 o'clock angle?

8. Are you permitting any line to escape through the guides as you put on the power, in the forward cast?

9. Are you in too much of a hurry and trying for the long cast before you're master of the shorter one?

10. Are you permitting yourself to tire in practice sessions?

CASTING AGAINST WINDS

There will be periods in your fishing experience when you will wonder if the winds are ever going to let up. There will be windless occasions but we forget them and recall only those days we suffered difficulty with the constant breeze or gusty winds. In fishing a winding stream we will have a sample of normal wind currents in every direction, but the prevailing wind will probably be in a down stream course.

I have fished in winds strong enough so that the casts were practically uncontrollable. I spent one afternoon in the Sierra Nevada mountains when a strong wind was constant and I was attempting to take advantage of that by fishing with it and letting the wind dap my fly on the water. For periods of minutes at a time my line was stretched out in front and nothing I could do would let the fly drop to the water. When it did it was instantaneous. Were I of a different frame of mind, I suppose, that would have been a time to affix a couple of buck shot to the leader. One or two experiences projecting a fly with a buck shot, in a strong wind, supplementing the weight of the line and it's usually enough. With the handicapping breeze that lead pellet is like a shot bullet singing around your head and I'm just too unreasonable to enjoy that.

Another hindrance that the winds place upon you is that not always does the fly travel the route in which you are directing it. It has a "pixie" inclination to fasten its hook into exposed ears, and other anatomical sections of your carcass, and unreachable (without unharnessing) locations of your shirt or fishing jacket.

Now that we've touched on the less desirable features of winds in fishing, I must also state that it is generally conceded that trout are prone to be a bit more cooperative in accepting your invitations to dine when winds are performing around you. That being the case, we want to continue fishing so what to do about it?

If the wind is at your back, your only concern is to get a good back cast into it. A bit of extra force, plus a bit of help from a single haul with the left hand, will do it. Care must be taken to be sure the forward cast clears you. It helps to tilt the rod tip some to the right so that the plane on which the line is rolling is far enough from you to avoid contact with you and also with the rod itself.

The wind from either side is a bit more easily combatted by leaning the rod WITH the wind so that your cast is forced into it. This applies not only to direct side winds but quartering winds also.

The head wind cast is the one you will need in the majority of cases if fishing the dry fly or nymph upstream. Your back cast is more likely to take care of itself in a head wind. The forward cast, it goes without saying, must be forced beyond the usual measure and the tip of the rod must be pushed ahead a bit more energetically. Instead of halting the rod at the 10 o'clock position, as in the normal cast, bring it down to the 9 o'clock angle before you release the pressure. An immediate lift again to the 10 o'clock position does not hamper the power traveling along the line. If the fly is not rolling out to the leader's end, as it should, give the line a short single haul as you exert the last of the pressure, just before the 9 o'clock position is reached.

SHOOTING THE LINE

Shooting the line is of much help in placing the fly on target. Also, the power given the "live" line is arrested and does not reach the fly, which lacking the thrust of impetus it would ordinarily get, halts momentarily, then drifts lazily down to the water as delicately as a "natural."

The procedure is easily accomplished. Strip four or five feet or more of line from the reel, holding it in loops in the left hand or dropping it loosely if you can avoid its fouling up. False cast enough so that timing is good, holding the line at its existing length, then when a good forward cast is coming up release the line as the forward cast approaches the end of its turnover. This "shooting" can be continued to the limit of the rod's power or to the limit of the caster's ability.

ROLL CAST (*See Fig. 33*)

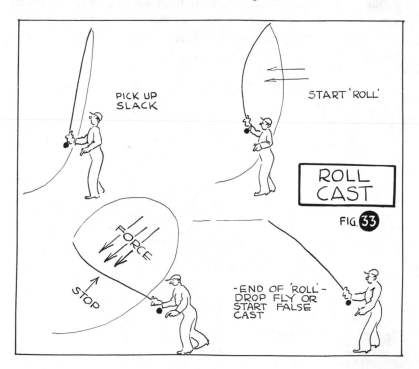

This cast, sometimes called the "switch" cast or the "straight spey" cast, is much easier than it looks or sounds. In fact, I've seen fishermen performing the roll cast fairly well, who couldn't drop their fly on a kingsize blanket in normal casting.

The roll cast is used, primarily, to pick your line and fly out of the water when conditions will not permit a back cast, also to lift the line from the water when the caster wishes to replace his fly up current again, with the minimum of water disturbance, or to lift the fly from the water to be followed by forceful false casts to extend the line in distance casting.

The correct procedure is to raise the rod to just past the perpendicular position. Hold until the slack is straightened by the pull of the rod and lifts gracefully almost straight up to the rod tip. Now slash the rod tip forward to about the 9 o'clock position. This maneuver will roll the line, leader and fly clear of the water, with little disturbance, and again send it out to the extent of the line. If false casting is the desired move, the back cast starts as soon as the line leaves the water.

The roll cast is particularly valuable when, at times, the fly has floated too close to you for a regular pick up.

CAST MENDING (*See Fig. 34*)

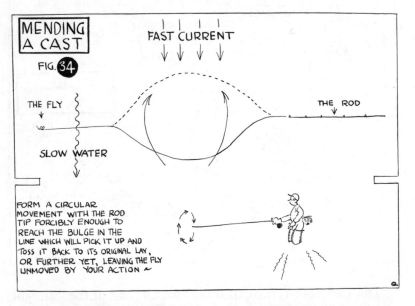

There are instances, while fishing upstream, when the line appears to be racing toward you much faster than your fly is drifting or on a cross stream cast the current between you and the fly is pulling a loop downstream that will speedily drag your fly. The "mend" is a mild roll cast that does not exert enough energy in the line to cause a pull on the leader or fly. It is done by lowering the rod tip almost to the water's surface, retrieving slack with your left hand, then throw an upward arc in your rod with just enough power to raise the section of line you want moved. This will toss the loop upstream again without hampering the drift of the fly. This cast is not difficult and a little practice will indicate just how much force should be exerted to perform a satisfactory "mend."

DOUBLE HAUL (*See Fig. 35*)

This act is performed only rarely by the trout fisherman. First, it is abusing a good fly rod and secondly its necessity is an acknowledgment that there is a lack of skill evident in normal long or regular casts. The double haul is used primarily by tournament distance casters, by salmon and steelhead fishermen, who have rods designed for this kind of rugged casting, and by a trout fisherman only when he needs just a bit of assistance in bucking a wind.

The procedure is a timing process in which the left hand, holding the line, more or less forcefully pulls or jerks down immediately following the beginning of both *forward* and *backward* casts. As the cast is on its way the left hand raises permitting the line which was pulled or hauled to resume its former position. This pumping action goes on with each cast. The movement accentuates the power in the rod tip giving it an unnatural starting force as it handles the line. The period between the start of the cast and the haul varies slightly according to the amount of line out, being worked.

SLACK CAST (*See Fig. 36*)

The major use of the slack cast is when it becomes necessary to cast a dry fly with, rather than against, the current although it is frequently used in both cases. It is also adopted when the fisherman wishes to scatter his line and leader between himself and the objective target with the purpose of avoiding a drag which would be almost certain with the normal straight cast.

The slack cast is a very simple operation, however if accuracy in placing your fly on a certain spot is required, you

START BACK CAST— PULL LINE DOWN WITH LEFT HAND 'LOADING THE ROD'

CONTINUE 'LIFT' WITH ROD AND 'PULL' DOWNWARD FORCEFULLY

HALT BOTH MOVEMENTS

KEEP HOLD ON LINE WITH LEFT HAND BUT LET IT PULL ITSELF OUT AS LINE REACHES END OF LOOP ON BACK CAST

START FORWARD CAST— 'PUSH' ROD AND START PULL DOWN WITH LEFT HAND **HARD**

CONTINUE MOVEMENT, ACCELERATING FORCEFULLY

HALT BOTH MOVEMENTS AND—

REPEAT AS ABOVE OR RELEASE HOLD ON LINE AND COMPLETE THE CAST

FIG 35   THE 'DOUBLE HAUL'

JIMQ

may as well forget it because if the fly drops within a couple to five feet of your target that would be an extraordinary cast and few can do it consistently. The only way I have heard or read of this cast being performed was to give the line a definite jerk either with the left hand or rod tip just before the line completes its straightening on the forward cast. This causes the line to return part way back towards you, falling loosely on the water. Another method was to make a higher than usual cast above the water, then as the line started to straighten on the forward cast to lower or drop the rod hand straight down from fifteen to eighteen inches.

SLACK CAST

FIG. 36

AT THIS POINT OF YOUR FORWARD CAST START AGITATING OR WAGGLING THE ROD SIDEWAYS AS THE LINE IS CAST

→AND THE LINE WILL FALL ON THE WATER IN A FORMATION LIKE THIS ↲

STREAM CURRENT

When I was in my teens I was fishing one day on the Black River in Michigan. I came up on a native of the area fishing a dry bug downstream. He had no reel, the rod was a cut stalk of some type of wood (could have been willow) about eight or nine feet in length. The line, as I remember, was about twelve or fourteen feet in length and secured to the tip of the "pole." This fisherman, as he worked the water, made one or two false casts then he would wave the rod tip two or three feet in span horizontally on the forward cast. As the line fell to the water it formed an almost perfect snake-like pattern between the rod tip and the bug. This permitted a drag free drift of the lure away from him downstream upwards of seven or eight feet, which is a generous float in any dry fly fishing without drag. I did not have occasion to try this method of slack casting for some time but I remembered and when I did use it, and effectively, it became my only "loose" cast practice. I called it my "lazy snake" cast.

You are not using a willow "pole" but the procedure is the same. On the forward cast wiggle the rod tip in front of you in a side to side motion and watch the line form a "snake" as it lays out upon the water.

This "snake" formation cast can be performed delicately by waving the rod just slightly or by exaggerating the movement, large "S" curves will form as the line drops to the water. The cast is equally effective on upstream casts where your line must cross varying currents. By the time the curves in your line have been straightened by the water's force your fly has traveled a long, drag free, journey. Many times when you think your apparently refused fly is moving without drag on a normal cast you might be surprised at the reception it will get by casting a few of those "S" curves into another cast to the same location. If you expect to place your fly on a dime with this cast you're going to be disappointed. Even though the cast is controlled to some degree, the minute you start the rod waving to create curves in the line the fly is going to drop only in the general vicinity of your target point.

STEEPLE CAST (*See Fig. 37*)

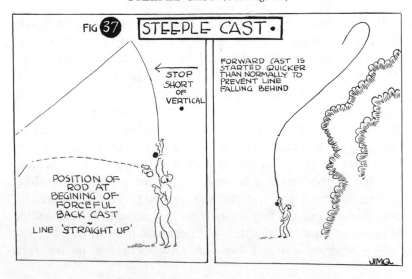

FIG 37 STEEPLE CAST •

STOP
SHORT
OF
VERTICAL
•

FORWARD CAST IS
STARTED QUICKER
THAN NORMALLY TO
PREVENT LINE
FALLING BEHIND

POSITION OF
ROD AT
BEGINING OF
FORCEFUL
BACK CAST
LINE 'STRAIGHT UP'

JIMG

This craft cast is a handy ruse when you are backed close to high bushes or other interference that may prevent the normal backward throw of the line. This, too, is a force action where, on the back cast, the arm and shoulder is put to use to raise the rod in a spearing motion, as you toss the line "straight up," and your arm extended fully up and slightly in back of you, but the rod itself must positively not go further back than 12 o'clock and short of that is even better. Beginning the cast it is advantageous to raise the rod on a horizontal plane, as slack is taken up, rather than raising the tip. When the hand is about at face level start the forcible upward cast. The wait for the line to straighten is reduced somewhat to avoid its dropping too far down. The forward cast, too, is stressed, the tip piercing the air ahead of you, but not lower than 10 o'clock. Because of the force employed on this cast the possibility is great that the fly may strike the water too hard. If it can be gauged correctly, the release of a foot or so of line from the left hand, as the live line straightens, will halt the energy of the cast and permit the fly to drop lightly.

CANYON CAST *(Galloway)* *(See Fig. 38)*

The canyon cast is a comparatively simple maneuver, occasioned by periods when you are fishing a stream and the foliage, trees or rocks form a more or less narrow channel in which your line must travel on the back cast. It is done merely by turning sideways and actually making a forward cast to the rear, to control the direction of your line. If your rod is not of the best quality it may be necessary for you to roll the grip in your hand so that the guides on the rod are facing in the direction toward which you are directing each cast. If the rod is a sturdy well constructed one this isn't necessary as the soft and hard planes are much less pronounced.

GRASSHOPPER CAST (*See Fig. 39*)

This cast is a craft exercise used when you wish the fly to alight ahead of the leader and is sometimes used in fighting a head wind to secure a fully extended drive. The action is performed by being more forceful than normally in the back cast and in the forward cast. Toss the line straight up as usual but raise the arm to almost its full extent, spearing the air with your rod tip. As the line in back of you straightens, drop your casting arm straight down just ahead of your starting the forward cast. Push vigorously on the forward thrust. The line in going out should carry a traveling inverted wave. This wave will strike the water, halting the line, causing the leader and fly to be mildly jerked and the fly will then descend to the water where you have directed it.

Another mild form of the grasshopper cast is performed by raising the rod only enough to remove the slack then whip straight down forcefully. This creates a wave in the line which should carry out to the fly itself. It is used more as a minor mend where you wish to jiggle your fly a few inches to the right or left of the path it is traveling.

SPEY CAST

The spey cast is merely a variation of the roll cast in that you actually make two loop casts in order to switch the line into another direction. As the line comes back to you after the first cast, swing your rod across your body in a vertical plane and slash downward to your right. This rolls the line in that direction at an approximate right angle. The same procedure is used to place the line to your left by slashing down to the left on your second roll or loop cast.

CURVE OR HOOK CASTS (*Sometimes called "Shepherd's crook"*)

This cast is not easy and there are few anglers, even those considered expert, who use it regularly because they just don't know how to do it. There are frequent occasions, however, when the curve cast is the difference between no action and a possible positive rise of the fish. Many skilled casters depend solely upon chance that their quarry will not be disturbed, or put down, by the leader preceding the fly over his rising spot. I know of two fishermen in the Middle West who use the curve cast eighty per cent of the time and their "luck" is just short of phenomenal. Both have been fishing and "practicing" this difficult maneuver for many years and rarely, under normal conditions, does the leader and fly fail to act as directed. In fact, it was in observing and studying the action of one of these sportsmen, on the Au Sable River in Michigan, where I learned how, after a fashion, to accomplish the curve cast. It did take many perspiring hours over a summer's fishing before I felt even practically qualified to try to show another how to do it.

I have never seen a plausible description of the curve or hook cast in print whereby an ambitious caster could understand what the writer was getting at. Neither have I ever read or heard of any other system that would consistently work. This is the only one that I know of.

The curve cast to your right, which is described first, is the easier of the two and I would suggest that this be practiced conscientiously until you are satisfied that you're doing it as nearly correct as possible before attempting the hook cast to the left. A longer, lighter leader with a full-hackled bushy fly is suggested in learning and practicing this cast.

You understand, of course, that as your line comes forward on a cast that it is describing a "U" shaped loop. As it approaches completion the "U" gradually, but speedily, is shaped into a "J" upside down (⌠). This is your curve. Now the problem faces us as to how to get this upside down "J" to drop to the water's surface in that position.

You have an objective point in front of you where the line would extend and the fly drop, if your cast were to finish. Now, for practice purposes, extend your cast by shooting out extra line so that the junction of the line and leader reaches that objective point. Your cast will then extend over, by the length of your leader. Strip back about five or six feet of line and hold in your left hand, with your left arm extended to grasp it at about its mid-point. Start false casting and lower your rod to the horizontal position or nearly so, directing your casts at the objective point. For clearer explanation I'm going to ask that you use the clock face system, and the face this time is up, with your rod acting as a moving hand. Your rod, on the false casts, as usual, is working between 10 o'clock and 12 o'clock. Watch this closely now. On your forward cast, as the reversed "J" is formed, which will be as your rod is about to the 10:30 o'clock position, RELEASE THE LINE FROM YOUR LEFT HAND. Continue the movement of the rod in its forward motion to about the 9 o'clock angle. Stop there and point the rod tip toward the "J" so that there is no danger of disturbing what slack exists and no danger of pulling on the line to break the formation on the water. The line, from your rod tip to the fly, is called the "Live" part of your cast. By releasing the dead line from your left hand, the energy or traveling force of the live line is halted immediately. The line will drop to the water in that position. There's no energy left in the line to straighten it out as on the normal cast. The inverted "J" starts floating in your direction, with the current, and the fly precedes the leader, to which it is attached, right over the nose of the wary two-pounder we saw rising there.

If there is a variation of stream current between the line and leader extending from you and the fly floating toward you, the belly of the line and leader will probably travel down and would eventually catch up with the fly and drag it, but there still is an interval of some distance where the line will have no influence on the fly and we get a drag free presentation.

If you are ambidextrous and can cast with your left hand, the formation of the left curve or hook, is just a matter of the same general action. But as few of us are fortunate that way, we'll have to do it the hard way.

The left hook or curve cast, in direct contrast to the right which was an unfinished cast, is a finished cast PLUS. More power on the forward cast, in the left curve, is injected than on a normal cast. Again, for learning and practicing this maneuver, I would suggest a shorter, heavier than usual leader and a fly that will not resist the air to any great extent.

When you halted the transmission of energy or force by releasing line in the right curve cast, you inject added force at about the same point in the left curve cast. The same extension of line, as in the previous action, is held in the left hand. Your rod is traveling in the same horizontal plane as in the right curve cast. You are aiming again at a target point. On the forward cast, which is to be extra forceful, you shoot your excess line through but still retaining a finger hold upon it. Follow it through to the first or stripping guide, on your rod, with the left hand. As the line *almost* completes its run, JERK THE LINE SHARPLY BACKWARD WITH THE LEFT HAND. This causes the fly to swing around to the left, forming your curve, as it drops to the water.

Although a difficult action, I have seen the left curve formed exactly as is done with the right hook by casting across the body with the rod extending to the left. Try it later on.

To possibly further clarify these "curve" actions you might proceed to perform the various moves in the normal upright rod casting position. In the case of the right curve cast procedure, done with the rod in its straight up, overhead operation, you will find that the fly will fall back on the leader. In the left curve cast procedure, the fly will complete its journey to the end of the straightened leader and then dive toward the water.

I must caution you now—do not become discouraged. If you can drop one good curve in your first ten casts you are a natural, yes a miracle caster. In your next fifty casts you should have an occasional success. Keep going, with intermittent rest periods and it won't be long until "occasional" becomes "frequent," then practice and practice only, will develop constant skill in this most difficult casting procedure.

An additional hazard that must be recognized in using curves in fishing is that many times when the fish takes your fly you have a few feet of slack that must be retrieved hastily if you are to hook and get a secure hold on your trout.

Another movement or manipulation to create a curve cast is that of rolling your hand from its normal position, on the forward cast, in a counterclockwise twist so that your thumb, which was on the top, will be on the bottom. Care must be exercised in performing this action that the rod tip continues in the approximate same plane of travel as normally. After quite a bit of practice this movement will do the job fairly well but is difficult to control.

Practically all other craft casts are combinations of those listed. Becoming familiar with them and the necessity of combining various maneuvers will come to you readily as will their successful outcome as you practice the different casting exercises given.

A great advantage in becoming adept in the normal casting movements and familiar with the craft casts is that you may then concentrate on your fishing, your approach and the presentation of your lure, rather than the physical operation of your tackle.

Chapter 5

Trout

Part I: Trout History and Families

NOT THE largest by far or necessarily the most beautiful, or the most edible, is the Salmonidae family of fishes. Regarded generally as piscatorial royalty the grouping includes the whitefish, the lake herring, the cisco, the salmons, the trouts and the chars. Some years ago many writers tied the grayling into the salmonidae picture because of their inhabiting the same waters and being considered a splendid game fish but the grayling, although related fairly closely, is a different family (Thymallus). It is of the trouts and chars with which we are concerned at this moment.

Nearly half a century ago a writer stated sorrowfully that his was the last generation that would relish the enjoyment of angling for the trouts in lakes and streams, and he was almost right in his prophecy had nothing been done about it. Trout hatchings, plantings and some study had been conducted but only as a sideline effort up to about that time. Since, concentrated work in company with scientific endeavor, restricting laws and conservation education has given rebirth to this important facet of trout supply for our recreational needs. In spite of the great number of anglers, which is constantly increasing, the work is pretty much in hand. Experiments and testings to still further improve our knowledge is a major effort of conservation departments of every state. The true wild trout is still with us in a few instances in this country, but his numbers are speedily becoming decimated. Hatchery spawn, when allowed time to become acclimated to their placement, will fast acquire all the traits of the "wild" fish with few of his shortcomings. Authorities declare that over ninety per cent of stream and lake trouts in the United States are hatchery plants and that is about the best ratio that the naturally spawned trout, under present fishing pressures, will ever reach.

The most logical theory as to the probable fount of the North American trout and char families was that they originally came from Asia. Only recently in evolutionary history, perhaps less than 100,000 years ago, these families of fishes migrated restlessly through the tumbling Arctic ice floes into Alaska. They extended their range southward to the Fraser and Columbia, then into the Yellowstone, the Missouri, the Snake, the Arkansas, the Platte, the Colorado and the Rio Grande. Other families reached Hudson Bay, then traveling coastwise southward and into the rivers and lakes of the eastern coast of North America. The theory holds water because we know the trouts and chars are anadromous by nature. Little difficulty is experienced in their shunting from salt water to fresh water and back again when the urge or impulse is upon them and when the salt water is available or open to them.

In traveling their various ways the trout groups became separated from each other. Biologically, isolated creatures have a natural tendency to change, to adapt themselves to fit the environment to which they find a liking. The trout species have proved to be particularly adept in this function. For instance, the rainbow trouts have been classified into seventeen distinct subspecies. The cutthroat trouts are next with fourteen designations. The brook trout (a char) is labeled in nine varieties and his cousin, the dolly varden, carries five scientific names. Those are the totals to date as near as can be determined. Tomorrow, or next year, there may be more.

In the lexicon of biology man is regarded as homo sapiens,

regardless of his color, habitat, personality and general physical characteristics. With the trouts and chars I won't say they've broken the types down so that colors and habitat, etc., is a criterion by which certain of them gets another signifying label, but it's close to that. Over a period of years the same fish, originally springing from the same batch of ova, becoming separated, or isolated, have definitely changed in appearance and in physical traits to fit the new environment, so they get another name. It is known that a planting of brook trout, all from the same hatch, a few months later in different sections of the same stream, had variations of color so pronounced that some looked like a different fish. It is also known that the Piute cutthroat trout has a chameleon-like ability in which he can change his outward complexion to fit the water or the stream bed he is coursing over. This, in a matter of seconds. Ordinarily the scarcity or abundance of food, its quality and type, the temperatures of the water and whether it is completely fresh or somewhat brackish, the sex of the fish, its youth or age, the color of the stream bottom, surroundings and general environment, all have a bearing, over a period of time, on the shape, the shade and placement of his identifying spots, and his basic general coloring.

A physical characteristic that is common to all trout, and to other fish, is the lateral nerve line, or sense radar, running along the side of fish at its approximate center. One often wonders how and why he can shoot through a complex cluster of boulders, logs or other impeding barrier-like forms, or why in thrashing about trying to dislodge a hook, he never bunts or rams into obstructions but seems to slide by without a scrape. The only answer is that this nerve line is the organism that guides the fish's movements and assists him to avoid touches even when traveling like a record breaking jet through the water.

Certain individual species of trout are considered by certain accusers as being of a stronger cannibalistic nature than others. The censure stems from just who is doing the judging and his present footing. The truth is that all trout, when they reach a size where food in quantity is necessary to keep them going, or where there is a lack of aquatic delicacies whatever the size of the fish, will resort to cannibalism as will practically all species of fish.

While it is true that all the trout of any one species cannot be expected to look exactly alike, act alike, eat alike or fight alike, each variety does have characteristics in common with the others which are important to the angler. Those we will cover later but now let's break down the several types of the better known kinds of trout and outline briefly some of their specific features.

BROOK TROUT (*Salvelinus fontinalis*)

If trout can be regarded as aristocratic (and justly they are) this member of the race is the aristocrat of aristocrats. In this country the brook trout is "Native" to the Eastern sea-board states from the Canadian border to and including the Carolinas, west through Michigan, Wisconsin and Minnesota and south to include all states between except those that border the Gulf of Mexico, and east to the Mississippi.

Since about 1880 plantings of brook trout have been made in states west of the Mississippi where suitable waters were available. Although other trout species are greatly in the majority he has caught on and in a few streams and lakes the Brookie is, speaking figuratively, the sole occupant. Michigan, Wisconsin and New York, for example, where the brook trout was once the only habitant of its clear sparkling streams and lakes now finds him strictly in the minority, having been replaced by other species capable of weathering the onslaught of encroaching civilization and its handicaps peculiar to him. The last remaining stand of consequence of his once expansive native domain is the Upper Peninsula of Michigan and the upper New England states, particularly Maine. As lands are cleared and his home waters become warmer his retreat is only to the North, where perhaps for a few generations yet he may fight off complete extinction. With few exceptions, in the interior of Canada, the brookie is still the dominating fish of the trout family.

The brook trout might be termed allergic to waters which

are not completely pure, that lack an abundance of oxygen and are not warmer generally than 65 degrees in temperature. This means that in the more southern states of the area in which he lives he will be found only in the higher altitudes unless the lower streams are amply fed by cold springs to bring the temperature down to his comfort range. He can and will survive in water temperatures upwards to 70 degrees but he doesn't like it.

Although salvelinus fontinalis is not a true trout but is scientifically listed as a char (or charr), which places him a rung above trout, the difference in the form of his vomer, or part of his mouth, and his scale structure is so insignificant that only a heritical scholar would insist on the discrimination between species. This salvelinus family, of which fontinalis is the more prevalent, breaks up into eight other classifications as oquassa, alpinus, marstoni, agassizi, stagnalis, arcturus and naresi. The nicknames by which they are more lovingly known are Eastern Brook, Brookie, Squaretail, Char, Springhole Trout, Red Spotted Trout, Eastern Char, Native, Rangely Trout, Speckled Trout, Mountain Trout, Silver Trout, The Wilderness Fish and there are probably many other local names.

In basic coloring the chars differ from the true trout. The trout invariably carry masses, or a sparse display, of dark spots on the skin in diverse patterns or arrangements. The char's body is covered partially with round spots, which are paler than the general coloration of the fish. This, of course, is in conjunction with other color fixes peculiar to each different type of char.

The brook trout starts spawning at about his second year and does this generaly during the fall months. Reports, however, have him spawning as late as March in some instances. The eggs, nested in cold currents, hatch in from 90 to 200 days later dependent to a great extent upon water temperatures. His growth rate is slower than with other trout species even under the best conditions. This might account for his being outnumbered in most hatcheries. With the older spawners the female lays from 350 to 2,000 eggs which are left to the vagaries of the current and nature to complete the job.

The brook trout is considered the best fighter, from the angler's view, in the trout family. Although there is little surface splashing and exhibitionism he thrashes around in a stubborn but exciting fashion giving the battle everything he's got and that's quite a lot.

Some brookies weigh upwards of a pound at the age of two years while others the same age may not tip the scales at an ounce. The largest brook trout, of record, was caught in 1916. It was taken from the Nipigon River, which empties into the north shore of Lake Superior, in Ontario, Canada. It weighed fourteen and one-half pounds.

SUNAPEE TROUT (*Salvelinus aureolus*)

A close relative of the brook trout, yet a distinct species. First found in Sunapee Lake, New Hampshire. Called the "Eastern Golden." More of a lake type trout than is the regular brook trout.

The Sunapee remains in that area in which it was first noted which includes New Hampshire, Vermont and lower Maine. The Salvelinus marstoni and naresi are considered by many to be closer to the Sunapee type than to the fontinalis, or brookie.

Some years ago an interested scientist regarded the Sunapee trout as an offspring of an imported species and not as a native, but this was never officially considered as a fact to record.

This trout is fished for much as is the lake trout and in many respects it is similar except in its outward appearance. The Sunapee trout is adjudged in the top bracket as a food fish.

DOLLY VARDEN (*Salvelinus malma*)

A relation from the other side of the tracks, to the princely brook trout. Regarded justly, or unjustly, because of its appetite for the eggs of all trout species, as the black sheep of the entire trout clan.

The dolly varden is native to the north western states and

Pacific coast from Northern California to Alaska. In addition to salvelinus malma other subspecies listed are spectabilis, pluvius, stenodus and leucomaenis.

The spawning period of the dolly varden follows closely the same pattern as the brook trout. Not a great deal of effort is expended to assist it in perpetuating its race but its depletion rate is slow in spite of it.

Dolly varden is known as Bull trout, Western char, Red Spotted trout, Silver trout (sea run specimens) and Dollys.

LAKE TROUT (*Salvelinus namaycush; Cristivomer namaycush*)

A quite distant relation in the char group. Resides almost entirely in cold, deep-water lakes. Its appearance is an olive tinged, drab gray or brownish in comparison to its other trout cousins and it sports a sharply forked tail in contrast to the more nearly square tails of most other trout. The lake trout is a bottom feeder and only rarely does it seek food in the shallower shore waters. Not regarded seriously as a game fish, but is in a top bracket for food value. Under some conditions the lake trout will exceed 80 pounds in weight.

It is known as Mackinaw trout, Lake Michigan trout, Togue, Longue or Lunge, Great Lake trout, Namaycush, Gray Salmon, Deepwater char, Forked Tail trout and Lake Salmon among others.

CUTTHROAT TROUT (*Salmo Clarkii*)

The "Native" trout of the great Northwest, the cutthroat is found in every suitable stream and lake on both eastern and western slopes of the Rocky Mountains, north of, and including the northern part of California, Oregon, Montana, Colorado, the Great Basin of Utah, Idaho, Wyoming, Washington and extending through British Columbia and Southwest Alaska to Bristol Bay.

This colorful trout, like the other members of the trout and char families, is classified, or divided, into fourteen groups. Starting with salmo clarkii lewisi we find it named salmo smaragdus, clarkii bouvieri, clarkii utah, clarkii stomias, macdonaldi, jordani, declivifrons, virginalis (Rio Grande), pleuriticus (Colorado), henshawi (Truckee River), regalis (Lake Tahoe), clarkii seleneris (Piute trout) and mykiss (some researchers say that this particular fish should not be in the cutthroat family but should be listed with the Brown trout, salmo trutta tribe). His better known "street" names are Silver trout, Black-spotted trout, Colorado trout, Red-throated trout, Red Throat, Yellow Fin, Spotted trout, Salmon trout, Rocky Mountain Brook trout, Native, True trout, Harvest trout and Bluebacks.

The cutthroat is a spring spawner, particularly on waters that empty directly into salt water. On the inland waters its spawning periods widen from March to early June in different localities. It is not too popular with the hatcheries. The slowest growing trout and one of the most troublesome and worrisome to raise, and plantings have not been too successful.

One strong identification that the family carries is the scarlet slash on the sides of its throat. It is considered second only to the brook trout in beauty of the four main trout species. It ranks low in gameness and fighting ability but above the rainbow and brown in edibility. Considered to be easily caught by general comparison with the other trouts. It is a good "Fly" fish.

BROWN TROUT *(Salmo trutta; Salmo fario)*

The welcome transplant from Europe. Eggs of this trout were sent from Germany by Herr von Behr to Michigan in 1883. Since that time the brown has been introduced to thousands of streams in over forty states.

The brown trout's faculty, or ability, of tolerating the civilized, warmer and dirtier streams which once were cold sparkling flows, has much to do with its increasing popularity inasmuch as it thrives, too, in even heavily-fished waters. Once planted and established in a stream or lake it would be an extremely rare instance that that water would ever lack, at least, a few browns. The brown just doesn't get itself fished out, which could easily be the case with brooks or rainbows.

Some confusion exists with relation to the also imported Loch Leven trout from Scotland and the commonly known brown trout. The argument exists in the fact that the Loch was originally the same race of brown trout and like those brought to this country were received in Scotland also from Germany. Here again the isolation factor is brought up. In Scotland the German brown, over a period of time, lost its red spots and accumulated the black spots. Interbreeding in this country of the two types is speedily eliminating the differences.

The brown trout spawns naturally from August to March, dependent upon temperature and water conditions. Certain observers have stated that they have witnessed brown trout spawning as late as May.

Its stream habits are much like the brook trout but it is a much more active surface feeder. This makes it rate high with the dry fly anglers. Its fighting ability, once hooked, ranks below other trout species—it gives up fairly easily. Its value as food isn't of the second helping quality by any stretch of the imagination.

The record brown trout is a 39½-pounder caught in Scotland in 1866.

RAINBOW TROUT (*Salmo irideus*)—STEELHEAD (*Salmo gairdnerii*)

Voracious and vigorous, the rainbow is considered the top western trout. It will garner a few additional votes from anglers about the Great Lakes where its "Steelhead" runs up the rivers from the lakes and is giving anglers a taste of a new angle to trouting in that area.

Native to the Western Rockies, principally the Sierra Nevadas, the rainbow has been successfully transplanted throughout the country. It is the hatchery pet, the fastest growing trout of all and the least troublesome to bring to planting size. The rainbow is not as hardy as the brown trout but is able to withstand warmer waters than can the brook trout or the cutthroat and is a welcome addition to any "Natives" the numerous trout regions have left. A strong spectacular fighter it jumps and leaps with abandon, with maddening regularity, particularly at the terminus of light sporting tackle. The rainbow loves fast, white water and favors the larger streams but is an eager and satisfying opponent when hooked up in the large cold water lakes.

The rainbow family of trout is divided into seventeen groupings with four distinct varieties. They are salmo irideus (the trout so widely distributed and the best known), salmo shasta (a variation of irideus yet definitely another branch), salmo gairdnerii (the steelhead or sea-run rainbow), and salmo roosevelti, aguabonita and whitei (the scientific names for the well-known and beautiful golden trout). Then follows salmo kamloops, stonei, gilberti (Kern River rainbow), rosei, crescentis, beardsleei, bathycaeto, declivifrous, evermanni (the dwarf), rivularis and nelsoni.

The steelhead is the regular migratory sea-run rainbow. Fresh from the salt water it is sharply silvery with hardly a trace of the lavender pink side stripe, which is the main feature of the rainbow family. The stripe, however, becomes constantly more visible as the steelhead travels up stream to spawn. It is found in all coastal, all year, streams from Northern California to Alaska. Only in recent years has its range been forced northward in California. The trickles that once were forceful rainy season rivers from Santa Monica north saw the annual steelhead run and only in rare instances now are these fighting fish caught in the infrequently formed estuaries.

The golden trout is comfortable only in real cold water, high altitude streams and lakes. It was first discovered in Volcano Creek (now Golden Trout Creek) near Mount Whitney in the Sierra Nevadas. The golden has taken well to hatchery transfers when planted in waters suitable to its taste and fancy. Rarely is it found in streams or lakes lower than 8000 feet in altitude. The golden is one of the most beautiful and picturesque of all trout and much the finest of the rainbow clan.

Many years ago the rainbow was regarded as an early spring spawner but civilization, I suppose, has affected these habits. Its spawning period now encompasses the whole year with the exception only of late summer and early fall. Perhaps in a few more of its generations it will bridge that gap too.

Lake Pend Oreille, in Idaho, has produced, at this writing the largest rainbow caught with hook and line. It weighed 37 pounds. Residents in that locality state that there are larger ones in this beautiful lake ready and waiting to be matched with an ambitious sporting angler.

Part II: Modern Hatchery Procedure

"Oh, so that's a trout hatchery! Nothing tough about raising fish is there? Get some eggs, let 'em hatch into minnows, give 'em all the truck they'll eat so they'll grow big and fat, then they cart 'em out to a stream, dump 'em and we catch 'em. What's so all-fired complicated about it?"

The author is sure he didn't hear you say that. In fact I cannot believe that any fisherman, anywhere, would be that naive. Many of us have visited trout hatcheries and, sure, we've been interested in observing the surface operations that might have been going on. We got a kick out of watching the gregarious little fellows in their troughs and channels. It was amusing to see the baby seven- and eight-inchers, and our fishing temperature jumped a few notches watching the twelve- and fourteen-inchers cavorting in their pond. But how many of us were curious about the internal background of these activities, the gears and the workings that makes what we see tick? Well, how about watching an egg come to life and following it through some of the intricate paths or channels it travels before it is introduced into the waters that we fish?

As we approach our first observation station allow me to state that this little trip will, of necessity, be as brief as we can make it. Some of the points will be broadly covered but we'll attempt to divulge most of the ground which should be of interest to us, as lay anglers. The possible "meat" of this digest, if brought out in its most complete and encompassing form, would require not one book but volumes and, although important, would be of vital concern only to those directly immersed in the activities and the workings of the trout culturists, the force we depend upon to keep our streams "alive."

Watch that worker so carefully strip the eggs from that female trout. Every precaution is taken to avoid any possible injury to the fish or to the eggs in the fish. He is wearing protective gloves and you will note the basin in which the eggs are being placed contains no water, it has been dampened only. When the eggs from three or four female or hen fish are in the container, the milt or sperm of the male or cock fish, which is similarly stripped, is placed with the eggs and stirred enough to secure coverage contact with every egg. This complete procedure must be accomplished in the matter of a very few minutes. Should there be any of the eggs broken in the transfer from the fish to the keg, in which they are placed, the batch will be reduced in the possible number that will be made fertile. It seems that the liquid content of the eggs spreads itself about covering the micropyle of many whole eggs and this prevents the entrance of spermatozoon to those eggs and they remain infertile. The stripper does not attempt to get the very last eggs from the female because this action is a contributing factor toward breaking the skin of the egg or of injury to the brood fish.

Immediately following the fertilization of the eggs they are washed carefully and placed in their receptacles where a current of clean water constantly flows over them, as it would in nature. They are closely watched from this point on until the "bumping" period which ranges from sixteen to twenty days away.

While we're waiting for this time to pass we might go back and explain briefly another progressive action that is beginning to be used in the egg stripping process. Many hatcheries are using anesthetics, where advisable, on the female trout before the eggs are taken from her. Incidentally, the same procedure is followed in many cases now, when trout are being fin clipped or tagged for identification. The trout are immersed in a solution of urethan for two or three minutes which puts them in a quiet, relaxed state. In the tagging process, following the operation, they also place the fish into another bath, a malachite green mixture, for a moment, and they are then returned to their regular water. We are told that the anesthetizing of fish is now being done by some hatcheries before they are plant dropped from planes into inaccessible lakes and water areas. The anesthetic is non-toxic and all experiments indicate that the fish are not harmed in the least.

In shipping fertilized eggs from one point to another they are transported in fifteen gallon containers, called "kegs," and generally are in batches of around 100,000 to 150,000. Water covers the eggs to a depth of six to ten inches and is changed regularly—as often as each hour.

Let's now observe the "bumping" of the eggs. In this process they are siphoned off from one container to another and as they pass through a short length of hose each egg strikes or bumps the finger of the individual conducting the operation. The fall of the egg is little more than an inch or so, they're quite delicate and it does not take much abuse to damage them.

About an hour after the bump the infertile eggs turn white and the batch, or "stack," of eggs is placed on a screening tray and cleaned of these infertiles.

Temperature is the important ingredient that determines the incubation interval of the egg. An old saw used to say, "Fifty days at fifty degrees." This, of course, isn't always correct but it does approximate the time. When the stack does start hatching it may cover a period of days before the process is complete.

There follows several days, after the hatch, in which the tiny new trout does not eat. The egg, of which the fish is a part, is still attached to his underside and his sustenance comes from this. In salmon trouts, the little fish is known as an alevin at this point.

When the fry or tiny trout, now with the egg completely absorbed, is ready to take food, and while learning to eat, he is fed a fine fish meal first, then finely ground beef liver or heart. As he increases in size to the fingerling stage the trout is gradually given other foods in addition to the liver and beef diets. During this early growth the feeding periods range from hourly down to scheduled dinner hours, still several times a day. This will finally terminate into one daily feeding when the trout reaches about the eight-inch stage.

Fish diets are under constant study. So many factors

enter the picture during the growth period that experiments
are being conducted unceasingly toward improvements. There
is, first, the initial cost to consider, then the compositions of
foods best fitted for the growing fish. Preparation procedures,
availability of the ingredients, the storage problem, the feed-
ability of the compositions, the quantity required and the
waste angle, among others, must all be analyzed. In the
composition of the foods, experiments are rigidly conducted to
determine nutritive value, palatability, adhesive quality of the
combined foods, the moisture content and even sizes of the
particles have to be determined according to the size-classes
of the fish being fed. Food that fits the fish, in the above
properties, results in faster growth and a lower mortality.

The feeding processes themselves are of major importance.
They must not be done hurriedly. The food must be so broken
up and apportioned throughout the area of the container or
pond that the weaker and smaller fish, in each class, is given
its chance to eat. Competition among these little savages is
great and can result in injury, disease and retarded growth.
Care must be exercised to avoid overfeeding as this could
very well terminate in a condition that would be extremely
unsanitary.

The foods themselves, in varying proportions, at this writing, consist primarily of meats, which are usually livers, hearts
and spleens from beef, pork and sheep, salt meats, fish meal,
fresh fish (carp, sea herring, whitefish, menhaden and others),
dried buttermilk and fresh milk, bran, oatmeal, cottonseed
meal, wheat flour middlings, cod liver oil, etc. New items will
be tried, found suitable and used tomorrow and next year. The
exacting ratios of these ingredients, to make up the menu for
the different sizes and classes of trout, is a technical, complicated probe and our hatchery is the laboratory.

During the feeding process careful observations are made
checking for odd or abnormal behavior which could indicate
the onset of disease or other conditions not desired.

During the growth of the various divisions of the trout there
is activity in thinning out the numbers, grading them and
removing individual fish for sampling and laboratory study.

This practice has been found to lessen the frequency of disease, the reducing of cannibalism and, of importance to a busy hatchery, the satisfying result of more rapid growth and a high percentage decrease in runty and poor quality fishes. This grading and thinning begins at about the two- to three-inch length stage of our trout.

Another big and significant activity, that is religiously performed by the modern hatchery, is the judicious, selective breeding of the trout. The objective, initially, is for improvement of the fish crop produced. The factors that are desired are those possessed by the wild trout, in many instances, and a plus not held, particularly, by those stream born fish. What is most desired of the trout, which will be planted in our fishing waters, is first, the ability to forage for himself, find his own food, to have a resistance to parasites and fish diseases, a vigorous "aliveness," ability to reproduce the species in the natural environment, to be fast growing, have good color and top physical and symmetrical characteristics. The speedy growth and disease resistant traits are those most sought from the hatchery procedure angle. The foraging ability and aliveness are best from the survival standpoint and every one of the attributes is desired by ourselves, as fishermen.

We will presume, now, that our trout has reached the required size mark and is scheduled for depositing in some stream or lake. The hatchery discontinued the feeding, of this batch, for from twenty-four to forty-eight hours prior to the time that the trout will be taken from his pond. They have been counted, graded and weighed some time before this transfer. The fish are netted and shifted to the tank, or cans, that have been prepared. If by truck, they are started on their way at once. Reaching the plant point, temperature of the water is or should be taken where the fish are to go. If too much difference is noted, water from the receiving site is gradually put in the containers until the carrying water agrees with that in which the trout are to be placed and the plant is made.

One of the major problems confronting the hatchery is that of diseases, fungus and parasites afflicting their fish stock. In many cases, with even as low a creature as the fish, many of the diseases, to which they are subject, have a similarity to the afflictions of man. Look at these: anemia, ulcers, cirrhosis of the liver, kidney diseases, gastric and gas disorders and dropsy. Besides that catalog the trout have to contend with fungus, worms, internal and external parasites, furunculosis, gill diseases, fin rot, trichodina and a form of virus diseases. Can you realize now the care that must be exercised in the sterilization of troughs, tanks and ponds and the cleanliness that has to be observed at every turn? Improper diet can cause some disruption but many of the ills are of a contagious nature and every precaution is taken against the spread should there be a break out of one. Disinfection must follow wherever there has been even minor cases of virus attacks or communicable maladies of any sort.

There are hatchery operatives who are skilled in diagnosis of the above diseases and from that determination can prescribe medicines and chemicals to counteract or cure. For instance, they know that glacial acetic acid, and formalin, will attack parasites, that malachite green is a remedy for fungus on both fish and eggs, that common salt is good for external infections. In addition to those chemicals they use calomel, merthiolate and sulfo-merthiolate, terramycin and much study is being made on the uses of other antibiotics in the treatment of fish disorders.

The hatchery also must constantly fight many other enemies of their precious babies. Birds, mammals, reptiles, certain insects, even vegetation is a problem. In their ponds they battle the submerged plant growth, also the emergent vegetation from water cress to cattails. They know that drying and working a pond helps much in the control of aquatic vegetation, that cutting of emergents below the water surface, plus a natural, or forced, bloom is effective in control. They know that poisons, traps and shotguns are necessary implements for eradication. They know that silt can be controlled or the condition improved by the application of hay, grass or manure directly on the water. Insects, such as water boatmen, back swimmers, dragonfly nymphs and diving beetles are a troublesome plague that needs be fought in every reasonable way.

The water used in the hatchery must be periodically checked. If too acid or too alkaline, measures to correct the condition have to be taken. The rearing ponds vary, naturally, in each location, so the temperatures of the water, its degree of pollution, whether the volume is constant or not in going through, whether the water has the quality whereby it can be re-used, all must be checked. The grade and kind of fertilizer, if necessary, and the type that will best fit the water to accomplish growth, in some instances, and the retarding of growths of both vegetation and aquatic life, in other instances, are details that must be considered and experiments executed to develop the right answers.

These men of our hatcheries know that there is a definite limit to the amount of trout stock, in the various sizes, that can be safely nurtured in their individual ponds or pools. Overcrowding results, just as it does in nature, in a reduced growth rate, severe rises in mortality and a generally inferior appearance and condition of the fish. For example, their data tells them that with trout, greater than seven or eight inches in length, they cannot give residence to more than a pound of fish per cubic foot of water, as a minimum.

The records that must be maintained, for and in each hatchery is a voluminous job. Statistics on production, on losses of the fish crop in every stage, the data on brood fish, detailed reports on growth of the trout and the rate, memoranda on foods and dietary supplements, complete and informative records on diseases, all must be kept. Then comes the cost accounting, which is so important, in every phase of each operation.

I hope I've given you a glance at the picture of what goes on at our modern trout hatchery. I know, in learning of this work, I regret that I have not appreciated the efforts of this helpful branch of our government as much as I should have. I sincerely hope my reader will vision it in that frame of mind, too. Maybe, those of us who are, won't be quite so critical.

Not unlike a normal classroom of students, some states are far ahead of others, technically and practically, in hatchery operation and procedure. Some, unfortunately, are dragging their feet almost lamentably. It would give me a lot of selfish, personal satisfaction were I to name some of them in both these ranges, but because these present conditions could reverse, could change tomorrow, or next month, or next year, either way, it might be embarrassing, so we'll forego that disclosure in the optimistic hope that all changes, which are inevitable, will be improvement.

Part III: Ways of a Trout

Never underestimate the instincts (or intelligence) of a wild trout. It can completely upset the studied theories of the most experienced of us. Without conscience, the trout is capricious, fickle, inconstant, fitful, crotchety, fanciful, eccentric, whimsical, variable, irritating, frustrating and as changeable as the mind of our loved ones, the feminine gender. He does the unexpected under normal conditions and sometimes the expected when we least expect it.

The innate impulse of the trout is first of all self-preservation. He wants food, yes, and although there are definite periods throughout the day when he is much more active in feeding than in others he will eat most any time *providing he feels safe while so doing.*

One must consider that every second of a trout's existence, from the time the egg is first ejected from the female until his last gasp, he is surrounded by enemies, natural and otherwise. Animals, birds and snakes prey upon him and to his larger comrades, even members of his own family, he is a tasty main course. To him, strange or moving shadows are sirens screaming a warning. Unnatural noises that vibrate to him are forewarnings of possible doom. Alien conditions of the water, unusual light circumstances—all are predictions of a potential liability to his comfort or being. And I haven't mentioned man, his most formidable antagonist.

Do you wonder why *fear,* in its widest sense, is the strongest intuitive force possessed by the trout? His life is figuratively crowded with signs reading "Beware," "Caution," "Look-out." His memory is all but non-existent, however his alarm system is as sensitive as a razor's edge.

"He was playing with my fly," sagely stated an angler. "He'd dive over it, maybe bunt it with his nose and then try to flick it with his tail. Probably wasn't hungry."

There are sound natural reasons for the fish acting as he did *and he wasn't playing*. Life is too serious an affair for him to waste his limited energy frolicking. As for not being hungry, I've observed fish that were so gorged with food that they couldn't take another morsel, then they proceeded to greedily take that morsel and look for more. Why the trout acted as he did is anyone's guess. We can advance suppositions and we can theorize but we're not sure and won't be until we can think like the fish or be infused with like instincts.

Most anglers, in their saner moments, are more intelligent normally than trout, and using that intelligence in a rational manner, many times, they can fool the fish into believing that the lure offered is edible and free from harmful after effects. The tid-bit trespassing the trout's domain becomes prey and there being no discernible circumstances to arouse his suspicion, and too much energy will not have to be expended, he proceeds to appease his constant craving for food.

Natural conditions of the stream such as wading animals rarely concern the trout. Nature's elements such as storms, lightning, thunder, hail and snow not only are of little consequence but generally trout are more active then, from the fisherman's viewpoint, than during other less turbulent periods. When an angler expresses an opinion that is contrary to the above it is probably occasioned, not from experimental findings, but from his personal discomfort and his desire to get under something.

Temperature of the water, I believe, has much to do with the trout's activity as it concerns the fisherman. Too cold or too warm reacts on fish just as on animals and man. The main four trout species vary, too, in their comfort requirements. The brook trout's comfort range is when the water is between 50 and 65 degrees; the rainbow and cutthroat feel better at temperatures between 55 and 70 degrees; the brown or loch likes water between 60 and 75 degrees. When the water is colder than 40 degrees trout appear sluggish and somewhat inactive. Fishing the shallows and riffles then, where the sun has had a chance to warm it a bit, is generally more resultful for the angler.

The temperature of the water as it relates to fishing types of flies, too, has a bearing on the fisherman's success or failure. In water temperatures between 33 and 45 degrees bait is the accepted and logical lure. Between 40 and 55 degrees the regular wet flies, streamers and nymphs work more successfully. The dry fly temperatures are best between 50 and 70 degrees. If it is your desire, in fishing, do not be reluctant to fish any type fly you choose regardless of water temperature. I have caught trout and have seen others take trout on dry flies when water temperatures were around 35 to 40 degrees, but these instances are really rare.

Trout are extremely sensitive to temperature changes in the water. A drop, for example, for any reason, as during or after a fall of rain, and usually all kinds of lures will be taken in a certain and deliberate manner. It was at such times, I am certain, that many fly patterns, born in the mind of the tyro fisherman and fly tier, were used with marked success and new "Specials" arrive to clutter up the scenery. But fortunately, or unfortunately, whichever way you see it, trout at these times will actually hit a hook with just a piece of yarn knotted to it—even a bare hook has been known to work. Small twigs, a cigarette butt, a piece of orange peel—everything in the trout's feeding range is tried and tasted before being expelled. (Many times, during these flush feeding periods, the novice fisherman himself grasps at the conclusion that he's quite a genius as a fly angler. What an awakening is in store for him come the next day.)

Generally trout, if feeding, have a one track mind—they relish one course at a time. When nymph feeding they indulge until somewhat gorged (providing food is ample) then take to the fly on the surface. Expecting trout to come to your floating fly when they're concentrating on underwater feeding is the equivalent of you eating a meal and taking a forkful of meat in one mouthful then a forkful of pie a la mode. You may do it but it isn't common practice. Trout, in feeding, seem to feed in unison the length of the stream then, as if on signal, they switch at almost the same instant to another diet or quit entirely for a time.

There has been much written of late years with relation to the angler's personal odor—that fish downstream can discern the presence of a human who has immersed his hands in the water and the trout react accordingly. Honestly I have not yet thoroughly tested out this observation but I am going to and I invite the reader to do the same then we'll both know for ourselves. Although I've never tried any of the liquid "fish lures" that are supposed to act magnetically in attracting the fish to your hardware lure, bait or fly when treated with the concoction, I've had a theory which I'm going to experiment with at a suitable opportunity. That is, that the oils and unguents or what have you which are offered us with attractive promises to catch more fish are merely descenters of the human odor. I could be as wrong as rain at a picnic but there might be something to it. I certainly cannot feel that some artificial additives, such as these preparations, are at all sporting except as desperation measures if they do what they say; but if they are merely eliminators of deterrent that might be on our fingers I say use them. Let's find out.

Rainbow trout and brook trout are more prone to venture out in the open water on bright days than are the browns or the cutthroats. Browns, for example, like to have the ready protection of a bank, a rock, a log, weed clump or an over-hanging bush. The brown, too, is no one's fool. He's as suspicious as a federal tax collector, as scary as a sentinal crow and as temperamental as a successful fishing guide. When the brown trout quits biting he really quits.

Rainbows like to locate in the current ahead of rocks or obstructions. Browns and Cutthroat are found on the down-stream area of obstructions and Brooks are likely to be found in either location.

Sizable trout will put up just so long in a pocket or hole that is unceasingly fished over and leave it to locate in a more private spot where their siestas will not be interrupted so frequently.

Another practice, in trout characteristics, is the reality in which a good spot, usually under tree roots or overhung bank, will hold a good fish month after month, sometimes year after year. When one resident is removed or leaves another replaces him within hours. Usually they are excellent channels that wash food right to their chin.

I have kept, for many years, a consensus record on some of the much discussed qualities of the various trouts as expounded by writers in both books and magazine articles. It is just one of those things that neither you or I can argue with. I don't say that I concur entirely with what the record discloses, neither perhaps will you, but here it is for what it is worth:

QUALITY RATING CONSENSUS ON FOUR PRINCIPAL TROUT SPECIES

	EDIBILITY	FIGHT	BEAUTY	EASE IN TAKING	ADAPTA-BILITY TO CIVILIZED WATERS	DRY FLY	SUNKEN FLY
1.	BROOK	BROOK	BROOK	RAINBOW	BROWN	BROWN	RAINBOW
2.	CUTTHROAT	RAINBOW	CUTTHROAT	CUTTHROAT	RAINBOW	RAINBOW	CUTTHROAT
3.	RAINBOW	BROWN	RAINBOW	BROOK	CUTTHROAT	CUTTHROAT	BROOK
4.	BROWN	CUTTHROAT	BROWN	BROWN	BROOK	BROOK	BROWN

The golden trout is similar to the rainbow in practically all characteristics. The dolly varden trout compares with the brook trout in most characteristics except much lower in scale. Under the heading of "Fight," this primarily covered stubborn resistance, strength and time required to bring to net. It did not regard the spectacular, in which the brookie and the rainbow would reverse positions on the chart. There will be arguments and contradictions on the ratings shown but the anglers who really should know from experience and test have rendered the verdict. For information purposes only, the fish regarded pretty generally as all tops in fight and spectacular exhibitionism is the landlocked salmon, "Ouananiche," followed by the grilse salmon, then the brook trout. In fourth place (hang on to your hat) is the bluegill, ahead of the rainbow and the steelhead (weights comparative, of course). For those of you who love bass fishing it might be noted that the smallmouth bass comes in immediately after the rainbow rating. The colder the water, in all instances, the more difficulty in subduing those leaders in their frantic efforts to escape. The brown trout and the cutthroat are prone to become discouraged and turn belly up much more readily.

The dolly varden was, and is, regarded by many as a destructive, not wanted fish. In fact it was considered a mark of distinction to take them from their waters and destroy them. This "bad character" term was given the dolly because of his custom of following breeding trout of other species and dining on their eggs. I'm in no wise defending the fish but I wonder why our highly regarded steelhead is not so characterized. In fact there are few trout that will refuse the fish eggs, even those of their cousins and sisters.

The prime lesson in this brief discourse on some of the trout ways and characteristics is that, under all normal conditions, they can be interested and caught if neither the fisherman or his terminal tackle or his presentation or some other unpredictable detail arouses the persistent, always present fear sense possessed by the trout and motivated so easily.

Some fish are brighter than a lot of fishermen! These are the smarties that you and I should strive to outwit because, during the course of the endeavor, many, many more gullible trout will find your creel, and well browned on a platter, no one can tell the difference.

Chapter 6

"On The Stream"

READING THE STREAM

ONE CAN state solemnly that in order to get the most from fishing you should know how to read the stream. This is a thoroughly complexing subject and in which many experienced fishermen (and fishermen writers) have hardly reached "C" in the alphabet. One who knows can take you in hand and travel a piece of water. He can point out exactly where he would stand and where he would place his fly and tell you why. Then you start out on your own and you'll hardly find the identical situations in months of effort. Everything looks different.

But you'll fish a spot that, to you, appears likely and you may have guessed right and had some action. If you did, and are wise, will you pause and try to determine why? What was there about that setting that made it good? Why did that trout pick that particular location . . . was it a good hiding site . . . was it near a choice food channel? Then again you may have failed in developing action. Will you ask yourself the same type questions, providing you feel that your presentation was satisfactory? That, my friend, is the schooling required provided, in your excitement or disgust, you remembered to file it away for a later recall.

True, there are certain pockets, certain descriptions of locations, certain type pools or stream edge hiding spots that can be outlined in a generally broad way, but no one can say do this and do that and you are immediately a discerning angler that can guess correctly more often than not. Beyond those more or less general situations, which will be described, you will be your own mentor. All other conditions being acceptable the harder you work at it, the more you puzzle it out, the better stream reader you will be. You will examine the flow of the current and determine the cause, in each instance, so that you can glance at the surface of running water and the "blocks" that divert it and at distances can presume fairly accurately what goes on underneath. There is a reason, directly within your vision, as to why these currents act as they do. No two streams or segments of one stream are alike, yet the water travels in identical patterns regardless of its location, whether through fast runs, at turns in the stream, over rocks, over weed growths, through slow deep pools, through whirling eddies or sluggish back waters and any other physical manifestations or conditions existing in that particular water. You will analyze and study the current channels through which the trout's food travels whether it be immediately underneath the surface, near the bottom, the middle or on top of the water. Numerous objects and particles are being carried by the moving flow in even the cleanest of waters. You will develop the ability to judge about where you should stand or kneel to exact the best or most productive float of your dry fly, your nymph, streamer, wet fly, spinner or angleworm.

So many varying conditions are possible on a certain outlined point that lengthy chapters could be written on one alone, and every spot is different. There is the water depth, whether the stream is high or low, whether it's clear or discolored, the season and the temperature of the water, whether the day is cloudy or bright and to what degree, the location of the sun as applied to your approach, the time of day and how it might affect your result, the type of fly or lure most appropriate and how best it can be presented. Can you see now what I mean when I say no one could possibly advance definite instructions to cover even a day on your pet river or lake? If they could, and would, your life would be wrapped up in reading the voluminous descriptions and you wouldn't have time to apply the teaching and do a bit of fishing anyway.

Throughout this book I've urged "observation"—that's the answer and only you can do the observing.

Now that I've told you why it cannot be done I'll reverse myself a bit and endeavor to briefly coach you on the basic situations so that you'll have a smattering or a beginning from which to start your own study.

First, remember what we've said about the fish. Their most important instinct is for safety (they'll leave their food source instantly if alarmed and their desire for comfort means little when the tiny mental bell tinkles danger.) So the hiding place or the locality where they're likely to be is screened to some degree. Secondly, it must usually be a place near the dining room or the food channel, and next comes his comfort which means about the same to him as to us . . . not too warm and having ample oxygen which is tied up with cooler quarters. That means, likely, shade. Bright light isn't desirable—he doesn't like it, perhaps because he feels too exposed and when on rare occasions you will see trout resting in the shallows, apparently sunning themselves, they'll scamper at the least provocation. Just the shadow of a falling leaf near them and away they go which indicates that they too have nerves. So our first guess is that we'll find him in a sheltered location. This could mean under any type of object projecting over the water. Overhanging bushes or shrubbery is a location often chosen because food morsels, young flies, bugs, spiders, worms, etc., many times lose their footing and drop on his table which amounts to an extra bonus not usually found in other residing places. Tree trunks extending from the land out over the water, if close enough to the surface, or partially submerged, affords an excellent hangout. If he chooses to hide himself in the water weeds it pretty generally is near an open channel where he can glimpse his luncheon tid-bits floating by, and those same weeds often supply him with tasty nymph and scud appetizers, secured with small effort, if he sees them. Rocks, large enough to permit a retreat under cover, is an apt site in which to find trout. The rocks break the current which forms into slicks and eddys where he finds it easier to hold his position and the food is carried by the current close enough so that he can dart out, grab it and get back hardly before he's been spotted by a real or imaginary enemy.

Where the stream narrows and the water flows through this neck, more or less unobstructed and as it again widens out and slows up one will usually find eddys forming at either or both sides. This is water softened of its force and a comfortable lie for the fish. From here they can see food traveling by, not difficult to secure and just a short, sharp movement back to the eddy.

The head and tail areas of stream pools are also good feeding spots if deep enough for protective cover or nearby to a protected sanctuary. Runs between white water, too, are favored locations from which many sizable trout are taken regularly if the lure is deceptive enough to allay suspicion.

At the bank edge, even in water only a few inches deep, when protected with overhanging grasses, reeds, etc., is an excellent possibility if the stream is not traveled too much by fishermen. Activity will scare the trout from this kind of cover because it is just "too close for comfort."

Edges of shelf formations in the stream where the depth of the water drops sharply from shallow to reasonably deep is a good course in which to present streamers and wet flies.

Just below spring outlets or feeder stream mouths, during the warmer weather, even if somewhat exposed, is always a good bet. Low water, warmed by the sun, is just a mite shy of the oxygen content demanded by trout, Brookies particularly, and as these cooler waters entering the main stream contain more of it that's where he'll be taking it in. In high water or during rainfalls don't hesitate to work these little feeder streams, if permissible, for a few yards. It's surprising where good trout will go sometimes for a snack of victuals coming at them in quantities.

Log or rock obstructions which form a dam of a sort as a pickup of nature's trash or a semi-holdback of the current usually have developed a more or less deep hole under or at the sides of the block. These are always good depths for all kinds of lures.

I've purposely held off mentioning what, to my mind, is the most productive location on any stream. It is my choice type of fish hideout and from which I've successfully lured many a sizable trout. This is the undercut bank. That kind of spot is not too difficult to work with all types of flies and lures. It is an ideal spot to "dap" with a dry fly which is fun and easy to do, and it gets results, if care is taken on the approach. These darkened areas seem always to contain trout when other locations are apparently displaying "vacant" signs. When fish are working only slightly, for every one feeding in the stream body proper three or four will be seen dimpling at the edge of undercuts. Being fully covered by a protective mass, completely out of the light yet able to see or feel any activity in the lighted area nearby and above, he considers himself safer than usual. Feeling that way he tends perhaps to take more chances with visible food floating by in or on the water that he is able to see.

There are numberless more minor areas which you will discover in your study of the stream. There are many variations of those major locations mentioned which may puzzle you for a time but a definite desire to learn, to want to be able to decipher the signs into personal stream knowledge, and you're well over the hump towards becoming a stream "reader."

As this knowledge becomes a part of your fishing you can go ahead and use your imagination. Put yourself in the trout's place. Just where would you be in the stream if you were hungry yet scared half stiff of a galaxy of "boogies?" Present your fly to the trout in that location and presto a fish on your line. (Sometimes it is just that easy.)

In Fig. 40 you are supplied with a bird's eye view illustration of a fictitious stream wherein is outlined some of the more general spots or sections of the water which usually are good producing areas, other conditions being satisfactory.

GENERALITIES IN FISHING TROUT

"There is no single BEST way of taking trout!"

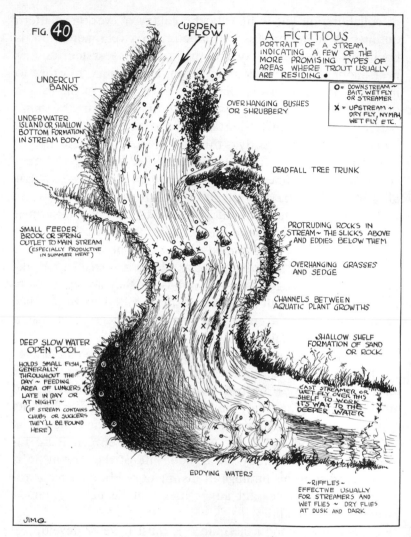

FIG. 40

CURRENT FLOW

A FICTITIOUS PORTRAIT OF A STREAM, INDICATING A FEW OF THE MORE PROMISING TYPES OF AREAS WHERE TROUT USUALLY ARE RESIDING •

O = DOWNSTREAM ~ BAIT, WET FLY OR STREAMER

X = UPSTREAM ~ DRY FLY, NYMPH, WET FLY ETC.

UNDERCUT BANKS

UNDERWATER ISLAND OR SHALLOW BOTTOM FORMATION IN STREAM BODY

OVERHANGING BUSHES OR SHRUBBERY

DEADFALL TREE TRUNK

SMALL FEEDER BROOK OR SPRING OUTLET TO MAIN STREAM (ESPECIALLY PRODUCTIVE IN SUMMER HEAT)

PROTRUDING ROCKS IN STREAM ~ THE SLICKS ABOVE AND EDDIES BELOW THEM

OVERHANGING GRASSES AND SEDGE

CHANNELS BETWEEN AQUATIC PLANT GROWTHS

DEEP SLOW WATER OPEN POOL

HOLDS SMALL FISH, GENERALLY THROUGHOUT THE DAY ~ FEEDING AREA OF LUNKERS LATE IN DAY OR AT NIGHT ~ (IF STREAM CONTAINS CHUBS OR SUCKERS THEY'LL BE FOUND HERE)

SHALLOW SHELF FORMATION OF SAND OR ROCK

CAST STREAMER OR WET FLY OVER THIS SHELF TO WORK ITS WAY TO THE DEEPER WATER

EDDYING WATERS

~RIFFLES~ EFFECTIVE USUALLY FOR STREAMERS AND WET FLIES ~ DRY FLIES AT DUSK AND DARK

JIM Q.

The author wishes, in telling you "HOW," that he could present you with a formula or prescription that would outline definite "one," "two," "three" steps upon which you could depend and that would result in a "never fail" action. Unfortunately, however, very few of the trouts do much reading and they are not versed in any expounded truisms of mine, or that of any other writer—thus, being uncooperative by nature, they can be depended upon to be obstinately independent.

True, on rare occasions, they will follow a general pattern

of collaboration but ordinarily the galaxy of working pattern outlines is more or less unlimited and experimentation is bound to be necessary to find that producing system or one near enough to warrant continuation, at the time, in order to net a few victims. This applies more particularly in the fishing of wet flies, streamers and nymphs. In dry fly fishing "working patterns" are extremely limited. You are either fishing a dry fly correctly or incorrectly—this will be covered later.

I trust the reader has seriously studied the basic casting procedures as outlined in a previous chapter. I must say that all good casters are not all good fishermen (there are other necessary requirements), but all consistently good fishermen are generally pretty good casters. I used the word "generally" because I have seen quite mediocre casters produce day after day but we find they always have either an excellent background of knowledge of the fish habits, or they are completely familiar with the water they are fishing. Good casting, other requirements being average, is a completely necessary first step to good fishing results.

When the student fisherman is confident that he can deliver his fly in the area for which he is aiming, and in any style or fashion he chooses, he can then devote his faculties to the investigation of the trout, the vagaries of the stream's flow, its hidden nooks, its shadowy undercuts, its mysterious pools, its sunny riffles and its moods. While resting between these investigations he can study the aquatic life of the stream he is fishing and store his findings in his memory library which will open avenues of pleasant adventures that he never dreamed would become realities.

To become a good fisherman one must have or develop:

1—PERSISTENCE
2—PATIENCE
3—OPTIMISM
4—AN INSATIABLE CURIOSITY
5—THE HABIT OF OBSERVATION
6—A WILLINGNESS TO EXPERIMENT

These qualities are possessed by each of us in a minor or a

major degree (without them we wouldn't have the desire to fish) and those in which we are weaker we must deliberately cultivate. If any one of the points is most important I wouldn't know which one it is. Each, too, must be tempered by reason and judgment—one could easily go overboard with any of the "six." For example, "Persistence" does not mean stubbornness. An excess of "Optimism" could become exceedingly boring, not only to those around you, but to yourself also. "Willingness to Experiment" doesn't mean that you make a cast without visible success then change your fly or the length of your leader immediately.

Now may I cover an ingredient that is commendable in many activities but in trout fishing it becomes a glaring negative. That is the quality of competitiveness. If you are obsessed with it, shed it by all means while you're fishing and it isn't so difficult if you want to. Hurrying to be first in line, hurrying for fear someone else might pass or precede you, hurrying to be first at the "Log Jam Pool" where you saw the big square tail yesterday—you are outwitting yourself and deliberately passing up really major opportunities to add to your fishing skill which in turn means added pleasure. You have no opportunity to observe any of the cardinal rules to make of yourself a better fisherman.

Working your hardest to catch the most trout or the largest trout, so that you can strut in camp that evening, not only is lacking in sportsmanship, but it doesn't endear you one particle more to your fishing pals—it merely increases the distaste they're building up for you.

Believe me when I tell you that following the six rules of a good fisherman will not only result in greater success on the stream but it will salve that ulcer of pressing competitiveness and give you returns in pleasurable fishing that you didn't believe were in the sport.

If a pursuit is too easy we get little kick from it. This truism is applicable to fishing, in particular. If you can take a single fish where the victory is gained under circumstances that are tough—where the obstacles, or conditions, present a real problem—where you are certain that most anglers wouldn't have attempted the objective, then you acquire a strong degree of gratification that can be gained no other way. The desire or urge to perform a formidable, ticklish task, in your fishing, as a challenge to yourself just because it is that kind of a handicap is an authentic sign of sportsmanship.

I firmly believe that trout can be taken on either flies or nymphs AT ANY TIME. At periods the trout's selectivity rises to the nth degree and it requires an ingenious skill and an ingenious system of ideas to interest them. Many times we fail and we tend to blame other factors when it rests entirely within ourselves. There is a method, a "stunt," if you will, that will arouse them. If we're lucky we hit upon it, if not we keep our creel odorless. I have spent hours of time and innumerable foot pounds of effort in trying to solve the mysteries of these periods. I have expended industrious hours in actively catching nothing. I have succeeded and I have failed, but over the years the successes have gradually increased and the failures become fewer. As I have sincerely recommended throughout this book that the reader experiment, try, analyze, test, investigate and experiment again, I am merely outlining what I do myself. It is at times like this that the six qualities of a good fisherman is of most importance. We must observe diligently, we must persist in experiments, we must try logical ways and we must try illogical ways, too, because sometimes the thing we ordinarily should not do is the successful answer to our problem.

There are three distinct phases of fly fishing:

> 1—Dry or floating fly.
> 2—Wet fly and streamer.
> 3—Nymph and Larvae.

Dry fly fishing is the easiest insofar as performance is concerned. Successful results is another factor. Nymph fishing enacted properly is the most difficult of the three and requires the most knowledge and know how. Wet fly fishing is the best known and at one time was practically the only manner in which flies were fished.

The dry fly simulates, primarily, emerged (hatched) duns,

spinners egging, spent spinners, hatched caddis or sedge flies, hatched stone flies, ants, bees, grasshoppers and other land flies accidently or purposely caught on the water's surface. The wet fly counterfeits nymphs and aquatic insects working to the surface to emerge as flies, aquatic or land flies damaged or dead under the surface and small minnows. The nymph fly imitates the true underwater stage of the aquatic fly in its living state preceding and up to the point where it is ready for the emergence as a flying insect. It is difficult to draw a line between the regular wet fly and the nymph fly inasmuch as the simulations overlap in many instances. The streamer fly, a type of wet fly, represents the minnow or "fry" period of the fish in the stream.

There are certain and definite periods in fishing when one of the three fly phases is dominantly the one to use for the most successful fishing. You hear or know of individual fishermen who confine themselves to one phase only and swear by it. He's eccentric and missing out on a lot of additional pleasure. Usually the fisherman who limits himself to this one phase and is not adverse to shouting about its merits is the fisherman who understands little or nothing of the other methods and doesn't want it known too widely. Use of any method of the group is as purely sportsmanlike as the others and the fisherman can class himself as a purist or stylist if he so desires.

I could supply pages of diagrams showing a section of a stream and outlining the various currents, where I stood while casting and indicating where my fly was placed as the pools, pockets and rifles were searched. I could tell you that I took two fish from position No. 1 and three good ones from position No. 2, but I only succeeded in taking one of three pounds from position No. 3. I could elaborate on what I did in each instance and expect that it would help you in your efforts to catch trout. It will not help you one iota and as for emphasizing my ego I only like to tell fishing "truths" when those whom I am belaboring with my saga have a comeback with their own "truths." Also, if I were strictly honest about the fictional diagram I'd probably have to tell you that not one rise occurred except at position No. 3 and he didn't stay on the hook. I contend that these episodes and stream maps make jolly reading but that it is extremely questionable whether or not you would ever be in that same location, under the same conditions, and if you were you wouldn't recognize it.

There is a tremendous pleasure in hooking into a fish at a time when, supposedly, they're not to be caught or at a spot which other fishermen have passed up because of its apparent lack of fish life or under conditions that others believe quite impossible. The very act or move that crowns your effort with a successful termination many times was occasioned by your doing the exact thing that you weren't expected to do. Concentrate on out of the way pocket holes that are irksome to get at right, particularly if it's one of those streams where a parade of fishermen has thrashed the water literally to a boil ahead of you. Keep in mind the fact that of that thrashing parade preceding you, nineteen out of twenty fished only the obvious, easily discernible, easily reached slicks and holes. I've watched successful, experienced fishermen deliberately overlook those evident spots, under the conditions mentioned above, and proceed to fish the tough spots only, as they worked the water.

When the sun is shining brightly, and in your maneuvering about, a shadow of yourself, your rod, sometimes even your leader and fly passes over a prospective pocket and you may as well waste little time attempting to work that spot. All but small or foolish trout are gone or downed for the time. As a youngster I was instructed, and believed for many years, that one, to prevent shadows ahead of you, should keep the sun in one's face. This made the surface of the water, at most angles of the sun, a confusing, flashing, moving glare which was unpleasant and difficult to penetrate in looking into the water. Later I found that there was distinctly a greater advantage, by being a bit more cautious with shadows, in keeping the sun at one's back—actually reversing my early training. For one reason, the fish looking in your direction would be facing the sun and objects within their vision would take on a fuzzy glare, tending to blind them somewhat, in that direction. The fisherman, too, is able to easily see down into the water ahead of him and determine the method he will use and the spot in which to place his lure. In casting your fly over a fish there is less likelihood of the shadow of fly or leader passing over the fish—the shadows are between the fish and you and a little care in casting will keep them there. Early day and late day shadows are long and sweeping. This is the time to get on the other side of the stream.

It probably goes without saying that the reader is more or less modern as it pertains to fishing clothing, hats, caps, etc. At one time, not too many years ago, it was considered proper to appear on the stream in a white shirt, a linen collar and either a bow or four-in-hand tie that matched the ensemble. Were it cool enough for a coat, your suit coat was the correct garment. This clothing didn't have to be your best, it could very well be everyday garments if they were clean and presentable. Nowadays wealthy anglers can look like tramps on the stream and a fisherman, who doesn't have a pot in which to cook his vegetables, resembles the tramp also. When I use the term "tramp" I am not trying to disparage that calling, I am but trying to bring out that most fishermen dislike new attire—they love the old slouch hat, the smeared fishing jacket, that has weathered years of fishing jaunts, and the dark flannel shirt, which is held together by shreds between the holes snagged by misdirected flies. These garments, whether old or new, are not of the flashy order. They are drab, never showing white, and that is as it should be. A fisherman clothed in drab attire, silhouetted against a foliage or rock background, is practically camouflaged and, to a degree, invisible to the fish.

In the same "caution" category it may be well to warn against untoward movements, if wading a stream, that will create wavelets which may pass over your prospective fishing pocket. This unnatural condition could be the warning signal to your trout to watch out, there's something in the offing that isn't exactly a situation recommended by the trout's safety council.

A trout that flashes to your fly and refuses to take it is a prospective fish in the creel. Something about your fly or something that flashed across his vision, has caused him to be leery. If you feel that it's the latter cause continue your casting, carefully placing your fly in or just above the same spot. If you are of the opinion that his rejection has to do with the fly itself you might do what most veteran anglers do. Change the fly to one of a larger or smaller size in the same approximate pattern. If that doesn't work offer your trout a distinctly contrasting fly. If you had been using a light-colored pattern change to a dark pattern or the reverse, but stay within the range of possible naturals.

On short rises when you have changed your fly to a pattern of a different size AND TYPE, hold off on your next cast for three or four minutes. Short rises are generally an occasion when the "lie" in your fly has been spotted. Splash touches and investigating hits both indicate short rises. In neither case does the fish actually come into contact with the lure. Another reason for pausing for a few moments, at the time of a fly change, is that if the fly is too much contrast for them or instead of the one they naturally expect to see, it gives them a shock surprise. This may lead their instincts into suspicion or may start the "fear" chain reaction.

When you think its the time or occasion to change flies be certain in your mind that it's the fly pattern that's at fault. Many anglers spend too much time changing flies trying to find the "lucky" one that will be a killer, when actually the fisherman himself is the direct cause of lack of interest by the trout, and caused by unskillful or careless presentation of the fly.

If a trout actually strikes at your fly and hits short and refuses to rise again to the lure and if you feel that your presentation was satisfactory, another change, should you wish, is customarily the thing to do if you want that particular fish. If fishing dry change to a wet pattern, similar, of course; if fishing wet, at the time, change to a floating pattern.

Never be hesitant about carrying the three or four types of flies to the stream with you. If you're going to devote your day to dry flies have some wets, some nymphs and some streamers along just in case. Maybe you won't use them but the time will come when you will wish you had come prepared.

Plan your fishing attack rather than tossing the fly dictionary of patterns at your trout. Select the flies with care and thought. Know them by name and the insect they simulate, if any. Pick the dry flies that should be emerging. Select the wet flies that, in your opinion and experience, might be effective, and choose your nymphs to generally match the possible "hatch." Streamers are fraud minnows and if you do not have your "pet" streamer chosen yet, you will eventually.

Fly patterns can be distinctly controversial. Nearly every fly fisherman who has analyzed and studied the subject has his choice dozen or half dozen and his preferred single pattern. Most fly fishermen, who have enjoyed considerable experience, have traversed the gauntlet of carrying and using, literally, scores upon scores of different fly patterns. After years of this experience their "pet" flies have dwindled in numbers of patterns until they can assemble those really needed for a day's fishing in one small box. I know of fishermen who actually will embark to the stream with just one pattern. However, many anglers, like myself, have their limited selections but will carry a rounded out assortment of several types and sizes just in case. A master fisherman in Maine may have his choice few as will another angler in New York, and the same applies to fishermen in Michigan, Colorado or California. Each group may vary but in the general consensus the similarity of patterns is surprising.

I earnestly urge the reader to traverse the experimental road and determine his own fly choices. It is, as mentioned previously, fun and an experience he should certainly undergo.

Generally, I use, according to various conditions, about six different fly patterns. Were I compelled to confine my selection to one wet and one dry pattern the decision would not be too difficult. It would settle, at this writing, on a Whirling Blue Dun, wet, and a Blue Wing Adams, dry. Other patterns in my list, not in order of preference because each, to me, fits a certain condition of season, of hatch on the water or the type of water being worked, are the Light Cahill Quill, the Red

Macaw, the Red Quill, the Hendrickson and the "All Purpose" fly, most in sizes 12, 14 and 16. In some instances, when I'm off the beam, when my casting is erratic, when what stream reading ability I may possess is fogged up, I might drop to sizes 18, 20 or even 22 to get desired action. In wet flies I favor the Royal Coachman (hairwing), the Gordon Quill, the Vampire Coachman, the Owen's Sedge and the Blue Wing Black Gnat in sizes 10, 12 and 14. I do carry, in season, cinnamon colored sedge or caddis patterns and a yellow-orange bodied Stone Fly in sizes to suit the area I am fishing. When I feel particularly adept I enjoy fishing with a regular "Nymph" fly. My top favorites in this class of fly are the Mayfly Nymph, the Coachman Nymph, Pott's Sandy or Lady Mite, the Hare's Ear Nymph, the yellow bodied Partridge and the Iron Blue Dun Nymph. Those patterns listed are my "confidence" flies and are used much more than any others. I am a rabid experimenter and when fish are coming too easily I experiment with other patterns—when fish are extremely touchy and wary, and hard to get, I experiment. I suggest you do that, too.

Several years back I pondered the problem of how to tell, from year to year during definite fishing periods, just what fly I should expect to see if a "hatch" occurred. In my study of the aquatic insects I felt that I could recognize the fly when I saw it. Having perused that data, which I could understand, outlining other fishermen's experiences and recordings of their findings, I was told to expect, for instance, iron frauditor to appear on about May 5th to the 10th. I noted that one writer's record indicated one period and another's would be a different one. I guessed that John Doe's findings were taken from a stretch of the Battenkill and Smiley T. Rout's was from the Brule. Their being a wide dissimilarity in the quoted emergence dates I deduced that perhaps the flies, for various reasons, actually appeared at different times even under similar conditions.

I carefully kept a record of my discoveries and those "hatches" that I spotted didn't agree at all with what was supposed to be. I fished hatches of the fly which we simulate in the Gordon Quill or the Hendrickson or the Blue Upright in May, for instance, and the son-of-a-gun popped up again in late August on the same stream. I determined then that a lot of fly tier's portrayals of certain flies were attempts, in many cases, to copy the same bug. Then I started to chart the insects by groups.

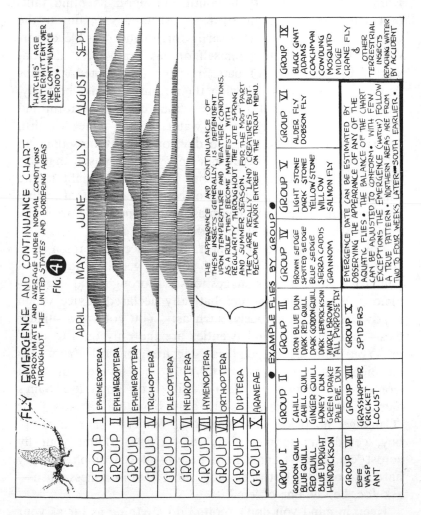

Fig. 41 shows the chart that was developed from this survey and is a composite of the writer's own notes, material sifted from other published sources and discussions with fishermen over the country. It will give you an idea of just what fly you'll find likely to work for you at the time you are fishing.

Regardless of the trust and confidence an angler has in a pet fly, it does naturally go against the grain for him to limit his fishing to its use, exclusively. Much of the pleasure derived from his stream activity is contingent upon its blind fallibility, its uncertain result, so if he restricts his angling to the use of one fly, he will necessarily forego the possible opportunity of complimenting himself on his shrewdness, demonstrated by the choice of pattern which is accepted, perhaps greedily, by the fish, following their refusal of his "best" fly.

The supposition that a fly resembling closely the form and color of the natural fly on the water, and to which the fish are rising, will be more apt to develop effectiveness than an odd counterfeit fly is logical, not only for the reason that this fly is likely to fool the trout, but it also looks right to the fisherman—it gives him a sense of confidence and that feeling is paramount to assured conquest. Faith in your lure is the greatest single ingredient toward fishing success.

Follow the guidance of honest, experienced fishermen as to your tackle, tactics and lures, if you can get them to council you. At least give their suggestions a thorough trial. Be suspicious, however, of the emphatically declared advice which is advanced too generously, such as: "You gotta use smaller flies—yep, eighteens and twenties are the only ones to use," or "You gotta use bigger flies—big flies, big fish. Yep, tens an' eights an' even sixes are th' only ones to use," or "You won't get no action on them Cahills, you gotta use 'Sam's Turkish Rug Specials,' it's th' only bug ther' a'takin'," or "Can't get no place with them long leaders—shorten it up, boy, get closter to your fish," or "Y'gotta skitter your fly acrost 'em. I didn't catch none t'day—guess I didn't try very hard, but one day last week, boy, did I haul in a mess o'fish— ask Joe, he saw one of 'em."

Keep in mind you don't "gotta" do anything as far as your fishing is concerned. A couple of trips on the stream, using what you can sift out of this book, and seasoning it with your own good judgment, and you'll fish rings around the characters who tell you, "You Gotta!"

A list of fly and fish axioms that I've picked out of my notebooks is herewith presented, again not as final, flat declarations, but as facts that I have found true and effective more times than not.

Tailing or bulging trout is the signal to tie on a nymph.

Large rolling fish are interested, usually, in a nymph or wet fly.

Dimpling may mean a tiny fish or a whopper—seldom of medium size.

As a rule, larger flies will catch larger fish more often than will smaller flies.

Success will be greater early in the spring, on any water, with large dry flies, streamers and nymphs.

Use darker toned flies in clear water and bright weather.

Use darker toned flies at dusk or evening. Exception to this rule is when it is extremely dark, with overcast sky. Then switch to light flies.

On dark days or in the evening, wet fly patterns with tinsel bodies, tinsel ribbing or tinsel tips are usually of greater value.

If you can see your fish and can ascertain whether he's large or small and you can control setting the hook, strike as fast as you can on smaller fish, but the larger he is, the slower the strike. (That's a lot to advise, and I know the complexes that hinder it, but it does work.)

During the heat of summer, except on extremely high altitude streams, fish are more receptive to flies during early morning and in the evening. The water surface is cooler than at midday and usually the fish are finding it more comfortable. This applies, of course, to those periods when there is no hatch on the water.

When food is scarce fish will take more chances than is ordinarily the case. If the food is abundant the trout are wary, wise and exasperatingly choosy.

Now, my friends, we come to the topmost requisite to suc-

cessful fly angling. Should every condition of the leader and
fly, its size, color and pattern be perfect, and the APPROACH
and the PRESENTATION be lacking in quality, the whole
effort is wasted to the degree of poor versus good in these
very important essentials. Regardless of the type fly you may
be fishing, if it is one that fits the day and the stream conditions, it will be taken, if at all, without delay if presented
correctly and never when not tendered properly.

Faulty judgment in determining your position, near or actually in the water, is one substantial condition that causes
inferior results and has a greater effect on your "luck" than
amateurish or inefficient casting of your fly. Do examine the
situation carefully—indifference is an attitude that is intoler-
able to success—study all the angles, then put yourself in the
spot that your judgment dictates is best, in spite of obstacles
and obstructions, providing it is physically possible without
endangering yourself.

Stream currents interlacing the water that may affect or
occasion a drag in your fly must be considered. Your shadow,
if visible, and that of your rod and terminal tackle must also
be taken into account. Winds, if forceful enough to make
casting more difficult than usual, too, must be borne in mind
and lastly does the background help or hinder your casting
action? All this must be judged, plus the fact that you should
approach your target out of sight of possible fish. The shorter
the cast the better the control, providing the trout's range of
vision does not encompass your point of vantage.

Far be it from me to even suggest that you make a serious
study of light refraction laws and rules as it concerns the fish's
vision cone. To some the subject may be interesting and of
serious content as it affects fishing. At one time I went into
the theme quite deeply, feeling that it was vital that I knew
all that my limited mental capacity could grasp. The only
visible result was a good old-fashioned headache and a realization that it might be a nice thing to know, but as it concerned
my fishing effort there was no particular benefit, merely the
fact that there is a vision cone and that it can be described
quite simply with a sketch, which has been inserted in this

book (Fig. 42), and a common sense statement of fact and we'll then drop the whole thing. The common sense statement is: "If you can see the fish, usually, he can see you, unless you are directly behind him or you've actually hidden behind a bush, a rock or the grass."

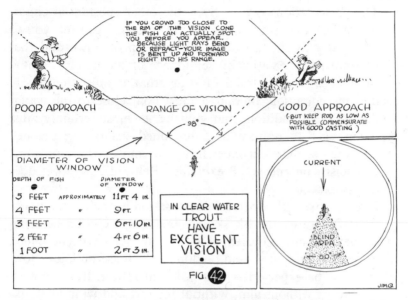

IF YOU CROWD TOO CLOSE TO THE RIM OF THE VISION CONE THE FISH CAN ACTUALLY SPOT YOU BEFORE YOU APPEAR. BECAUSE LIGHT RAYS BEND OR REFRACT—YOUR IMAGE IS BENT UP AND FORWARD RIGHT INTO HIS RANGE.

POOR APPROACH   RANGE OF VISION   GOOD APPROACH
(-BUT KEEP ROD AS LOW AS POSSIBLE COMMENSURATE WITH GOOD CASTING)

98°

DIAMETER OF VISION WINDOW		
DEPTH OF FISH		DIAMETER OF WINDOW
5 FEET	APPROXIMATELY	11 FT 4 IN.
4 FEET	"	9 FT.
3 FEET	"	6 FT. 10 IN.
2 FEET	"	4 FT 6 IN.
1 FOOT	"	2 FT 3 IN.

IN CLEAR WATER
TROUT
HAVE
EXCELLENT
VISION

FIG. 42

CURRENT

BLIND AREA

60°

JIMG

Do not be hesitant about crouching, squatting down, fishing from the knee position or casting from an actual belly crawl. All good fishermen go into these positions when the need is evident to avoid being spotted by the trout.

It is true that calendar pictures or illustrations, either drawn or photographed, show the fisherman standing tall in his boots waving his rod on high like a tournament caster, however on smaller waters you'll see your good fisherman portraying a skulking Indian in tall grasses, casting from the protection of a bush or a rock, kneeling in the water or tip-toeing in a crouch. Factually you'll find him in many unromantic postures that are rarely illustrated except in the comics, which generally are closer to the truth.

You've watched a common domesticated cat stalk a bird that has trespassed on his range. That is the correct procedure in your fishing approach many, many times. Stalk your fish whether actual or potential—sneak up on the spot which is your objective casting target—your trout may be away visiting friends but, all things being normal, he's usually home and, as I've mentioned before, is pretty generally receptive to luncheon invitations.

The presentation of your fly is the other substantial condition that has a bearing on successful results. I can tell you to lay your dry fly on the water like a wisp of down and that the fly must deliver a cocky semblance of the natural, that it must float without a trace of drag, that it must float high, under one condition, or that it must float close to the water, under another condition, that your leader most certainly must be submerged to prevent that magnified shadow on the bed of the stream, that you must fish upstream or that you must fish downstream and you'll exclaim, "Beloved cow, what does that lug expect?"

I don't expect it! A perfect presentation is one for the book, they're so rare even with skilled and long experienced trout fishermen. What is to be expected is that every cast you make, every fly you present should be done as well as you know how. What is to be expected is that you will refrain from careless casts thrown without aim, without interest and without thinking. When you get to that stage it's time for a siesta and a cigarette or a pipeful.

If ten per cent of the fishermen fishing trout would average ten days of fishing during a season and would, throughout the day, make almost perfect presentations of their flies with a faultless approach, then were compelled to keep all those over ten inches, for this example, every stream would be stripped clean of trout. You might ask what about the little ones? The other ninety per cent of the fishermen, those with faulty or mediocre approaches and presentations, would have all those trout running up to ten inches in their creels by July 1st. Those are the kind they generally bring home anyway. When these fishermen do snare sizable fish it's because of an accidental, unplanned, suitable approach and presentation.

I haven't outlined much on what a good presentation is. This, too, is an essential that must be determined somewhat by the fisherman according to the conditions under which he has to present his fly. In fishing the dry fly, of course, a chief necessity is NO DRAG. The fly must float, looking much like natural insects to the trout, and the natural insect floats freely, unhampered by a leader. The fly must be directed to, and placed above, the potential fish immediately beside the channel which carries his food to him. The leader, attached to the fly must be away from this channel whether your fly is drifting to the right or left of that food channel line. If fishing the wet fly, or nymph, it too must make its journey as would the underwater natural, whether the natural be insect or minnow. There are other methods of presentation which will be covered later under the specific suggestions for fishing the various types of flies.

"They aren't taking flies today!"

Ever heard that statement made by an angler? As you attain skill and knowledge in your fishing you will sprinkle more and more salt on pronouncements of that character. The angler should have stated, "They aren't taking flies today FOR ME!"

Were the truth known the angler, above, was, in all probabilities, incapable of artful fly fishing—he really didn't know too much about it. There are times, as I have mentioned before, when trout will avariciously rise to almost any fly cast almost anywhere. It could be that our angler needed periods like that for his fly fishing. It could be that he had better luck with worms or salmon roe, or dead minnows, or cheese, or dough balls, or chicken "innards." There are some days that fly fishing results seem to come harder than on others and maybe it isn't the reluctance of the fish, it could very well be us. We could be a trifle weak in our knowledge as to just how to go about it. I can say, with emphasis, however, and hundreds of fishermen will bear me out, that there never was a day, sans earthquakes or tornadoes, that trout could not be induced to take some fly, or some nymph, if offered judiciously.

In the following sections, in which we concentrate on certain ways and means as it pertains to that particular method, we perhaps repeat ourselves and for that we apologize now.

The reason it may be necessary is that many of those methods, in each particular type of fishing, actually have enough similarity to others as to cause procedure overlapping.

DRY FLY FISHING

Dry fly fishing is by far the simplest, also the easiest, method of fly fishing for trout and many other fish. You can, usually, see the fly on the water—you have a pretty good idea as to whether it's a good presentation or not—you can see the fly taken and you can see whether it created interest in the fish and was then rejected for some reason. Less knowledge of fish habits is necessary and less knowledge of the stream itself is needed to successfully fish with the floating fly.

Your major objective in the use of the dry fly is to sell your prospective fish into the idea that the tiny feathered creature, so jauntily bobbing down his food channel, is a toothsome tidbit that he should grab off. Invite the trout to smite the fly but do not insist by placing it directly at his nose. Tease a bit, your success will be greater.

Although dry flies can be fished downstream or across stream on occasion when necessity requires, it is almost imperative for favorable outcome that the fishing be done against the current. The fish has his back to you and is not suspecting that a villain is sneaking up on him with murderous designs and directing his deadly fraudulent enticer right smack dab where he can most easily gulp it down. An amusing fact, considering the way we fish now, is that previous to circa 1850 the upstream cast was regarded as unsportsmanlike an abominable act, a heresy, a sin and a shameful practice.

A flush "hatch," or emergence, and the dry fly enthusiast is in his heaven. Strangely, the height of the hatch is, more often than not, the least productive period. There are sometimes so many floating naturals on the water that the angler's lure is lost in competition. The most favorable periods of the rise or hatch or emergence, is as it is getting underway and during the tapering off interval. It is true that some hatches seem to start as if on signal and terminate as abruptly. The observant fisherman, however, will have expected the emergence because he had spotted bulges and swirls in the water where the trout were feeding on active nymphs for upwards of an hour or two preceding the actual surfacing.

During the season of fly "hatches" there is hardly a spell when some aquatic flies are not emerging, even if few and far between. The fish instinctively know this and are not shocked to detect a single occasionally floating down the channels if the fly is not too much in variance with those that same instinct tells him are O.K. Also during the warmer season land flies and insects such as ants, beetles, grasshoppers, deer flies, cattle flies, house flies, blue bottle flies, mosquitoes, spiders and many others, are active and are frequently falling into, or being blown onto, the water surface. Trout are not going to completely ignore those occasional aquatic and land flies traversing their dining room so we see splashes and dimples when there is no general rise in progress. Incidentally, the fisherman should lay particular heed to those same dimples in an otherwise undisturbed surface. They could foreshadow the lair of a sizable fish.

When a working fish, or one that seems to be feeding, is observed, that's when our dry fly angler goes into his act. This is the time to pause and plan his attack; this is the time to put into effect the best judgment he may possess in approaching his objective. Then comes the careful presentation. If his fly is a reasonable facsimile of a natural that's in season and his approach has created no apparent disturbance, then he can be accurately judged by an impartial critic on his presentation. If the trout attacks the fly without hesitation he can mark up 100 per cent. If the trout ignores the invitation or does a disappearing act, the angler can ponder on his failure to pass the examination.

Some energetic fishermen deliberately go along the stream in search of working fish. You will see them crawl or creep to a point where they can, unobserved themselves, view the water for a space upstream. Then they retreat back to a safe distance, move further along the stream, and repeat the performance. A fisherman wallowing along the stream's bank in constant view of the water will be able to expose many working fish, too. Fish working diligently to get away from that area as fast as their little fins can propel them.

In meadow type, open water streams, when trout are not rising, when you can observe no evidence that there are actually fish in the stream, they are in all probabilities quietly resting under or close to the bank or in shadowy haunts near rocks, overhanging bushes, ledges or logs. In this instance your first move is to carefully start bumping the bank where you can, with your fly, close to the water. Short casts in the beginning and gradually working upstream with the fly to the limit of accurate casting. The fly hits the bank and tumbles or bounces to the water almost at the water's edge. Permit the fly to float down toward you until in safe territory before you lift it for the next cast.

If no action is forthcoming start again close to you with shorter casts and drop the fly eight or ten inches from the bank, working up-water again in successive casts to the limit of your normal fishing distance. If there's no action, commence the procedure once more but this time place the fly two or three feet from the bank. This latter cast is likely to be effective if the overhanging bank is heavy or deeply undercut. The two previous spaced distances were protective measures performed under the supposition that the trout may have been close to the edge or actually in open water but near the bank. The two- or three-foot interval from the bank's edge will ordinarily permit the fly to come into the vision range of the trout. If the fish is back in the dark recesses of the undercut, as they many times are, the close-to-the-bank floats would not be visible to him.

While following this potent procedure always permit the fly to complete its float back to you or past you before lifting from the water. This suggestion should apply to practically all your upstream casts no matter what type of water you are searching with your lure. There are times when the disturbance caused by the "lift" will scare your trout into fasting for hours.

You will notice, or have seen, fish taking midges on the surface. Duplicating the midge, even vaguely, in a fly is a highly ambitious endeavor that, to my knowledge, has never been done to any degree of effectiveness. The midge is a tiny insect that, were it simulated correctly would have to be on a size 50 or 60 hook and neither of those sizes are, at the moment, available. If they were and it would be possible to affix a semblance of a fly on them, which isn't likely (there are not more than five or six fly tiers in the country that could satisfactorily dress sizes tinier than size 40 which is the smallest I've heard of being tied), the bite in the hook could barely snag the slime in the mouth of a fish, let alone getting hold of a skin layer. Anglers, being what they are, will generally try anyway with the smallest flies they have, which are giants compared to the natural, or they tie on spider flies which are as good as any, usually better, for this effort. When the trout continue with their midge snack, paying little attention to the fisherman's tempter, the fisherman, usually reluctantly, gives up.

If you will notice carefully, the midges, being gregarious, fly in groups or perhaps clouds would be a better description. The trout rarely rise to take ONE from the surface but will slash with his tail into a cloud splashing a number of them under where he leisurely sucks them in. Here's a game you can play, too. Affix the smallest dark fly you have in your box. Cast into these clouds of midges and draw the fly under the surface, if you can, so that it floats just submerged. If your fly should pass through the area where midges had been slapped down, your trout probably wonders how he ever missed gulping that nice big one and the likelihood of its being taken is good.

In the rougher sections of the stream you are fishing, regardless of how turbulent the water is, you'll spot smooth glides that are almost glassy in appearance. False cast for distance and drop your fly at the head of these glides. The fly ordinarily will give you a drag-free presentation for a foot or two and these spots are dynamite to feeding fish. You'll see glides, too, at the head of pools just ahead of rough stretches. These are excellent feeding grounds as a rule, particularly the spots just before the turbulent water starts.

Do not be hesitant about permitting your fly to hit the rough areas also. They may not stay on top long and supposing they do go under, they're certainly no worse off than a high wet fly and may develop some unexpected slashing action for you.

Where the water is heavy and mostly rough and turbulent I would advise the use, entirely, of the variant high floating patterns, if you're sticking to the dry flies. Although not too close a resemblance to the natural insects they will withstand considerable tossing about by rougher water and will stay on top. The character of the water precludes the necessity of delicate simulations of natural flies which are needed when trout are choosy. One nice feature of this type of fly is that they are, by far, the easiest of the dry flies to present. Even the most inexpert amateur has little difficulty in securing satisfying action with their use. But where trout are extremely particular, or as some say, "educated," these heavily hackled flies are just excess baggage except late in the day or at night.

We haven't touched on the "abomination" subject for quite a spell now and I hope you will seriously catalog this issue in your mind. DRAG causes more unfilled creels, more actionless days, more heartbreaks in downing fish than any other cause in normal dry fly presentation. Natural insects rarely skate around on the water's surface leaving a discernable "V" wake behind them and trout instinctively know this. If the insects knew it they'd make it a point to develop this prank, then they'd all live their whole life rather than suffer violent extinction before they have a chance to meet the boy friend. The aversion to dragging flies is one of nature's gifts to the trout clan. It's an ideal protection against the trout's toughest enemy, us!

If we've taken every precaution, as far as the stream currents are concerned, against possible drag, then we must never cast too tight a line. If the line were cast so that there was some slack then that slack must ordinarily have to become straightened so that it could do some pulling on the leader to move the fly unnaturally off its course, causing a drag wake. So the answer to the problem is to, within reason, put some slack in the line and leader. In other words postpone the drag as long as you can.

I've seen others do it and I've done it myself—that is, in making more or less extended casts and not applying the required amount of power, have the line get itself thrown about by a blast of gusty wind and dropping in a very amateurish disorder then have the fly, in amongst this jumble, be taken very deliberately by a trout. I cannot suggest that this performance become a part of your fishing practice. You won't have to try to do it, it'll do itself. All you'll need is a desire to put out a nice long cast coupled with a nasty unexpected burst of breeze and there you'll have it.

I know of one fisherman who resides on a ranch in the Sierra Nevada mountains who fishes some practically every day during the season. He knows his water well and he knows fish. He is not a champion caster by any imagination stretch but he uses an extremely lengthy leader (14 to 18 feet) and he deliberately drops an exaggerated slack between himself and the prospective fish. He keeps few of them but, man, can he catch them!

Now that we've touched on the "drag" problem from the negative side let's cover it on another, sometimes successful, procedure from the positive or intentional drag angle. Actually working a variant or a somewhat bushy fly over the surface in jerks or bounces, as if a large fly were trying to get off the water will, at times, bring out a savage appetite in your trout. This is usually done on a downstream or cross stream cast where the current will assist you in your manipulation of the fly. Instead of a straight drag, try to jerk the fly a few inches so that it will bounce on the surface. Keep repeating the maneuver as you retrieve the line. On broken surfaces or rough water, drag is no particular problem but the worked fly will at times secure action that a "no drag" float will fail to accomplish.

Here's another procedure in dry fly fishing that is easy to do and will, many times, turn an otherwise mediocre fishing occasion into one more successful. It is that of dapping your fly on the surface in likely spots and, providing you are comparatively out of sight, working the edge of the water near you. An extremely short leader (3 or 4 feet or less) is necessary if you're going to indulge in this practice to any extent. Some line must extend out from your rod tip to prevent the lack of any weight at that point, which being the case, the leader would slide back through the guides, pulling the fly right to the rod tip-top. The bit of added line weight will tend to prevent that action. Hovering the fly straight down from the tip of the rod, you lower it so that the fly touches the surface where you're going to dap it. Raise and lower the rod giving the fly the motion of flying near the surface, dropping down to touch the water then up into the air again a few inches. Performing this dapping operation is "dynamite" when the angler is safely hidden behind a bush, a rock or lying flat on his bread basket on the bank.

The greatest satisfaction that a dry fly fisherman can experience is that of carefully securing, on his leader, a well tied fly of his own fashioning and choice and deliberately and accurately presenting this feathered lure repeatedly over a hiding lair of a known sizable trout and inducing him to eventually rise to the fly in this false "hatch" created by the fisherman himself.

Your fly cast skillfully and repeatedly over a contrary, apathetic, inactive trout who is apparently abstaining from all food will, if he isn't scared, ultimately motivate him into an interest in your lure and a highly probable hook-up.

This supreme method of dry fly fishing was perhaps used by many early dry fly enthusiasts, either consciously or unconsciously, but it remained for H. G. McClelland, a noted English fisherman, writer, fly tier and sportsman before the turn of the century, to recognize that the action was, to all purposes, creating an artificial "hatch." Since that time a number of authors have described it in their writings. George M. LaBranche, the No. 2 dean of dry fly men in this country (no one can take "No. 1" from Theodore Gordon), the angler who created the famous "Pink Lady" patterns, and one of a few known, outstanding sportsmen of all time, made much of this method of fine dry fly fishing. He described it as the ultimate in skill and deception. At this moment I know of no other thrill that is so satisfying as the successful accomplishment of this fishing performance.

If you have fished with companions much you'll know of those anglers who insist on shorter leaders with the claim that it makes no particular difference providing the tip of leader is fine enough. A longer leader, having no particular weight, is more difficult to cast and you'll find that those who do not or will not use a leader longer than nine feet have discovered that fact. Knowing their casting limitations and having no wish to improve their skill they stick with their six, seven and eight-foot leader lengths and blame failure to catch as many fish as they could on other factors usually outside themselves.

There are streams and there are occasions when the shorter leaders are the ones to use but generally a longer one is of greater advantage to the fisherman if he is able to handle it satisfactorily. In performing craft casts, particularly the curve, or hook casts, a shorter leader is of assistance in getting the accuracy that's sometimes imperative if your efforts are to be crowned with results. I am not, however, alone in the experience of fishing with a seven to nine-foot length leader tapered to a suitably fine tippet and having only mediocre or no success and by extending the tippet three or four feet have the action pick up surprisingly. Why this fact is so, is problematic. With a nine-foot leader the line rarely gets into the trout's direct vision range but the extended leader does result in more rises to your fly. One reason could be that in using the longer and finer leader the dragging line has less effect on the action of the fly.

With an abundance of varying conditions occurring during the fishing period it is not too easy to experiment with different lengths of leader in an attempt to determine just what footage is best. Over a period of years these same experiments should have given us some idea of the facts that we want and my conclusion, which is by no means final, is that the twelve to fifteen-foot leader will secure more resultful action for you while using the dry fly on normal dry fly water.

Should it be quite windy, the longer leader, however, is not the easiest thing to control with any degree of accuracy. In rough heavy water the length of your leader, generally, has no particular bearing on your fishing success providing the leader is at least seven feet long. In this type water, too, the tippet does not have to be quite so fine. In fact one can drop down to as coarse as .010 (1X-3½ to 4 pounds) if the water is not too clear. If low and clear water is the case .008 or .007 (3X-2¼ pounds or 4X-1¾ pounds) would be satisfactory. These latter tip strengths vary as to quality of the material but are probably considered over one and one-half to two pounds providing the knots are correctly formed and tied and that is ample. A one-pound tippet (approximately .006 or .055) in open water, with the bend of your rod, will successfully subdue any ten-pound fish without reaching a breaking strain, if the fish is played right, which is not too difficult if you don't become impatient or panicky.

In fishing dry flies on smaller streams which are open, and allowing the angler to play his hooked fish, leader tippets of one pound and less will hold satisfactorily if the leader knots are right. Most anglers use, however, 4X (.007) and 5X (.006) as the minimum in fineness, and 2X (.009) and 3X (.008) for rougher going.

You have noted that we stress the quality of the leader knots. Just any old connecting tie won't do. Where a leader crosses itself in a knot is definitely a weaker link, sometimes reducing the strength in half. Care should be taken to learn and make the correct knot which will provide the strongest possible tie in the weakest locality of your terminal tackle. Follow the recommendations in Chapter Three for your leader knots.

You've heard fishermen complain that the fish just snapped the leader and got away. That was not the fault of the leader in nine out of ten cases. The reason the fish got off was because the angler wasn't prepared, either through ignorance or carelessness, so the fish turned out to be a better man than he was. The angler might have been using too fine a leader for the water he was fishing or his leader knots were faulty or he permitted simple overhand knots, which will occasionally form in the tippet, to remain and weaken that part of his leader to a great degree.

An interesting and sometimes an extremely effective variation in dry fly fishing, when circumstances warrant it, is "windapping," sometimes called "fly bouncing" and "blowline fishing." This scheme of fishing is best done from a boat on a lake, but can, in cases, be conducted on a stream.

One has little control of exactness in the presentation of the fly but with the conditions under which the method is pursued there is not too great a need for it.

The tackle, for best effects, is more or less special. The longer the fly rod, within reasonable bounds, the better the job. I like to use one at least nine feet long and longer is better, even up to twelve or fourteen feet. The lighter the rod the more fun and pleasure you will get. The reel can be almost any kind commonly used for trout fishing, whether it be the single action type, an automatic or a casting reel. The line should necessarily be ultra light. I like to use two- or three-pound monofilament and one should have, at least, one hundred yards on the reel. The fly itself is optional but should be a good floater and well dressed with floatant because there is no opportunity to dry it with false casts. It goes without saying that the fly too, should, after a fashion, resemble something that looks edible to the trout and not a concoction that would scare the daylight out of a cranky wolverine. I would suggest a twelve or fourteen badger bivisible, an Adams, a full-hackled black or grizzly spider, a full-hackled Cahill or Hendrickson, or whatever fly, in your judgment, could best fit the season or the possible "hatch" and that can be seen by you, the fisherman.

The conditions under which this windapping is feasible is an open water area, not too deep, where there is a good possibility of trout residing or traveling through, and naturally we must have some wind, at least a breeze strong enough to carry the fly in intermittent gusts.

Personally, I'm not a stand-up caster in a row boat or canoe. I like to work from a sitting or kneeling position. A flat-bottomed boat or scow or raft is a different matter . . . .

one can stand with reasonable safety if careful. Anyway the higher one can get their rod the more distance will be accomplished. The angler holds his rod up at approximately arm's length and feeds out line. The wind will tote the fly, holding it in the air and dropping it lightly for an instant, lifting it again and between gusts permitting it to touch the water and float for from periods of an instant up to seconds. The line, if light enough, does not, usually, touch the water. Just the fly alone is visible to the prospective fish and there being nothing in evidence that looks out of line (your stand is anywhere from 80 to 200 feet away), what do you think he will ordinarily do? I've seen trout leap twice their length from the water to get at one of these teasing morsels of fly. Other times I've seen the fly completely disappear with hardly a visible disturbance on the surface.

In fishing running water the operation is the same. If the stream is large enough or wide enough, there will be little trouble encountered in keeping the fly over the water but on smaller streams, hook-ups in grasses, bushes, or trees is likely because wind is rarely in one exact direction and the speed with which the fly is sometimes whipped around does not permit a pull back to avoid its contact with objects or terrain not particularly the target choice of the fisherman.

Needless to say, using this extremely light line, you will not "horse" your fish. He will have practically total control until such a time as he tires and you're able to gently bring him your way. Two-pound line, with knots and all, will assure you of a pound pull anyway, and whoppers can be brought in with that much strength, if you're careful and have just a bit of luck.

Should you be on a stream or a lake with your regular fly tackle and a wind comes up which is difficult to combat with the equipment you are using, get out your tippet material and build your leader out to twenty or thirty feet. Put on a fly such as described for this kind of fishing and put it to work windapping. It may not perform as well as the tackle described but it will give you an opportunity to fish effectively.

Windapping is almost as much fun as taking the tip section

of your "second" fly rod, fasten a few feet of "D" line to the tip-top and put on a ten foot leader tapering to 6X or 7X, then a size 20 or 22 dry fly. Fish this from the bank, preferably, over an area where you've seen rising fish. If you're concealed well, you'll see action like you never dreamed of. It's a swell way to kill a little time while you're waiting for the fish you caught today to be cooked up and served.

Suggested dry flies, and sizes, which are generally considered standard types and which could be used pretty much throughout the country at most times during the season. Those indicated with an asterisk (*) are the author's favorites any place.

ADAMS, spent wing	10-12-14	IRRESISTIBLE, natural	8-10-12
(male & female)		CROSS SPECIAL	8-10-12-14
*ADAMS, blue dun wings	12-14-16	BADGER BIVISIBLE	10-12
(spent or upright)		BROWN BIVISIBLE	10-12
ADAMS, yellow body	14-16-18	GRIZZLY BIVISIBLE	10-12
GORDON QUILL	14-16-18	BADGER SPIDER	14-16-18
GINGER QUILL	12-14-16	BROWN SPIDER	14-16-18
*LIGHT CAHILL	14-16-18	BLACK SPIDER	16-18-20
CAHILL QUILL	12-14-16	FLYING CADDIS	6-8-10
*HENDRICKSON	12-14-16	JOE'S GRASSHOPPER	8-10
BLUE UPRIGHT	12-14-16	GREEN DRAKE	6-8-10-12
FLIGHT'S FANCY	12-14-16	(deer hair body—size	
MOSQUITO	14-16	according to locality	
*RED QUILL (Art Flicks')	12-14-16	and size of natural)	
(blue dun hackle)		GRIZZLY WICKHAMS	12-14
BLACK GNAT	16-18-20	*RED MACAW (JimQ)	14-16-18
PALE EVENING DUN	14-16	SIERRA CADDIS	14-16-18
GRAY HACKLE, YELLOW	14-16	PINK LADY	12-14-16-18
WILLOW	12-14-16-18	RENEGADE	8-10-12-14-16
ROYAL COACHMAN	12-14-18-20	TOBIN'S GOLDEN SPINNER	8-10
(hair wing)		*'ALL PURPOSE'	10-12-14-16-18
DONNELLY VARIANTS	6-8-10-12	CATHY B SPINNER	
		(JimQ)	14-16-18

WET FLY AND STREAMER FISHING

An old-fashioned, not quite so sporting method in fishing of using two and three flies on a "cast," attached by snells to the main leader, is fast losing favor. It actually went out with the snelled flies. There are, however, still some anglers who insist that it's quite the proper procedure. There are still anglers, too, who demand snelled flies for no reason except that it is the kind they used last year and the season before and also in 1910.

The triple or the double fly "cast," for one thing, is an easier mode of fishing in that the additional weight on the leader does not require the exacting skill needed for the more modern single fly "cast." In actual fishing the multiple fly fishing takes just a bit of advantage of the fish and heaven knows the fair thing is to render him just a bit of that advantage. Why should we take it all? My last word on the difference between these two ways of fishing wet flies is that, all conditions being equal, I'd wager my lucky fishing hat against an old brittle gut leader that the single fly fisherman, with only a moderate amount of skill and a moderately fair presentation, will take as many if not more fish than the old method and he won't have to sneak the extra flies off his leader before he enters camp. He has no reason for being just a little ashamed.

Now if the angler, maybe not to his admissible knowledge, has a lack of skill in casting (I've seen published pictures of so-called experts in action and their rod, on the back cast, was approaching the horizontal behind him—need I say more?) or a decided lack of knowledge of fish habits and stream characteristics, then I say may he use whatever procedure he desires to possibly equalize, in his opinion, his chances with others. Enough of this, let's get on to fishing wet flies.

Wet flies are generally fished with the current, however, fishing upstream can be highly effective. The most common maneuver is where the angler casts to either side almost at a right angle (called quartering) and permitting the fly to drift down with the current until directly centered in the stream to the limit of the line and leader. An important action to take, as your fly is drifting, is to stay with it, pointing towards the lure with your rod tip, releasing more line or retrieving it as necessary. It is best at all times to have your line just short of the point of being taut without hampering the natural movement or drift of your fly or nymph. This is not the easiest way in the world to fish but the procedures of value to you, the real "know how" of trout fishing, the little things that mean the big difference in superior fishing "luck," are all on the difficult side. Any fisherman can do things the easy way and most of them follow that course most of the time.

Some anglers release more line, if fishing downstream, permitting the fly to drift with the water's flow a few feet more before the retrieve is made. The retrieve itself is sometimes a jiggling done with the rod tip as the line is stripped in— or in foot long jerks by pulling line in with the left hand and by reeling in or by coiling in the hand as retrieved—or by skittering the fly gently over the surface as the line comes in —or by recovering line by the hand-twist where line is looped over the fingers of the left hand as the hand is twisted to gather it in—or by palming line which is a most effective practice. This latter is accomplished by holding the line with the first and second fingers, then the third and fourth fingers reach up and grasp the line packing it in the palm under those fingers. The hand is swung to and fro in an oscillating fashion as the line is regained and palmed. The line can be then cast and the loops released without difficulty, through the guides, as needed. This is an efficient process for regaining line, used with streamers and nymphs also. The handtwist retrieve is just slightly different. The line is held between your thumb and index finger in a normal position. Turn the hand over so that you regain a few inches of line. The hand is in a stationary position, the forearm and wrist are not moved in any direction. The thumb and index finger, with top of hand uppermost, are near the butt of your rod. In twisting the hand over, between the third and little finger, get hold of the line. Twist this under then regrasp the line with forefinger and thumb. Keep repeating the operation until the lure is back to you ready for another cast. The excess line retrieved may be packed into your hand or looped, holding with the right hand against the rod butt, or just let drop as you collect it. Either of the above retrieve methods are used at any time but are almost a requirement when fishing in lakes or in slow water pools in streams to give the fly or streamer traveling action.

In working the wet fly one should experiment as to the depth which will bring the best results. At times you'll fish as deep as possible, other times shallow or half way down. One good scheme is to let the fly go right to the bottom. Then jerk the rod tip upward a short distance a few times. Retrieve a foot or so of line then go through the same spasmotic jerking or twitching of the rod tip again. Follow through with this repeated action until line has all been taken up ready for another cast. Like other retrieving operations the angler should try faster and slower motions until the successful method is found.

If you're fishing a pocket or a pool where you're pretty certain there are catchable trout residing, and they refuse your offering after tempting them in the customary fashion, hit the spot from other angles. Practice the different retrieves on them and with varying rates of speed in the movements. If no action at all is secured and you're still certain there are trout in the pocket, carefully leave the water and detour around the location and come up on it from the opposite direction. Change your fly to another possible effective pattern and give them the "upstream" treatment. If the stream is low and the water comparatively slow in the pool you're working, try retrieving the fly in long, sweeping pulls as fast as the rod will permit without throwing the fly from the water. If still no action, it could be the pool needs a rest. Between five and ten minutes will often serve as an ample resting period. Try another pocket in another location then go back and try it again.

The slick, at the lower end of a pool, in low water, many times will be found a productive spot to work. If there is a lack of disturbance by a hooked fish, at these points, you may take a number of trout before the pocket is exhausted. A hooked trout will sometimes, by his escape antics, put down all other fish in the immediate area and at other times the remaining trout are as unconcerned as youth is to unasked advice. Fishing these slicks or glides the fly is generally more effective when it is traveling just under the surface. Trout will strike at a fly which is surfacing and skimming the top but usually a just submerged lure, in wet fly fishing, will accomplish greater results. Also the fly, just under the surface should seldom lag along. A more or less fast journey, as if the lure were trying to escape, is regularly of greater worth than with a loitering fly.

If a trout is on the feed in a pocket or pool he will, in most cases, go for the fly on the first cast providing all other conditions are favorable. Very rarely will he wait to attack the lure on subsequent casts. However, never neglect fishing a promising looking area thoroughly. Trout are unpredictable and may want to be coaxed.

Although possessing quite different characteristics from many angles, we have learned that the average salmon is caught only after about five hundred casts by the salmon fisherman. When we consider the wariness of trout and their tendency to scare easily; which is not possessed by the salmon, it would appear that trout, too, should have to be cast over at least a fifth of that number or one hundred casts per good fish. I've seen "put-'em-down" anglers in action on a stream where a thousand casts would never result in one reasonable keeper. One hundred casts, each carried through or followed through to some extent, would take upwards of thirty minutes to an hour, perhaps longer, so do not become discouraged if the first pool results in just fishing exercise. The next pocket or pool might be a different story because this is the case in many instances, for no particular logical reason. Fish are often active and can be taken in one spot and not in another. One of the enjoyable features of trout fishing is the suspense and the optimistic expectations.

Striking a trout as you see him rise to your fly, when fishing wet, will in too many instances pull the lure away from him, possibly scaring him into departing to elsewhere. When you feel the tug is the time to get a tight line on him. Four times out of five when a trout hits a wet fly, if he's hooked at all, he has hooked himself.

It goes without saying that each cast or maneuver should be completed and do not allow the fly to come to a standstill at any time. Either you are moving the fly or the current is controlling it. It just wouldn't be natural, in moving water, that the object would halt in its travel unless an outside influence was tied to it.

In wet fly fishing on small or medium streams the line should always float and the leader should be submerged along with the fly, if possible. In fact the connecting knot of leader to line should cut the surface and be visible to the angler. On larger waters many fishermen use a heavy line, undressed, to purposely get it down. The depth of the water and its rate of speed would otherwise preclude your placing the fly near the bottom where the fish are. A deliberately weighted fly or weights on your leader should be avoided wherever possible in downstream fishing. Natural movements of the lure are next to impossible when hampered by unnatural weighting. When you consider it absolutely necessary to add a shot or two to get your lure down, secure it to the leader, at least, eighteen inches from the fly. Two or three feet is better. Clamp the shot directly on the leader or make a small loop and drop the shot from a fine snell, three or four inches in length. If it is your wish to secure a shot or a few turns of fine lead wire directly on your leader and if that leader is of the knotless variety, do not make an overhand knot to hold the weight from sliding down. If your tippet knot is too far away, or you're not using a tippet, it is best to cut the leader at the point you wish the weight and retie it with a barrel or blood knot. The overhand knot reduces the strength of the leader too greatly to risk it. In all cases use the minimum weight necessary to accomplish the action.

Wet fly leaders used in clear low water should be long, at least nine feet and longer is better, and tipped with a fairly fine gut or nylon: 5X-(.006) and 4X-(.007) tippets are not too fine and they should be from three to four feet long, at least. On heavier, rougher waters, roily or semi-roily water, when limiting your fishing to larger fish, or for evening and night fishing, the leader can be shorter, if you want it that way, and heavier. The tippet, in most cases, should not exceed, however, 2X-(.009) or X-(.010) in diameter under the worst conditions.

Suggested standard wet flies, and sizes, that usually are effective in most waters and pretty general throughout the

season. This could be a list to start on until you have determined your own favorites. Asterisked (*) flies are the author's
pets.

*GORDON QUILL	12-14	GRIZZLY KING	8-10
*WHIRLING BLUE DUN	10-12	WICKHAM'S FANCY	12-14
GREENWELL'S GLORY	12-14-16	BEAVERKILL	10-12-14
*BLACK GNAT, dun wing	12-14	*HENDRICKSON, dk.	10-12
PROFESSOR	8-10	*CAHILL, lt.	10-12-14
GRAY HACKLE, yellow	12	MARCH BROWN	8-10
GRAY HACKLE, peacock	12	*OWEN'S SEDGE	12-14-16
HARE'S EAR & G. Rib	10-12	*COACHMAN, vampire	10-12-14
ALEXANDRIA	10-12	*R. COACHMAN	10-12-14
CAPTAIN, black	10-12-14		

STREAMERS

Fishing streamers is in many aspects the same as fishing wet
flies. Streamers are simulated minnows. Minnows move with
the current and dart about exactly as you sometimes manipulate your retrieve in the wet fly procedures. In using the term
"streamer" we include all the various types of this lure as the
feather streamer, the feather and hair streamer, the hair
streamer or "Bucktail," the squirrel tail series and the maribou
streamer with its variations.

Inasmuch as the streamer represents the smaller edible fish
and inasmuch as they are in the stream at all seasons it would
seem that there would be no "best" time of the year or time
of the day for fishing this fly. Those anglers, confining the
major part of their fishing to streamers, claim that early season
is a bit the better. Extremely low water is considered an effective time also. A fast increase in the water level, an increase
or decrease in water temperature has been known to start the
larger trout actively feeding on the minnow and most times no
excuse at all is necessary to encourage the fish to dart out and
take a mouthful of a small fish.

Most streamer fishermen fish the customary cast of quartering across and permitting the line to swing with the current
until directly below them. Some start the retrieve from this
point but others feed out line to allow the fly to go further
down before beginning to bring it back. The retrieve of the

streamer is performed in various fashions and the angler should try different ones until he hits on that one most effective at the time he is fishing. An important thing to remember is that experienced and successful streamer fishermen rarely, if ever, let the lure stand still. It should be moving at all times, either with the current or on its way back. This applies equally to stream or lake fishing. If trolling, keep the fly moving, but slowly, if you wish better results.

In performing retrieves the angler should never attempt to induce the interest of the fish by artificial movements which no small fish or minnow would ever make in its normal state. The fish you're after, in using streamers, are not the little yearlings, they're the kind gauged by pounds rather than inches and they have a highly developed and suspicious instinct—they're the fish that got larger by avoiding unnatural temptations. The way you bring your fly back to you should simulate, as much as possible, the way a minnow acts in the water. Spare the time, at your first opportunity, to observe the movements of these little fellows under various conditions. The time won't be wasted, believe me. If you think that movement is of lesser importance than the streamer itself, try fishing it as you'd fish a worm, for example, in still water. If by chance it should get some attention in its static mode it will be from a fish that was probably dropped on its head, quite forcibly, during its transfer from the hatchery to the home waters.

One effective procedure with streamers, particularly the bucktail variety, is to fish upstream. Holding your rod low to keep the fly as deep as possible, use this action: jerk and pause, jerk and pause, much as a minnow would act, picking up line as the fly nears you.

The jerk and pause method, in nearly all instances, is the productive procedure but the way in which it is done is the determining factor. For example, one angler will "jerk" in say two feet of line then in the "pause" release half of the line, or about one foot. That is one way. Another will jerk in the two feet then permit it to go back a few inches followed by a minor jerk and another minor release before he sweeps up again with the two-foot pull back. Another will sweep in say three feet of line, for example, then release just a few inches followed by the three-foot sweep again until the line is brought in close for another cast. Another streamer fisherman will swish his rod from left to right as he retrieves, getting in an additional side darting action. I know of fishermen who merely jiggle the tip of the rod as they use a hand twist retrieve, much as the wet fly is brought in. I haven't had much luck with that method. One further deception formula is to develop a palsy-like shake of your rod hand (if you don't already have it)—this is just an added feature which gives the streamer minnow a nervousness that has an appetizing appeal to your cannibal customer.

The same series of experiments may be necessary as to depth in which your streamer should be fished. As a rule, streamers, particularly bucktails, are worked near the surface, probably not more than ten or twelve inches down, but if no action is evident at that distance you may find that near the bottom is the proper range. In this case, if the streamer refuses to get down there, it will probably be necessary to add a shot or two immediately above the lure on the leader. Try the BB size first—if a couple or three of the BBs don't do it, add buck-shot, or number sevens. When trout are really on the feed for minnows they usually are prowling about in relatively shallow water and generally near the shore or the bank edge. I have seen large trout take streamers when the trout's dorsal fin was out in the air, in waters only five or six inches deep. Shallows are the areas that minnows frequent and if you and I were hungry trout we'd go where the food was, wouldn't we?

The colors, pattern and type of a streamer is, to a great extent, a personal choice of the angler. All streamer fishermen have a pet lure, whether it be the feathered type, a bucktail or a maribou lure. Some will swear by the Ghosts, others the Tigers, some will use only bucktails or squirrel tail flies, and the maribou user chuckles over his secret formula. All are good. At times some colors or patterns do have precedence in arousing action, but here again the presentation, or the play of the streamer, is the most important element contributing to successful fishing.

Discolored water, to some anglers, is the signal to tie on a streamer with a tinsel body or at least some of the flashing metal to attract his fish. Some go to the lighter colored patterns and what makes it interestingly complexing, some drag out the drab, dark, even black, patterns and will use no other. I, personally, like the brown and white bucktails or white maribous, under this condition, but I'm only one.

As to the best time of day I believe the dawn to bright sunlight, in the morning, and late afternoon to dusk, and even darkness, are the most productive periods. Dark cloudy days and during and following a rain can be disastrous spells for the fish.

The leaders used in fishing streamers should be from seven and one-half to twelve feet in length but the tippet end need rarely go finer than 2X-(.009) and X-(.010) and heavier is still better. Large trout don't, as a rule, nibble at a minnow. They're pretty savage when they hit. They're out to kill and swallow fast, so too fine a leader may not be able to take the positive shock strike. Never let the rod point directly at the lure if the line is near taut. Keep the tip up or at enough of an angle sideways so that the shock will be partially absorbed by the bend of the rod.

It may be of interest to you to note that streamers, themselves, are not new. How they actually started is problematical but it's a guess that ragged, strung out wet flies were the beginning. The bucktail streamer, no one knows how far back they went in fishing history, but Emerson Hough, a noted and respected angler, I understand, brought samples down from the North country which were tied by natives, and their use could possibly have gone back centuries. This example is not unlike many of the known deer hair and bucktail dry flies we now use with definite labels. Many of them were used by the Indians in Canada and some of the Northern states before the creators of these named flies were born. Emerson Hough could very well have tied up bucktails, with a slight change over those he saw and had his name go down in fly history with his name tacked on all bucktail flies. He didn't and may the gods have granted him, from that moment, taut lines the rest of his fishing days in appreciation.

A few suggested streamers that have proved effective, not only in one locality but in waters across the country:

Those marked with an asterisk (*), in the author's opinion, are good ones with which to start.

*BLACK GHOST
BLACK DACE (primarily eastern)
*WHITE MARIBOU
*BLACK MARIBOU
MICKEY FINN
BEAN SPECIAL
GRAY GHOST
CHAPPIE (yellow-orange)
BABY FARIO
*NIPIGON BELLE (D Gapin)

*COCK-A-TUSH, (D Gapin), muddler minnow)
EDSON LIGHT TIGER
SUPERVISOR
*BABY GAIRDNERI
*VAMPIRE COACHMAN
*BUCKTAIL PATTERNS
*SQUIRREL TAIL PATTERNS
*BABY FONTINALIS

FISHING THE NYMPH

The nymph's life, up to the time he feels the urge to get out in the open air, is spent under rocks, covered with silt or in a case constructed of gravel, sand or sticks. When this latter type nymph, the caddis or sedge, has the desire to move he drags his house around with him. As he grows in size he builds an addition to this case house. In the instance of the ephemoptera or the commonly called Mayfly nymph, he likes mud and spends his time covered up with the stuff. As he grows older he is found, too, sometimes under rocks and stones on the stream bed. The real rock and stone inhabitant gets his name, the Stonefly, from his inclination, at this stage of his life, to keep himself protected and out of sight of his chief enemy, the fish, by living under stones.

Just preceding the Mayfly nymph's emergence into a dun, on the water's surface, he is a pretty active creature. (See Fig. 43.) A fast mover in the water, he makes a number of trips from the stream bed to the surface. It looks like he cannot make up his mind. The latest theory on the cause for this behavior is that his respiratory system is undergoing a fast change and until this alteration has been completed he has to impatiently exercise his swimming muscles and keep moving.

During this interval when he's in midwater darting around the trout have a banquet. We can place this activity in its later stages by observing swirls and bulges in the water made by fish feeding on this nymph. The earlier stages take place much closer to the stream bed. This period is the big dinner time for our trout. Activity continues, but somewhat abated, into the mid waters, then to the upper strata where we can visualize the action.

NYMPH ACTIVITY PRECEDING EMERGENCE ~ TYPES OF PATHS TRAVELED

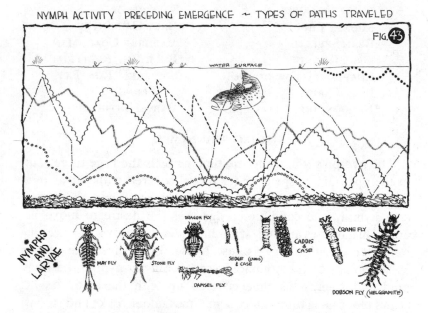

Sometimes we see parts of the tail of a trout breaking the surface intermittently. They seem to be trying to stand on their head but they actually are nosing around on the stream bottom moving stones about to expose the nymphs. We call this action "Tailing." I've watched trout do this, then slip back in the current and wait for the nymphs to be washed down to them.

An English fisherman and writer, G.E.M. Skues, may have been the originator (some writers credit him with it) of nymph fishing as we know it, but at least he popularized and promoted it a long time ago. It was his conviction that true nymph fishing was the topmost rung of sporting fishing, supplemented by dry fly fishing as the secondary method. It was his claim, and most experts concur, that nymph fishing as it should be done required much more skill and much more stream and trout knowledge than any other order of trout fishing.

Some of the maneuvers in nymph fishing are very similar to the fishing of the standard wet fly upstream but true nymph fishing is not "chuck and chance it" by any means but is a skilled exploration of the water, based on the scientific application of experience and knowledge of trout habits, aquatic feeding, aquatic insects and stream currents. Fishing nymphs, skillfully, will result in more and larger fish day after day than any of the other fly practices. This method takes fish when the other methods are practically dormant in action.

If you should be fishing a representative looking nymph fly during the trout's nymphing activity you'll have little difficulty inducing them to taste what you have to offer. Your major difficulty is in knowing just when they are mouthing the lure.

In fishing nymphs you are bound to make many fruitless hooking maneuvers when you think you've felt a touch. Nymph anglers try to develop the habit of watching the knot to which the leader is affixed to the line. As this knot drifts toward you it should precede at an even tempo. A pause in its travel indicates that the nymph has been halted for some reason. That reason might be that it was delayed by dragging itself around a rock, on the bottom, or it might be a trout. So you set the hook. Raise the rod easily, but swiftly. A tug with the left hand is advisable, too, if there seems to be more slack than the rod tip can straighten rapidly. I have heard of other nymph fly anglers casting their lure into a large pocket, which would supposedly hold good trout, determining or guessing when the fly had reached the feeding area, count three and set the hook. It sounds crazy but it works oftener than you would think.

If you are fishing a stream in an area where small birds abound you will notice, sometimes, that they seem to be gathering and holding fairly close to the stream. They have ascertained, by observation or through the bird's grapevine, that the nymph life is becoming restive on the stream bed and they seem to know instinctively that it won't be too long before an emergence is going to take place. They relish duns that leave the water and clumsily fly to bushes and grass at the stream's edge. This signal of nymph activity is your signal to go down after your feeding trout.

One of the most opportune times to fish your nymph fly is during and immediately following the run off after a high water period. Whether the high water was occasioned by rainfall or a man-made changing of a water level in a dam above.

A nymph fly fished deep and near an overhanging bank is one of the most resultful areas in which to find feeding fish cruising up and down on the lookout for just the kind of an insect you're showing them. Another good site is in runs between weed beds. Smooth, quiet water that flows between faster, rougher water courses is an apt locality in which to try your nymph, as are points in and around eddies in the stream.

Drag in fishing wet flies, generally, is not a serious point but in fishing the nymph correctly drag is as much an odious plight as it is in dry fly fishing. Although there is a tendency for the line and leader to form a tension pull on the lure it is not quite so prevalent as the creation of a wake on the surface of the water. To avoid the drag under water it is well to keep the rod well up permitting the least possible amount of your line to stay on the water to create a surface pull against the leader and fly. Another method is by fishing an exaggerated slack line which, by the time it has straightened out to do its vicious pulling, allows the nymph fly to complete its searching journey. With the slack line method, however, by the time you usually get around to a taut pull to set a hook, the fish has hit, tasted, spit out and, it being so long ago, has almost forgotten the incident.

If in starting on the stream to fish a nymph and you're doubtful, at the moment, which "bug" to select, a good general rule to follow is to pick one which somewhere near matches the color of the stream bed where you are to fish.

Another broad formula is, in choosing a fly to fish, if the stream or the section, which you are to fish is quiet slow moving water, put on an Iron Blue Dun colored nymph. If the stream is fast, riotous, rough over gravel beds or rocks, use a brown toned fly. If the water is just medium, between the two mentioned, use either an olive or fawn nymph fly. These suggestions are only general, they might work and they might not but they have proved successful more times than they have failed.

Every fly tier and manufacturer of nymph flies, like the blind Arabs feeling the elephant and guessing what it is, seem to see the little fellow in many different ways. Every tier believes his formula to be superior and he wonders how it is, how it can be, that the other fly tier's interpretation seems to work equally well. There again we are trying to see the nymph as we think the trout sees it. Several years ago a fly tier and writer, by the name of Louis Rhead, attempted to influence fly fishermen to the theory of exact imitation or exact reproduction of the natural fly just as closely as skill and materials would permit. The theory displayed feet of clay in that we didn't include the fish's viewpoint, which as it turned out, the impressionistic patterns secured better results. We see little of the Rhead theory in modern fly tying. Over a period of time, and of hundreds of fly tiers making minute changes, which are accepted after trial, the flies simulating the various naturals have evolved into comparatively definite standard details. The nymph fly, like the various methods of fishing it, is now going through the stages of trial and error. Later on they, too, will evolve into a semblance of accepted, proven patterns, or models.

The next suggestion is a closely held secret of a number of successful anglers who, in their experimenting practices, discovered it. Rarely does it fail. When nymphs are known to be working, at the onset of an emergence "hatch" and during the hatch, pick a matching nymph fly from your fly box and treat it with your dry fly oil or floatant. Fish it as you would a dry fly. It might be well to have a modest assortment of nymphs tied on fine dry fly hooks for just this purpose. If the presentation is carried out with care and precision become alert to the surges of taking trout. If the presentation is incorrectly handled, however, you must accept the fact that exercise only, and just being outdoors, too, is beneficial.

Some fishermen frown on the use of weighted flies. In the case of the nymph, however, in order to reach the lower feeding strata of water, it is sometimes necessary. The added weight should ordinarily be built into the nymph when it was tied. A weight added to the leader will work but some difficulty is encountered in manipulation and in hooking your fish. Unlike the wet fly fished downstream where the leader only is weighted, the nymph, being fished generally upstream, would be hampered by a weight on the leader. G. E. M. Skues, who fought so energetically to have nymph fishing recognized as the acme of sport in fishing trout, when confronted with the "weighted nymph" question, argued successfully that weight added to a nymph fly, to assist in its effectiveness, was identical to adding oils or floatants to a dry fly so that it, too, would be at its best.

I have used nymphs both with weights added and unweighted also, as conditions demanded. I have also placed a couple "B" shot about eighteen inches above my nymph when I wanted the fly to go down after them. I cast upstream and slightly across, or if it was an undercut bank edge the nymph was dropped as closely as possible to the bank and allowed to sink to the bottom. I gathered in line as the slack was formed by the fly drifting in my direction. When it passed my position, in the stream or on the bank, I cast short loops, without disturbing the drift of the fly, to force some of the line I had retrieved back out the guides. When I judged that the cast had reached the control limit I permitted the line to tighten and the nymph arose toward the surface. Watch this point! That's where the fish is most likely to take it and he usually hooks himself.

Before we go further in this subject permit me to advance a strategic suggestion that may appear to be superfluous but that has paid off when the excitement of the battle prevents your doing it. As you start to fish or work a pocket, observe the shore and the water around you. Plan where you'll stage the fight, if you hook one and then have anything to do with where it will be fought. Determine the spot where you'll lead your fish for netting or beaching. This little precaution seems unimportant but it could mean the difference, under certain conditions, between success and failure in each fishing adventure.

To acquire a comparable degree of skill, in taking trout, that one can grasp in the matter of a couple of days fishing the dry fly would demand, at least, a couple of seasons of fishing the nymph fly. Discouragement is the greatest bane to the angler first attempting the proper, and resultful, methods of using the nymph and it should not be so because there are thousands of accomplished fishermen working these nymph flies that are doing no better than first-timers—fishermen that are convinced they're doing it the right way but with results proving otherwise.

To the best of my knowledge I would estimate that there are probably less than a dozen nymph fly experts in the country. To be successful constantly, and it is very possible, requires a high measure of casting skill, a pretty thorough knowledge of trout ways, a fair comprehension of stream currents and flow and a familiarity of the aquatic creatures and of the simulated frauds being used at the end of our leaders.

As to the leaders to use in fishing nymphs, follow the same suggestions advanced for fishing the wet fly. Go to even finer tippets if you feel that you can successfully handle your fish.

Suggested nymph fly patterns. Those marked with an asterisk (*) are, in the author's opinion, the best with which to start if no other evidence of type is available.

*MAY FLY NYMPH, (general pattern)	BLACK NYMPH, (D. Marteniz)
"VIC CRAMER" NYMPH	*IRON BLUE NYMPH
STONEFLY CREEPER	OLIVE NYMPH
*HARE'S EAR NYMPH	GINGER NYMPH
*HENDRICKSON NYMPH	*CAHILL NYMPH

MARCH BROWN NYMPH
*PARTRIDGE, YELLOW
MOSSBACK NYMPHS
(D. Bailey)
STRAWMAN NYMPH
(Paul Young)
*COACHMAN NYMPH
(grizzly hackle)

ROCK WORM-CADDIS
CARROT & BLACK
NYMPH
*POTT'S "MITE" SERIES
(both plain and
palmered)
*FRESH WATER SHRIMP
(not a true nymph
but fished much
like one)

BAIT FISHING

Paraphrasing a saying by the great Indiana poet, J. W. Riley:

"Speakin of artful bait fishin' I once knew a man, in Boyne Falls, Michigan, who could cast out his angle worm an' spit on it 'fore it hit th' water."

ONCE A fisherman gathers a little skill in fishing he will rarely turn to bait because the kick seems to be lacking. There isn't a truthful expert or experienced fly fisherman but who must acknowledge the use of bait in his earlier fishing days, so there are none who can go high-hat or look down on the user of bait by those less skillful or by the youngsters just starting.

The most popular standby throughout the country is the good old garden hackle of nostalgic memory for most of us. Fishing the worm successfully is not the easiest kind of work. The worms must first have been prepared by toughening in moss and in impaling on the hook do not pierce him in several places to make a lumpy mass. Get one good hook hold either in his middle or at the larger end and let him squirm. Read the nymph fly fishing procedures and follow that pattern of handling your worm. The natural bumping along the bottom is by far the finest and most efficient exercise to follow whether fishing upstream or downstream. Grubs, rockworms and live nymphs are fished the same way.

The salmon egg is the most popular bait in the far west, whether used singly on a salmon egg hook or in clusters. The cheese baits are next in line and becoming increasingly popular because if luck is bad one can eat the bait. The method of fishing salmon eggs, in states or areas where this bait is permitted, is the simplest possible performance and requires little or no knowledge of trout, of water currents or of fishing generally. It's merely a matter of dunking the lure and keeping it in the water. In lakes it's fished just off the bottom and it's pure "chuck and chance" wherever used. I heard a salmon-egger reporting at one time why the egg must be kept off the bottom. He said, "We salmon-eggers mostly chum a bit with eggs or canned corn before we start to fish. Well at Lake Crowley (in the Sierra Nevada mountains) the whole bottom was paved with chum and to make our egg look different we had to raise it up a few inches."

If you do prefer the use of salmon eggs and must chum before you fish them I hope you're not a canned corn user. I saw a couple baby rainbows washed to shore that had died from eating chummed canned corn and I never could forget it. Nearly all states, that are at all modern, and with the interests of future fishing in mind, prohibit chumming. In all fairness that's the way it should be. The use of salmon eggs in some states is against the law and eventually, as those others remaining, where eggs are used, awaken, they too will clamp down. Egg clusters are used primarily for larger trout and steelheads in the streams, although lakes, too, get their share of "cluster" fishermen.

Crickets, grasshoppers, large caddis flies, stone flies (called salmon flies in some localities) impaled on the hook or caught through their collar are fished floating or sunken, either upstream or downstream. These baits are most effective if fished during the period when your trout are accustomed to seeing them and feeding upon them.

Minnow fishermen usually have their own pet way of handling this lure and if one got them altogether in a group to outline their secret we'd find practically a consensus of like methods. There's no secret in minnow fishing. Make your lure act like a minnow and you're in. Read the chapter on wet fly and streamer fishing.

Miscellaneous baits, and they're legion, each have their adherents. Cheese balls, dough balls, liver chunks, bacon chunks, beefsteak pieces, fish tails or fins, fish eyes, cut bait from fish flesh, shrimp, clam and oyster baits, crawfish, crawfish tails, caterpillars, other bugs of all kinds and fat pork are but a few of the grocery listings used to entice trout. The top secret of their success is to keep them in the water and try varying depths until the right fishing depth is found.

In fishing bait a general rule to follow, which works in the majority of instances, is, on feeling a touch, to let the trout have the lure a while before striking. Small trout pick at the bait—larger fish are more deliberate, more positive.

'HARDWARE'—ARTIFICIAL LURES

Many otherwise confirmed fly fishermen, to be able to garner enough trout to form a layer in the frying pan, have, for one reason or another, resorted to their pet spinner or spoon or other artificial lure to accomplish the feat.

In nearly all instances these "hardware" lures are fished, as are wet flies, downstream and in the same general manner or trolled slowly in lake fishing.

The common spinner, used with or without the supplementary fly or bait, is perhaps the most popular artificial enticer. Anglers who have experience in using the spinner also have their favorite shapes and their theories on which kind fits best or works best in fast water, in slow water or in dead water. The more choice shapes are known as Colorado, Indiana, Bear Valley, June Bug, Willow Leaf and the somewhat different Aeroplane propeller blade spinners. Fishermen use their spinners naked in some instances and in others they attach their favorite spinner fly, streamer, pork rind, pork chunk, chamois strips, meat strips, etc.

In gathering factual material for this chapter I went into a huddle with an old-timer from Kentucky who had a reputed know-how for catching, not only trout but every species of sweet water fish he put his mind to. The knowledge and skill that he possessed and demonstrated was worthy of praise yet he claimed it was only horse sense.

"They ain't nothin' mysterious about it," he stated, "Any water splasher could do it as good as me if they'd jes' listen. No, they gotta go on the way the latest magazine article told 'em—so, they don't catch the fish an' I do."

His method, which was no secret, was in using strips of fish belly skin, preferably white, hooked on and trailed behind his spinner or spoon lure. I gathered from his instruction that the strip should be narrow and not too long. The skin strip should be scaled and scraped almost clean. A little meat left on, near the hook end, would be advantageous. He said it would impart more "flavor" to the lure. He varied the shapes, for no particular reason except a hunch, from a long narrow triangle to a snaky wave cut, a narrow oval and one that had finger-like streamers cut into the piece. I was also informed that pork rind, chamois or white kid skin strips were also good but not as effective as the real thing which had action and also exuded taste and smell.

The spoon lures, which flutter and wag their way through the water are a popular decoy when metallic; weighted lures are the type chosen for use. Spoon lures come in a number of varying patterns. Some are shaped like a modified dumb-bell and some are pear shaped, triangular, cone shaped, diamond shaped, oval shaped, egg shaped, shaped like a fish, circular like a tin can cover and quite a few are spoon shaped. Like the spinners, all are not metal. They show up in plastic, bone and mollusk shell, among others. The metal spoons are usually nickel or chrome, copper, gold and brass and the large majority are enameled or partially enameled in striking colors and patterns, some of them fantastically futuristic.

I've seen tandems of spinners running to as much as five and six feet long, ahead of the trailing baited hook or fly. These tandems consist of from two to a dozen blades, sometimes all the same size but generally tapering from extremely large to smaller ones. I'm told these are "attractors" to point out the lure to interested trout. These tandems are used only in trolling behind a boat. Paul Bunyan might have been able to cast them but you and I would look mighty silly trying to fling them around.

Both the regular spinners and spoons, with or without the additional skin strips, require current or forced pull to bring out their action. In a stream they would be worked similarly to the methods used in fishing a streamer fly. In lakes, they are generally slow trolled and are more effective just short of the bottom or close to aquatic foliage patches or weed beds. If casting or using spinning tackle try the cast out—let sink— wait three or four minutes—then retrieve slowly, method. A couple of successful experiences doing that and you'll wonder why you used to be so impatient and anxious to start reeling in. You had the lure back to you before the fish you were after had recovered from the scare of the splash, occasioned when your bait struck the ceiling of their dining room.

A tremendously effective artificial lure is that of the curve shaped wood or plastic wobbling plug of the Flatfish type. There are many lures patterned after this enticer and some of them are pretty good. It is the opinion of many experienced fishermen, including myself, that these light-weight, under surface plugs will get the desired action out of a trout when other lures are not getting the response you'd like to expect. They must, however, be handled and fished carefully against the current and the current will force them to deliver the movement for which they were designed. These little artificials troll well if done just as slowly as patience will permit. If they are not running deep enough, pinch on a shot or two of lead two or three feet ahead of it. If placed too close to the bait you may lose some of the desirable action which tantalizes the trout into a frenzy of vicious savagery. In striking this type lure usually the fish is not fooling. He bangs it hard and either hooks himself or he doesn't. The angler has little to do with it. His job is to keep a taut line and hang on.

One procedure to follow with a small lure of this character, in the stream, is to work from the bank and fish it close in as slowly as the current will permit. If the water is fast, keeping the bait too close to the surface, it may be well here also, to attach a shot or two to the leader as outlined above to pull it deeper into the water. Even though the lures are constructed to bite into the current, if it's too fast the lure turns and rides the top or just spins, twisting the leader ahead of it. If the plug isn't acting right examine to see if a hook is caught over the leader which sometimes happens and this kills the effective movement.

Many anglers fish the lure across stream to cover the middle waters just as a streamer fly is used, most times. If wading the stream and fishing from the center this is the right procedure. The lure will swing around until directly ahead and this is the spot where strikes generally occur. Some fishermen like to work the bait some distance ahead of them, if the water is deep and this, too, is a productive method.

Although a fly fisherman, being accustomed to light leaders, is tempted to use these artificials on that same leader which he would use in casting the fly, he should be cautioned to step up the tippet strength to approximately a minimum of three pounds (.009) or four pounds (.011), which means a heavier leader throughout, or use a level monofilament leader inasmuch as casting is no problem as in the use of flies. I've gone to as high as six-pound tippets (.012 or .013) where the water was rough and the fish large. The lure itself carries enough weight to straighten out the leader and I might pass on the warning that sometimes, unless the cast is perfectly executed, the lure can sing by, overhead or "nearhead," too close for comfort. It may even strike pay dirt. Although small and light, the tunk that it delivers is sometimes severe even if one discounts the danger in the dangling hooks.

There are many different types of "hardware" lures for both trout and other fish species. In addition to the fly rod baits, the regulation spinning lures and the well-known "bass" plugs all have their place in trout fishing. Then there is the galaxy of miscellaneous plugs and lures of diverse shapes, sizes, construction and action. One example is the balsa wood or plastic, pear shaped, fluorescent "cherry bobber," created by a fisherman barber in the state of Washington. The tie clasp Super Duper lure invented by an angler in Southern California, and now being manufactured by a major tackle concern, is another. Lures which carry batteries and light up, lures that bleed, lures that are purposely noisy, lures that emit fish odor and lures which do everything but find the fish for you, and even that one might hit the market next year. Those are additions to the old stable standbys. Many of these enticers are presented to us each year. Some, figuratively, like the rockets, shoot up, flare momentarily, then fade out. Some continue their effectiveness, in varying degrees, from then on.

Trout appear to develop odd characteristics when it pertains to odd lures. They might go for them like some people go for money and then again, on certain days, they'll shy off and hide from them or deliberately ignore them. The fish actually seem to become familiar with certain lures and wisely are not tempted by them after a brief acquaintanceship. I'm certain trout have quite a limited sense of humor, but at times they seem to laugh at us for trying to fool them with what we think is a real killer. This "pig in a poke" uncertainty with what will happen when we cast out our appetite tempter is the objective which makes fishing so much fun.

SPINNING

This comparatively new method of fishing, in this country, is becoming increasingly popular for the reason that even amateurs can learn the procedure in a few minutes and become adept and fairly accurate with a few hours practice. Many authorities are of the opinion that this method of fishing attained its popularity because it permitted the unskilled children and women a fishing occupation while the "boys" coursed the riffles, with their fly rods, around the bend.

Spinning or threadline fishing serves a somewhat definite need between the fly rod and the plug casting rod. It is primarily for use on lake waters and larger streams. It is definitely an effective and accepted method for salt water fishing and is being used in just about all types of this sport. The only exception is that it is not too efficient on the big game fish, but this will probably come. The type of construction of the reel and the rod permits casting artificial lures to as small as one twentieth of an ounce with extremely light delicate tackle and with heavier spinning equipment the bait or lure can exceed ounces.

The major attractive feature of regular spinning is the fact that it can be done with your back to a wall or a clump of shrubbery. Because of the frictionless stationary reel distances are remarkably easy to reach.

Spin lines built like miniature big-head or torpedo lines can be used to cast flies, after a fashion, but the rod must be manipulated as is a fly rod with a back cast or two to start the line in motion. Another popular means of fishing the fly with spinning tackle is the use of transparent plastic bubbles containing water or mineral oil for weight.

In consulting a considerable number of anglers who use or have used both the fly rod and the spinning mediums, coupled with my own humble opinion, the conclusion is that for fishing pleasure and fishing results, there is no method even comparatively close to that of fishing flies with a fly rod by one who knows a little something about it. That "something" I have endeavored to give you. Spinning is here to stay, of that there is no doubt. For certain kinds of waters, and for certain kinds of fishermen, spinning is the answer to a long sought means that would enable us to match the skill of the fly caster, in some instances, and provide a measure of successful fishing.

Fish, and in any reasonable amount, can be caught so easily by the spinning method that the sport loses, for many, much of its fascination. Using spinning tackle on a number of occasions, the thought kept running constantly through my mind that I was wasting good fishing time, that if I only had my fly rod in hand I could really have some fun.

Chapter 7

The Little Brooks

And this our life, exempt from public haunt,
Finds tongues in trees, books in running brooks,
Sermons in stones, and good in everything.
I would not change it.
            Shakespeare—(As You Like It, Act II, Scene I)

THE AUTHORITATIVE angler who drops his fly on the Esopus, the Beaverkill or the Ausables in New York, the Penobscot in Maine, the Mad in New Hampshire, the Pere Marquette or the Jordan in Michigan, the Brule or the St. Croix in Wisconsin, the Brodhead in Pennsylvania, the Housatonic in Connecticut, the White or the Ompompanoosuc in Vermont, the Gunnison in Colorado, the Skokomish in Washington, the Snake, Salmon or Silver in Idaho, the McKenzie or Metolius in Oregon, the Owens, Feather or McCloud in California or the Little Colorado in Arizona, may and most often times does doff his fly draped hat to the blue jeaned youth who, with his cut pole, his earthworm or dap fly, snakes his silent way along the brush topped and meadow meandering baby "cricks" and takes his mess of eatin' trout when he chooses, while foreigners to his water come up with but a brace of eight inchers or fail miserably.

These tiny lotic rivulets, many just capillaries to the well-known arterial trout streams over the country, were and are

140

the schooling grounds of many of our millions of trout anglers. And of these millions a great majority seldom or never have the adventure of feeling the surging throb or experiencing the flashing struggle of trout in the well publicized streams. Many dream of the day or resolve that they will shape their future so that they will taste the thrill of wading or coursing the banks of those waters little realizing that they, when they like, are on the home base of the true sportsman, the land of the little brooks so imbedded in the nostalgic memory of most of us.

I recall a small stream, tightly fringed with jealous brush, guarding shadowed pools, carpeted with fontinalis moss, no larger than a dish pan and where the few open areas were choked with crisp, bitter-sweet water cress, where miniature rapids boiled over diatomic, varnished pebbles and gurgling riffles charged into undercut banks, where pocket holes of mysterious dark water swirled under sunken dead falls. Some sections of this run were hardly wide enough to dip a bucket of water. This was the headwaters of the Boyne, located in a lumbered-over district of Northern Michigan, but the description, with few alterations, pictures literally thousands of similar flows and feeder streams across the country. Alike, yes, but no two ever were identical. Every turn in their course is a mysterious promise even to those who claim familiarity. In the lower lands these streams just move happily along and in the hills and mountain areas we add more boulders and the water roars with laughter as it races down slopes or leaps from rocky steps to rocky steps and boiling pools. This gentle, diminutive brook, I remember, was where my cousin Eddie and I cut our incisors on trouting and where we learned, nearly always, to garner a few keepers to take home and show. On rare occasions we met another angler, usually a grown up (14 years of age or older), from whom we may or may not have secured a bit of trout lore. I recall one instance when a kindly fisherman told us of a whopper that made a certain undercut bank pocket his home. He related that he had had him on a couple times before but he couldn't interest him this trip. How could he when Eddie had him safely buried in damp moss in his basket?

He was all of eleven inches in length and we sagely kept still about it. Eddie had seduced him with a dapped Montreal fly.

Whether these little brooks are headed for larger waters in the White, Green or Berkshire mountains in upper New England, the Adirondack or Catskills, the Alleghanies, Blue Ridge, the Smokies, the Cumberlands or the Ozarks, the Canadian border states or in the Rockies, the methods of fishing them vary only slightly. Whether it's a barefooted youthful nomad or a renowned surgeon seeking relaxation or the village plumber stealing a couple hours between jobs, they must, if they wish a modicum of success, pretty generally follow a few natural rules, augmented with their own secret formulas. The fishing procedures and methods, too, are quite a stretch from the customary and repeatedly quoted designs for working the larger streams. The fish in these larger streams may, as a rule, run to more length and weight but certainly are no more wary or wiser than the habitants of the little streams. Emphatically, no less skill is demanded in inducing the smaller stream trout to partake of your offering and in many cases the effort needed to place your lure, in the best way, where it might do the most good, is a most discouraging process. These tiny creek trout have to hustle to satisfy their hunger but the environment with even fewer visitors tends to emphasize their self-preservation instinct.

Whether the angler is a fly tosser, a worm chunker, a salmon egg or cheese soaker or a "hardware" devotee, weaving the lure through a snarl of brush to reach a presentation point is no job for a nervous individual. The successful fisherman of the little brooks must copy the stealth of an Algonquin, develop the monumental patience of nature itself, have the energy of an ambitious ant and the curiosity of a detective. Possessed with these traits in more than average abundance all he then needs is the perseverance of a spider trying to build a web bridge from table to phone in the home of a feminine teen-ager, and a studious obsession to learn the water he is fishing. From there on it's merely a natural skill and some experience.

The fishing tackle required to work the little streams can

encompass an almost complete outlay down to an economical
set-up costing just about nothing. I have observed boys and
men carry their stuff in a pill box and it consisted of a couple
of bait hooks, some split shot, a chunk of leader and a few
feet of level fish line or just a piece of strong kite string. Maybe
it was an extravagant outfit and boasted of a few flies and
spinners, too. Their rods were supplied at the point of action
from nature's bounty and their bait, if used, was found under
rocks, off the bushes, in the grass, from the soil, or nymphs and
muddlers from the stream itself. On the other hand, he who
enjoys the use of good rods and fine equipment can go as far
as he chooses in outfitting himself. In the meadow flows the
angler may please to use his finest rod, his double-tapered fly
line and his trout net but in the "bush" they're out of place.
The sweetest fishing rod for thicket maneuvering is one from
four to six feet in length and it shouldn't be too delicate or too
limber. In this type of fishing one rarely has the opportunity
of playing his fish—that would be quite one-sided in favor of
the fish. When a trout has been caught, usually the fisherman
lays to and, if the alders permit, throws him skyward in hopes
he'll land where he can be found. I built a very serviceable
rod from the tip and mid-section of a discarded bamboo three
piece that didn't have too much of a set. Building a new grip
with cork pads, using the old reel seat, increasing the size of
the guides to allow more freedom in letting out line and I had
the ideal instrument for the brush. A trout net is just a troublesome luxury when crawling on hands and knees through a
copse of cedar, scrub oak, alder or laurel . . . every protruding twig grabs hold of it with intent to keep forever.

The lure or lures to be used is pretty much an opinion
matter and I'm guessing that about three out of five resort to
worms, grubs, nymphs and of course grasshoppers when in
open runs where the hoppers are in evidence. Many use
cheese, fresh meat pieces and salmon eggs where it is legal to
do so—some even employ the use of small minnows. Then
there is another fifth that use spinners, small spoons and fly
rod and spinning lures. The last fifth use artificial flies both
wet and dry. I know of anglers that are good fly fishermen

and that feel that the use of bait is a fall from grace. I can make that statement without hesitation because I went through that phase. Most of the time, in brook fishing, bait or spinners is the only lure that will attract fish for some fishermen and more power to them. I've used both and will again if I have to when I want action and my flies won't produce. Because I belong to the fifth that use flies is no sign that I believe it's the only way. I do it because I selfishly enjoy it above all other methods and because I, personally, have found that I can do better with flies under every condition that I have encountered so far.

Now that we have the prologue out of the way let's take a jaunt up "Lost" Creek or over on Perkin's pasture and see if we can't snare us a mess o' trout for supper.

As we leave the dirt road, heading downstream, there is a discernible path of sorts winding along the banks of the brook on each side. You'll note that the twisting track is much like that made by cattle, following the line of least resistance. There will be worn patches, off the path, at stream's edge where a fair sized pool is easy to reach but the path will completely circle areas of tough going like "hard to get over" deadfalls or rocks or solid barricade thickets of streamside brush. You'll also note that there are no worn patches near the water where the overgrowth makes it work to fish or where the chances of possibly losing the hook on snags or river weed is great. Too many fishermen have the optimistic attitude, in fishing the little waters, that up ahead a ways it probably is easier to work so they'll pass up some of the finest opportunities, scrambling along the beaten trail until tired, semi-discouraged and impatient. In that frame of mind they'll never add to their exhaustion by toting a creel weighted with trout.

The first thing we must do, and believe me it's very important, is to lay aside any thoughts that arise that the stream we're fishing is probably fished out or that there are none but little fellers to take our bait or our fly. Believe as strongly as you can that each place you choose to drift or sink your lure is holding a good one and that he's hungry as usual. If he doesn't take, blame yourself and be a mite more careful on the next hole. Be alert every minute as well as completely confident.

We aren't going to float our worm out or dap our fly without first carefully looking the water over to find the best spot in which to do it. We'll fish the usually fished pools, sure, but we'll also fish those tough locations that the other nine didn't fish. And we're going to stay out of sight and we're going to tread lightly, lightly, lightly. You must have observed or heard of incidents where two fishermen worked a little stream and one caught one or two seven-inchers and the other had a phenomenal day. You can be assured that the second fisherman was not seen or heard or felt until it was too late and that could very well have been the reason for the difference in results. The first angler was unlucky, the second created his own luck, if one believes in that superstition.

There on your side is a good looking pocket. You can't see it but the water swirls under the bank and it looks dark and deep. The alders are as thick as cultivated bushes in a nursery but if you pull your lure right to the tip-top of your rod you can ease it through. Now let it down gently and release all the line that you can. Ah, see? I was sure you'd connect. A nice one too. He's only about nine inches but brook trout are big for their size, and isn't he beautiful? They can spout off about goldens, sunapee or piute trout but give me a brookie every time. Try the same hole again, his brother is probably waiting for his chance and maybe his grand-dad is lying in there, too.

I've a good looking little pool right ahead of me. If I can just dangle my fly over this bush without showing myself. What'd I tell you? Did you see that flash? No, he didn't touch it . . . . probably wrong color or something. I'll try a different one. I've got an Adams, an Irresistible, a Black Gnat, a Wickham's Fancy, a Beaverkill and a Black Spider, all in size fourteen. Incidentally the type of fly or its silhouette isn't too important here if it's not too large or too small. I had on a Badger Bivisible, I'll try the Adams. It has plenty of hackle so it will dap good. See, I touch the water, raise it again, touch the water, let it float a second, up again. If there is a

slight wind it works even better as the breeze lifts, flutters and
drops it back, making it act like an insect trying to take off
and having difficulty. Another little ruse with the dry fly is
to crawl up quietly about your rod's length from the bank
and dap the fly on the edge so it will tumble naturally into
the water. On bright days this trick can be dynamite. If the
pocket you are trying to reach is under a bush or an overhanging log, and the area won't permit even a limited horizontal back cast you might "sling-shot" it in. Grasp the hook
tightly with your left hand and spring the rod tip to give you
a bow-like tension, aim and let it go.

Just for the fun of it I'm going to try a small, slender wet
fly, one that vaguely resembles a "fry" type minnow. This
could be a ten or twelve wet Gordon Quill, Ginger Quill,
Chappie, Mickey Finn, Cahill Quill, Whirling Blue Dun,
Professor, Alexandria, a sparse natural Bucktail or Squirrel
Tail pattern. I might even use a regular streamer as long as
it isn't too large. A size eight, ten or twelve would be about
right and almost any steamer pattern may be effective. One
of the surest ways to work a wet pattern is to get it as deep
as possible with the rod tip close to the water's surface then
work it back with a jiggling retrieve or pull and drop back
recovering line gradually as the lure is worked toward the tip.
The taking trout pretty generally hooks itself. So I caught
a couple on the Whirling Blue Dun, not large but nice pan
size. Anyway they were put back to grow some more.

We're coming up on a different kind of terrain. Here the
brush growth is so thick that fishing from the bank is out of
the question. We notice too that some parts of the stream are
almost dammed up with the jumbled deadfalls and leaning
cedars that look nigh impassable. We also note that the path
veers completely away from the stream and heads directly for
the open pasture that lies a couple hundred yards ahead.
Many anglers realize right here that they are just a bit worn
out so they take the passage to the clearing where the fishing
will be of a more civilized nature and easier. (They think!)

We're after some brookies and we turn our longing eyes
away from the tempting sunny expanse we can spot through

the trees and gingerly mince our way into the chill water. Quieter now because we're completely exposed and we're going to have to work our lure farther out ahead and as best we can close up. This is ideal water for worms, wet flies, spinners and flat-fish type light lures that work in the current. The flow here pours over submerged logs and sucks under another not quite so low in the water. My fly follows this water draft and disappears from sight. Then the delicious, surging tug tells me that this isn't the normal pan size, this is a real trout, maybe a specimen to mount. There's no tossing him upward—in fact he has the rod tip almost between the two logs and he's insisting on more line which I grudgingly release through my fingers. For a full minute or two he's the boss, then the throbbing tow eases and I get back my line inch by inch. I have no net, I cannot beach him so that means I stay where I am and tire him completely. He surfaces, then savagely bores down again. The next time up he rolls weakly and allows my fingers to get a grip on his gills. He's mine. Not a trophy in size, as he felt when he hit, but a beautiful fourteen-incher. Brilliant scarlet dots circled in sky blue. Pink, white and yellow dots fixed in round gray fields, the whole set in an iridescent olive, shading into orange and white on his belly, into sharply defined vermiculate, curly-que markings, almost black in tone, on his broad back. The lower fins of scarlet-orange contrasting with white frontal borders. Him I keep!

I examine the leader for frayed spots and the hook gets a lick or two from the sharpening stone. I'm ready again and my next interesting spot is where the water glides over a partially submerged stump and circles about, flecked with foam, before it takes off again. The fly sinks through the foam and starts to circle with the water. The trip around was never completed. This brookie was mean, confused and very excited. There was never a let up for rest. When he quit sashaying about the area he was all through and easy to creel, almost the mate to the other.

I had my imposed limit of two in my basket so now the rest was for fun. I noticed shortly that I was standing on coarse gravel and the brook spread out just below me into a quieter silt bottomed pool of a sort. What a place for a try with the nymph flies so I acted on the impulse. I put on a fraud mayfly nymph almost black in color, dropped it into the water at my feet and let it drift out into the pool. I guessed right this time. Action was immediate. After I released him, and he was all of ten inches long, I changed to a straw colored creeper. No action. I bent on a brown toned Vic Cramer nymph. No action. I tried an orange bodied grouse fly and took a small one. A yellow bodied grouse was good for a couple. I tried a rock worm fly. No action. I replaced with the dark mayfly nymph and took another before I moved on.

The stream coursing through the pasture or meadow was quiet—almost still in spots. The footing where we stand was muskeg spongy. This meant that every footfall would be radioed far ahead of us. If we used bait or spinners we would crawl as close as possible to the stream, right smack on our belly, reach out to the water with the rod and try to let the lure out to travel yards below. If we wanted to work the water close up we'd wait several minutes before we let the lure touch. Give the trout time to get over their scare.

I'm going to try dry flies so I'll be back some yards from the bank. I'll also be low enough so that my view of the stream will be only that open area between the sedge banks —I won't see much water. I'll necessarily have to false cast to get my fly located right . . . . this is good . . . . looks like bugs flying around. A slight twitch on the rod tip just before the fly alights may give me enough loose leader so that, I hope, I'll get a few inches of drag-free float. This would be an ideal situation in which to use spider flies. Besides being an effective bit to offer, no matter how presented, there will be less harm if there is a bit of drag or if the fly submerges. If my casting procedure doesn't work I'll do a crawl, too, up within a few feet of the water and dap my floaters just like I did back in the woods.

Ah, here's an old bridge . . . . probably used by the farmer to and from the fields or by cows, horses and sheep who dislike getting wet feet. The brook narrows and swirls as it leaps under the crumbling, rotting log beam. You can just know for sure that there are trout a plenty under there, particularly if it's during the heat of the day. Did you see that grasshopper hit the water just as it slid into that bridge shadow. I'll bet my tackle he'll never see daylight again.

The return to the road, fishing upstream, was a bit more difficult in the handling of our lures, but we knew the holes now, after a fashion. With the flow heading towards us we had to keep our line picked up. When the lure halted we set the hook. Usually it was a rock or moss or a twig but we had to be sure. Being just as careful and of course being less visible to the current-headed trout and we found the little brook even more productive than the first enjoyable coverage downstream. That is exactly what the man said would be the case.

Chapter 8

Lake Fishing

FISHING FOR trout in lakes, ponds and dams resolves itself into five major methods. These are, casting from a boat, casting from shore, trolling, drifting and plain old bait dunking.

This latter mode of fishing is that of nostalgic memory. Just bait fishing is one so often pictured portraying an individual comfortably snoozing, with his "pole" secured at an angle near him, and the bait immersed in the still water, hoping to attract some passing fish. With the huge majority of fishermen, bait dunking was their initiation into the pastime of luring fish. When we graduated from that practice into working for our fish we gave up the relaxing, peaceful pursuit to which we dream someday of returning, even if only temporarily.

Lacking experienced guidance in that very simple manner of fishing we usually placed our large hook with the heavy sinker two or three inches above, baited generously with a gob of closely packed angle worms. We varied the worm menu with grasshoppers, crickets, grubs, cheese, fish eggs, doughballs, pieces of meat or a very dead minnow. As we gathered experience we eliminated the sinker, then the bobber, and we started to use a leader, then smaller hooks. We performed jiggling motions and we cast the bait further out and slowly moved it back toward us.

150

Finding that the moving bait attracted more fish we worked from a rowboat or raft permitting it to drift where it would. If there was a slight wind we traveled in its direction as far as the shore then we'd row back slowly to the point of beginning to start the drift again.

The rowback was the first actual trolling we had done. It too secured fish for us. Then we tried the "hardware" lures— they worked (and still do) and so did wet flies and streamers. We didn't have to concern ourselves with the securing of live bait or of bothering with other messy ingredients. We could carry our trolling lures, spinners and flies in a box always ready for use.

When we became a bit adept in casting we worked the shore from the boat using streamer or wet flies or we used our plugs or spinners. If we didn't have a boat we cast from shore and were almost equally as successful.

Many of the same procedures in fishing a lure on a stream can be adopted in fishing still water. In the use of wet flies and streamers we create the current's force by either drifting the boat or working the lure by hand as we do on the stream.

In fishing dry flies, and the flies should be good floaters, our line must float or as it sinks it will pull the fly back toward us or pull it under the surface. After a cast and the dry fly is placed always leave it rest for at least a half minute, or even a full minute or more, then twitch it gently and let rest again. Repeat this action two or three times before you begin to twitch the fly, in jerks and pauses, back for another cast.

Fishing trout in lakes requires, for best results, some knowledge of the lake itself. If you cannot secure reliable advice as to where their feeding grounds are or where they usually can be found you must spend some time searching. Underwater vegetation will often disclose where fish are because the vegetation probably is the habitat of shrimp, nymphs and other fish food. As a rule where you have secured a strike or a fish there will be others in the neighborhood. A drift troll either dragging a lure behind the boat or casting as you drift will many times put you over a spot that may be just the type of fish water you're looking for.

Fishing a nymph is comparatively a simple exercise in lakes. It is important that a long fine leader be used and that the nymph be permitted to actually reach bottom and rest there for a moment. Then start a slow, slow, slow hand-twist retrieve. If you are in the vicinity of fish this manner of fishing is pure dynamite. Generally the nymph used in lakes is larger than those you would adopt for stream fishing. You must be alert for the vaguest "touch" and act speedily to hook your fish. Rarely will they strike a nymph as they will a traveling wet fly or streamer fly.

The wet fly is also permitted to go into the depths and the retrieve can be a normal hand-twist retrieve or a more rapid movement of lifting the rod tip a few inches, lowering it and taking up the slack and repeating until the fly is near enough to you to pull up and re-cast.

The streamer is fished similarly to the wet fly. Keep in mind that you are imitating a darting minnow or one supposedly trying to get out of that danger area. Sometimes an effective procedure is to cast and retrieve fast with the streamer near, or cutting, the surface of the water. As a general practice the trout hit a streamer more or less savagely. If they are tempted, and want it, they take without fooling. Streamers most resembling the minnow, or the young of the fish in the lake, are of more value than fancy patterns, yet there are times when the colorful "fancies" seem to be the only thing to which they'll pay any attention.

In the early part and the late part of the fishing season the shallows are usually most productive. During the more heated part of the season, particularly when the sun is bright on the water, the fish seek deeper parts of the lake. The shallower sections and shore areas have their innings earlier in the mornings and later in the day and at night.

Summing it all up, there is but one outstanding difference in fishing a lake or fishing a stream. On the stream you have a water current which assists you in working your lure. On the lake you must work the lure yourself. And the slower you work it, within reason, the better your results will be.

Chapter 9

From Strike To Creel

OVER HALF the trout you catch, deliberately but certainly not intentionally, hook themselves. You can take the credit should you wish because your listener believes you, as all anglers are traditionally truthful. Aren't they? The hooked trout, those which might have again become free agents and in which you had a finger in snaring, were caught because you delivered the twitch at the proper time and not too forcefully. The trout mouth is not too bony and hooks penetrate without difficulty. If you feel that the fish is caught merely on the hook point, twitch the rod tip two or three times until you're certain that the barb has penetrated the flesh or gristle.

Now that he's securely (we hope) connected to you do not follow your natural instinct to get him in fast. Never hurry, do not get panicky or impatient. If you're using ultra light tackle or any other kind of tackle keep a taut line, never release the rod pressure—maintain a bend in the rod to the degree which your judgment dictates is short of even the slightest danger. It certainly is a possibility that he may escape you, you don't know for certain how securely you have him hooked or where the hook is lodged. If you've failed to hook him properly it's a cinch that hurrying will separate him from you quicker than by patiently taking your time. Even if the contact is fragile, which you don't know at the moment, be

153

content to take it easy until he tires. Merely hold him as steady as you can during his first two or three sashays which will certainly be forthcoming if the fish is at all alive. Should the trout head for the sunken logs, rocks, weeds or underwater brush (if there's any in the close vicinity, that's where he'll try to get, for sure) you'll have to gamble a bit on something giving 'way, and hold him back using the bend of the rod. Refuse to let him have line unless you want to chance entanglement with those sunken obstacles or the sharp corners of rocks that might serve to part your leader. Naturally if the fish is large enough and strong enough to make you give ground to avoid breakage of some part of your tackle (broken rods have broken more hearts than loss of a mountable trout) you will have to grudgingly let him have his way with you temporarily. Should everything hold, work the "bugger" into open water where you can follow his escape maneuvers and circumvent them, where you'll have your best opportunity to fight back, and never permit him to rest if it can be avoided.

If the fish wants to run and is of the poundage that gives you assurance that he'll do as he darn pleases for a few moments, at least, the only advice anyone can give you is, "let him." If you're bank fishing at the time and the terrain permits it go with him—if you're stymied and have to stand pat let him have your line (I don't mean by this that you should relax —make him struggle for every inch) and hope that you have enough on the reel to discourage him.

Experience alone will tell you how to counter the moves of a struggling trout. For instance if a trout leaps clear of the water and falls on the leader it might pull the hook loose or even break a fine tippet if the line is held too tightly so we slack off just a little to prevent that occurrence. Some fish roll on a leader and manage to wind it around them in their floundering. The safest course to follow in this event is let him have line, he's just making it tougher on himself for the movement may wind himself up to the stronger parts of the leader. Always keep in mind that every leap, every run, every frantic move he makes brings him closer to the exhaustion point. Should a fish get himself entangled in weeds there isn't much that can be done. Hold on, sometimes the weeds part enough to permit the line to free itself, sometimes the fish himself will backtrack out of the weeds. Sometimes you may have to take all pressure off and see if the trout will drift or pull out on the other side of a weed clump where you might be able to net him. Sometimes you may have to chance it a bit and try to net the trout right out of the weeds.

Some hooked trout will, at times, come obediently right to the net (you can see yourself showing him off to the neighbors) then he spots the net or spots you and zowie he's off like a streak or he does a jump right in your face. Woe to you if you have an excessively tight line on him. Should your trout pull this ruse, and if you are not too surprised to act, release your hold on the line, or the reel if that's how your're fighting him, and point the rod in his direction. He'll take up any slack you may have without hesitation. Let him perform his acrobatics or his run without too much strain except a bend in the rod, keeping the line tight. When he's through he will likely come to you on his side. Don't hurry to get the net out. If you can, lift the trout's head out of the water a few times so that the water will back through his gills. He'll tire much quicker.

Anglers, of all grades of skill, are divided almost equally on whether to fight a fish from the reel or from free line stripped in and caught with the finger against the rod grip. Both systems have advantages and both have disadvantages and I recommend that you experience trials at each. The fact is, I am in a spot because I do it either way that comes handiest at the moment and for no particularly logical reason. Strive, if conditions permit, to guide your scrappy fish into quieter water. The trout's resisting pressure is reduced greatly when he loses the force of the current to press against in his struggle to get off the hook.

When the fish is ready to net or to beach, and that means he's an exhausted creature that has little or no fight left, lead him carefully to the spot you've picked for this move. If netting him never, never scoop him unless he has actually become detached from the fly and is getting away. You might succeed a couple times in a hundred in a case like that and it's worth the effort. (Probably shouldn't have mentioned that last because you'll do it anyway; the most dignified and most unemotional angler alive will take a swipe with the net in hopes of snaring the fish he almost had). If you can, lead your fish so that he will drift into the net head first. If that seems out of the question, get the net under him and lift it to encase the whole fish, or as the last resort let him drift tail first into the net, if it seems to be the only way. That latter procedure is the most dangerous because sometimes the fish revives enough to give a final swerve with that powerful tail, if any part of the net touches him, and it may be just that one last move that separates him from you.

Consider your net as a necessary adjunct or tool to use in preference to your hands, as a device or implement to assist you in safely landing your trout and then in handling him with the mesh between your hand and the fish whether it is your intent to release him or kill him.

If beaching the trout, care must be exercised and you should move slowly. If at all possible to get him to shore without grabbing hold of the leader do so. That gives him something stable to suddenly pull against and, if not too solidly hooked, he may tear loose. Use the bend of the rod, by all means, if the rod is of a quality or strength to take it, to draw the fish to the shallows where you may have the opportunity to grasp him behind the head or with your fingers in gill covering to pull him to safety. I've seen fishermen actually boot them to dry land and it isn't such a bad idea if it's a heavy fish.

For the sake of the tackle, let us mention here, in landing your fish, even baby fish of six to eight inches, never intentionally lift them bodily from the water with your rod. Free of the water cushion their weight is intensified greatly and many times it's just enough to permit a lightly hooked trout to drop off.

You've heard anglers complain, "Boy, oh boy! I lost a gorgeous brown today. Had him on for ten minutes and he got away. My luck's gone sour, I guess."

Do you think the fisherman blames his luck, the conditions

under which he fought the fish or the quality of his tackle? In ninety-nine cases out of one hundred it's one of the three. The one hundredth fisherman is brutally honest and blames himself. Were he not lacking in ability and skill, or his lack of alertness, the conditions under which he fought the fish would be of no particular concern. If the trout was poorly hooked, only one person in the world can be at fault. Poor hooking is faulty timing and is no accident unless the fish hooks himself, and our angler can take no particular credit for even catching him. Does he blame the leader strength? Who chose the size he was using—who checked it for faulty knots and possible weaknesses? Was the fly too small for secure hooking? Who selected it and put it on? One can run through all the excuses and the cause gallops directly back to our angler. He claimed, too, that he "lost" the fish. One cannot lose something he hasn't got! The man just had a struggle with a fish (probably one-tenth of the fisherman's weight, or much less) and because the fisherman, himself, "missed" on something the fish gave him a licking. It's tough but the good sport swallows the bitter pill and gives the fish credit.

When once you have your trout in hand, or on shore, and it's your intent to creel him, kill the fish at once by rapping his head sharply with a hard object (I use my fisherman's knife as a "tunker" when I'm keeping a fish). Anglers used to carry, as part of their stream equipment, a small replica of a leaded shillelagh, called an "Itchomaniac's Black jack" or "Priest" or "Fish Billy." If you don't choose to put him out of his misery with that coup de grace, break his neck by forcing his head backward with thumb in his mouth until the backbone noticeably cracks. If the fish is large, a cut just at the head severing the backbone will do the trick.

Fish will keep fairly well in your shaded creel if kept reasonably dry without cleaning but for the most adequate preservation, until you can put them on ice or in a cooler, clean your fish as soon as killed—do this DRY preferably. This leaves the protective slime coating over all parts and has a tendency to add hours to the keeping quality. Cleaning the fish in water washes away the coating, permitting active bacteria to start their spoiling action at once. After cleaning the fish thoroughly and certainly removing the gills and the kidney, which is the black bloody section along the spine, wipe the fish as dry as you can before creeling. I mentioned several chapters back that I was a "junk carrier" and part of that junk is a pad of absorbent paper toweling and a few sheets of wax paper. The purpose of this material is, I believe, self-evident. If the trout is wrapped dry, securely in wax paper, you can use dampened moss or grass in your creel and this makes quite a suitable stream refrigerator.

Never let the fish become even moist if you can avoid it even in ice-box refrigeration. Keep him dry, in wax paper. These admonitions apply, of course, to those fish that must be safely preserved and "freezing" is not an available service.

In transporting the fish that you're keeping, from camp to destination, iced certainly is the surest safe method. If icing isn't convenient or possible, do this: When ready to pack the fish, and this should be the final act in preparing to head homeward, remove them from whatever receptacle or place you had them to keep cool and wrap your wax papered fish singly in a sheet or two of newspaper or more wax paper or aluminum foil. Then in one or two groups, or in single batch, wrap the bundle in more newspaper and then some more. Wrap this whole bundle then in a heavy blanket or your sleeping bag and store in the car away from direct sun's rays. This system has safely kept trout cool and fresh, in many instances, for from eight to ten hours, and much of that time driving through the Mojave desert in July at midday.

Chapter **10**

Sportsmen's Ethics

WHETHER CALLED formality, good form, civility, etiquette, manners, courtesy, or ethics, one could fill a modest volume on things one should or shouldn't do in the opinion of real sportsmen if one wished to be regarded, himself, as a sportsman or just a real man on the stream.

I could plead that you do not walk up to the bank's edge if another fisherman is working in that spot. I could suggest that the fisherman working downstream, and meeting another angler fishing upstream, leave the water and circle around at a suitable distance before re-entering the water. The same procedure would be applicable if fishing from the bank or the stream's edge. I could advise that a fisherman wading the water and coming up on another angler fishing a particular hole, either from the bank or wading himself, wait until he is finished or get out and go around. I could urge one, if having fished a pool or a good pocket for a reasonable length of time, with others patiently waiting for a crack at it also, to pass on up- or downstream, at least temporarily, until they move on leaving the spot open for one to go back. However, I won't admonish you on any particular situation but will cover it in one sweeping Golden Rule plea:

> TREAT THE OTHER ANGLER AS YOU, IN ANY SITU-
> ATION, WOULD WANT TO BE TREATED!

159

If you are a cantankerous, obstinate, self-willed individual who feels you should, for any or no reason, be given preferred exemption and you won't, by gosh, give an inch, you have no business or right on a trout stream. The Creator gave us a heavenly privilege of fishing trout and he who deliberately cheats or purposely acts contrary to accepted sportsmanship practices should be toted on a knotty rail three times around the earth at the equator and I'll furnish the tar.

MODERN FLY TYING

Photo by Dean Vannice

THE AUTHOR

Dedicated to the army of piscato-rial philanderers who love the gentle art of throwing a make believe tid-bit into the menu area of colorful gamefish in an attempt to prove the absurd theory that hu-mans are smarter than they are!

Foreword

I NEVER did take a great deal of interest in fly tying until I was almost ten years of age. Before that, however, as far back as memory serves me, I have fished for trout. In this phase of my youth, a vivid imagination and a faith in the reality that water meant fish, I diligently pursued the piscatorial occupation in sump holes, open wells and ditches. The fact that when I was fishing with my father and had a mild degree of success never struck me as strange. Even now when fishing a stream, invariably I work all the water, that which is not completely out of reason, and it doesn't affect me as odd that so many times, in pockets that would hardly seem to shelter a hiding chub, I have hooked into satisfyingly sizable trout.

Since my first cast I have fished quite an expanse of water. I have experimented with just about every lure, both natural and artificial. I have, however, never used live minnows or dynamite, not because they aren't effective or perhaps illegal, but I just never could bring myself to it. Neither do I like salmon eggs or cheese, but where it is legal some of my most conscientious fishing friends use them on occasion.

I have the firm conviction that where fish, and I'm referring principally to the trout and char families, can be caught at all, they can be caught on either wet or dry flies. I could be prejudiced but a forty-year avocation endeavoring to deceive

163

crafty trout into tasting my offerings has not given me the slightest evidence that I have been wrong.

I have studiously read, I believe, every published book on the subject of flies and fly tying. I have read, also, hundreds of essays, sagas of instruction and revelation stories on the same subject in periodicals over the last quarter century. In fact my morgue of selected, clipped items and complete articles would, if baled, bring joy to the heart of a waste paper dealer. Throughout the entire perusal of this reading matter the one definite conclusion I reached is that the varying opinions and conflictions in methods, materials, etc., is all but explosive. Many of the writers are or were nationally known fly tiers and some of them I know were entirely sincere in their presentations, while others MUST have advanced their theories with tongue in cheek.

I cannot say that I learned fly tying the so-called hard way. I had the best teachers in the world. Starting with Halford, from whom I learned much, I absorbed the writings of McClelland, Bainbridge, Harding, Skues, Leonard and Williams of England, then Gregg, Cross, Sturgis, Young, Hyndman, Jennings and Bergman of this country. Later came other intelligent treatises by Leisenring, Flick, Blades, Laurie, Marinaro and Edson Leonard. I picked up helpful suggestions from scores of individual fly tiers including guides, professionals, experienced amateurs and even novices, whom I was teaching the art, and I tried everything. Of greater importance, which all the above would grant, I was curious about the actual living flies themselves. I went to the streams and lakes for true samples of the nymphs, the duns, the spinners, the caddis and sedge, the stone flies, the crane flies and of the land insects near the waters.

Seeking further knowledge, I purchased dozens of patterns tied by or supervised by noted fly tiers. These I carefully untied to discover methods. Here, too, the conflictions were evident but not so alarming as in the published expositions. Some of these flies were honestly tied and well worth the fee. Others produced by just as noted tiers and presenting an equally excellent outward appearance would, as soon as the finish knot was loosened, spring apart completely right down to the bare hook in many instances.

I have had serious-minded students come to fly tying classes, which I was conducting, who were supposedly in the advanced stages of acquiring this art. Their knowledge of materials and their efforts in fly construction were all but pitiful. Some of these individuals obtained their limited proficiency from other amateur tiers, tiers who apparently didn't know ephemeroptera from diptera, but most of the willing advanced pupils gained their know-how from books . . . . books, many of which, in my humble opinion, I thought were pretty good. Is it because manifestly many of these presentations have missed their target or are still advancing old-fashioned, out-moded methods, are incomplete in description, are too complicated in description or are too opinionated without divulging logical reasons? I was told that was the case! Anyway, this writer, his student fly tiers and his fishermen friends feel there is need for another treatise. This is it!

Without the slightest notion of depreciating the ideas, writings and teachings of other noted and excellent fly tiers and writers, without any thought of disparaging the use of almost sacredly traditional materials and methods of structure, I state frankly that these chapters will deal with the pleasurable art of fly tying only in the attempt to portray my findings, my methods, materials I have found to be most efficient and equally, or more effective, following actual stream testing by many fishermen friends and myself, than many of the old standard ties of many well-known patterns.

Myriads of fishermen are compelled to purchase and use flies, and I use the term "flies" loosely, because they cannot secure the result getting, exacting productions that are a pleasure to have and to use. There are not enough good fly tiers to go around. I sincerely hope that what I have to say here will help, in some measure, to bring a few new producers of good flies to the front. Good luck!

JIM QUICK

Chapter 11

Of Flies and Their Use

ONE COULD get oneself seriously enmeshed in this somewhat controversial subject and I present my findings and recommendations with temerity even though I have sincere convictions.

I am presuming that you are a trout fisherman. You would hardly become seriously attracted to the construction of usable flies unless you were, or at least had the desire to be one.

Part of the pleasure of fly fishing is experimentation. Were we to have discovered that "Killer" fly which all of us, since the days of Walton, have searched for, fishing would become mechanical and monotonous. At some periods of fishing we may believe that we've found the fly but a few hours later it seems to have become poison for all the action it develops.

Follow the suggestions of writers and friends, if you will, not as a statement of finality but as a personal experiment. There is hardly a thrill comparable to the discovery of how wrong an expert can be at times, particularly when it concerns the idiosyncrasies and contrariness of the trout species.

One fisherman-writer might state that he uses no dry fly larger than a sixteen, another that he uses nothing smaller than a twelve. Both are probably correct in accomplishing the maximum result. The fact is, the actual sizes of the same species of the aquatic fly varies in different localities and in

166

different altitudes. The proper procedure to follow is to match, if possible, the size of the fly emerging or "hatching" on the water you're working. I said, "If possible," and many times it isn't. However, this is not a serious matter. SIZE of the fly, within reason, is probably the least of the fly fishing requisites.

Many years ago, on the Manistee River in Michigan, I overheard a statement made by a fisherman, who in my humble opinion ranks with Halford, Gordon, LaBranche and Hewitt in fishing knowledge, in skill with the rod and fly and in sportsmanship. The more I have thought about this assertion over the years the more convinced I am that he was right.

He said, "Forget everything about your fly except in its presentation to the fish. Make it alive—not by movement, but by realistic placement on the water, in the right channel and without any more drag than a real fly has. If you're skilled enough to do these things consistently use any size fly you choose, but if you cannot present it accurately and with finesse, you must use smaller and smaller flies. The faults in your presentation and in your fly are much less noticeable as the size is reduced. The less skilled you are, the smaller the fly to get a modicum of action."

Summing up this "size" subject, I must concur with the above declaration. I believe that a small fly, correctly presented, receives little more attention than a large one, correctly presented, if as much. However, one of the complexities with which we must contend is that on one stream a size eight would not be considered too large and on another piece of water a size fourteen would be regarded as a big one.

Up the ladder of importance is the fly PATTERN. Its form or design or silhouette, as you will. One could hardly expect top action from his simulated mayfly if there is a caddis hatch on the water.

There are three major classes in the trout fly patterns. These are the impressionistic "naturals," the impressionistic "fancys" and the true copies of the insect as closely as we can duplicate them. This latter type has been tied and tried at periodic intervals ever since the advent of artificial fly tying, but our crude efforts to exactly copy the real fly has, in the past, resulted pretty much in only mediocre results as far as their successful use is concerned. The impressionistic "naturals" do, if you have a good imagination, look something like the fly you're apt to see on the water or fluttering around your ears. These are the flies generally most effective both in normal fishing and during a rise. Example patterns are the Gordon Quill, Ginger Quill, Adams, Hendrickson, spiders, variants, etc. The examples of the "fancys" include the Royal Coachman, Wickham's Fancy, Silver Doctor, Candy Fly, Flight's Fancy, Professor, Jock Scott, Pink Wickhams, Butcher, etc. These flies resemble a natural about as much as Theodore Gordon resembled Cleopatra.

Of greater importance than either size or design is COLOR. Do not commit the error of believing that fish are color blind. They just are not! I believe they discern color and shades of color better, in their element, than we mortals. Science has not yet determined exactly just what fish see in our lures, why distinctly gaudy patterns are favored in certain regions and in others only the subdued colors are accepted by the same species of trout under comparitively identical conditions.

I have, throughout many seasons of fishing, experimented by using two different shades of color in the same fly pattern. For instance, a light blue dun quill bodied fly alternated with one of a darker shade of blue dun. The same experiment with a light Cahill type fly alternated with one of a darker pattern of the same structure. Invariably, my notes indicate, one of the shades of the same general color was superior to the other in upwards of ninety per cent of the tests.

In selecting a fly, or tying a fly, to represent an insect you have observed on the water, consideration must be given to the colors used by you to match the natural. Remember this, many materials change color when wet or when treated with an oily floatant. Match the natural with a wet or treated material, then you can hardly go too far off. Remember, too, that objects dancing along on the surface of a shallow stream reflect the color or shade of the stream bottom, in the degree according to the object's compactness. If the amount of light filtering through is great then the reflected color is less. If the object or fly is opaque, or nearly so, then the reflected color is strongest. The ephemeroptera is a fragile insect, seemingly almost transparent, thus the reflected light from the bottom is extremely limited whereas your fly, with a body constructed over a metal hook, is opaque and will render maximum reflection. Under these conditions, choose slightly lighter tints than the natural seems to be. This same reflection factor applies to any kind of fly or object on the water.

Another step upwards, in the rating of the cast fly, is its ACTION. It would perhaps be more apt to say, "Its lack of action," because this pertains to naturalness of the fly on the water. It means, in other words, that there is a complete lack of drag, the fly presenting a cocky realistic form. (Naturally, I am assuming that the fly is a well-tied quality creation. There is a tremendous difference in the "action" and efficiency of good flies over the common so-called market productions.)

The chief requisite relating to the fly itself is its POSITION on the water. This means accurate placement in the natural food channel. It means, perhaps, a delicate bump off the bank to ride closely along the water's edge where naturals might also travel. It means a delicate drift over that open area, in a close-to-the-surface weed bed, it means a float just slightly to the right or left of the line in which you witnessed a rising fish, it means, when conditions warrant, a curve cast which permits the fly to precede the leader over a prospective fish location.

The two most vital essentials of all, I firmly believe, are not particularly concerned with the fly or the cast, but to the PRESENTATION by the fisherman and his APPROACH. These requisites are developed, not from careless fishing but from a conscientious desire to improve and from successful, studied efforts to carry them out in the best possible way you can.

I like my flies sparsely tied as to hackle. Just enough to float the fly is sufficient and in well-tied, high quality material flies the small amount needed to float them is surprisingly limited. (After all the insect has only six legs.) And I want wings on my flies. I have an aversion against fooling my fish with crippled simulations even though they are impressionistic copies of the naturals. Certain hackle flies tied wet are O.K. with me inasmuch as many nymphs, before rising to the surface, have no discernable wings. I prefer and insist upon hackle tip wings instead of the old-fashioned English type cut wings from flight quills. These latter wings are opaque, unlike the naturals. They will not stand even mild abuse and as for resurrecting them following a clash with the mouth of a trout, it is practically impossible. Hackle tip wings and also wings formed of the flank plumage of woodduck or mallard are sturdy, will withstand maximum abuse, are easy to put back into shape (they rarely get out of shape), and they are far and away a better copy of the natural's fine transparent wings. Regardless of statements to the contrary, and to the so-called excuses for eliminating wings, the winged fly is more efficient, will give you more action and because it represents the insect form better the positive results are better. A thorough series of tests has proved this fact to me and an honest test will prove it to you.

A fallacy that took me a long time to see through is that a ragged, chewed up pattern was superior to one of the same species or type of good physical condition. A fisherman may have struck on a certain Ginger Quill, for example, and found it so desirable to the fish that its constant contact with the mouth and teeth of those fish rendered it a sorry object but it still continued in efficiency. When things were going along in an exciting path few fishermen would take the fly off and replace it with another. Had they done so they would have found, providing the fly was an identical pattern and size, that the action would have continued unabated or even increased. I've done it. The fallacy developed, by the fisherman probably losing the fly and replacing it with another *almost* like the original and his surge of successful activity tapered off—so the old ragged lure becomes the model and another "truism" comes to being. The only possibility of their being a factual superiority in the chewed up fly is that the fisherman, perhaps unknowingly, happened to be handling the lure as a nymph is sometimes fished and that could be what the trout calculated it was. Too, the chewed-up fly has become a "sparse" type and gets deeper into the water where the trout wants it.

In the almost unending list of fly patterns you will note that, aside from color variations or uses of different materials to accomplish the same end, there is but a surprisingly small number of basic models for the few species of aquatic and land flies used in fishing.

As we mentioned before, many fancy flies resemble nothing in nature. The outstanding examples of this are the old type salmon flies, the steelhead flies and in trout flies one well-known fly is the Royal Coachman. This fly has been a leader since 1878. Until we think like or experience a like instinct of the fish we will never know for sure what they see in this attractor fly.

The increasingly popular "Variant" tied flies, which are coming into their own more and more at this date, actually were developed over 75 years ago by Dr. William Baigent of England.

The Gordon Quill is over 50 years old. The Cahill is over 70 years old. The Hendrickson was tied first about 1916. Those flies have stood the test of time and are among the first ten with the great majority of expert and experienced fishermen. Our youngest fly, which is destined according to a consensus of leading sportsmen to rank with those flies mentioned, is Leonard Halladay's Adams. The Adams was created in 1922.

There are, we hope, "local patterns" in use now that will become as great after they have been put through the mill for a few years and found not wanting. With few exceptions great flies were based, not on the imagination of the creator, but were designed as his effort to simulate a "natural" the way he thinks a fish likes to see it.

Anyone can tie just anything on a hook merely to have a different pattern or to make a so-called good looking fly. This is the distinguishing mark of the rank amateur. Don't do it! There will be times, however, after a long session of tedious production of regular patterns when, to take off the pressure, it is advisable to go all out on a crazy concoction. Do it with intent to see how far off the beam you can get. It will relieve you but it probably won't be an original. Halford, Hardy, Hewett or Haily, no doubt, tied the same pattern back in 1880 or thereabouts for the same reason you did.

I cannot emphasize too strongly the necessity of observing and studying the insects in and on the fishing water. Not necessarily from the technical, diagnostic standpoint of an entomological student but with the idea of outward appearance in an attempt to solve the riddle of the fishes' viewpoint. By no stretch of the imagination am I depreciating that technical knowledge. On the contrary I firmly believe that the more one knows of the aquatic life from every conceivable angle the better fly tier and better fisherman he will be.

My suggestion for the beginner is to secure samples of the natural flies and nymphs from the water. Instead of chucking them in your fly box, or other container, take a moment to observe their coloration and mentally make a comparison of the insect's color to something you can connect it with later because in a very few minutes those sparkling true colors of your captured fly will be gone. Note its natural silhouette, the length of its wings, of its tail or tails and the position in which they are naturally carried.

There is your perfect model—far superior to the finest artificial fly you could lay your hands on. While its colors are fresh in your mind construct the fly mentally, as you will later in your vise. Try to visualize it as the trout would see it. What materials do you have that will best simulate it? Can you think of other materials that might be suitable? The time involved, although precious when fishing, believe me, will be well invested if you have any intent or desire at all to build better flies and subsequently hook into more and better fish.

Delve into the silt on the stream bottom, examine the tiny living creatures on the weeds growing under the surface. Carefully lift or turn over stones in the riffles. You will be astonished at the number of varied forms of live organisms you will find. This is the bread, butter, meat, potatoes and gravy diet of your fish. Eighty percent and more of the volume of the fish menu is under the surface. Were it not for the existence of these tiny creatures in the streams and lakes there would be no fish to fish for.

Many of these living forms are tied artificially as nymphs and wet flies. Many are too complicated to permit even a reasonable imitation that is effective with the materials and procedures we now use. Some day, however, some fly tier will come up with the answer.

There are actually no hard ways to tie a fly but, using the old cliché, I must admit that some ways are easier than others. Consistent, careful preparation of materials and consistent tying of proven patterns will effect constant improvement and skill in tying flies.

Permit me to emphasize one important action here. If you are new at fly tying or just starting, GO SLOW DELIBERATELY. Make every move and every operation of the procedure as perfect as you possibly can. Be brutally critical of your own work regardless of the complimentary platitudes of your friends. Be wary of the head turning remarks such as, "That's a beautiful thing," or "How can you possibly make such perfect little flies," or "Boy! If that won't take old Mac-Donald up in Hot Creek nothing else will."

Never, never be completely satisfied with your own work. It could have been done better by you. If the tip, the tail, the body, the wings or the hackle isn't just right do it over and over again until your own standard of perfection is reached or you are ready for a straight jacket. When that latter point is reached it's time for a cup of coffee or a Coke.

Believe me when I tell you that if you work in the attitude of demanding perfection and are consciously deliberate in your material portions, the improvement in your productions will be startlingly fast and with it will come increasing speed in tying.

It is amusing to me and will be to you to observe the tactics performed by some anglers in testing flies to determine their quality. I've seen fishermen drop flies on a showcase to see if they would bounce. Their theory was that if the fly bounced it was a good one. The truth is, the only thing this procedure proves is whether or not the fly will bounce on a showcase. If you should happen to have a discarded, sloppily tied dry fly in your collection, just take your scissors and clip off the nice fine ends of the hackle all around the fly. It will probably bounce lively enough when dropped. I've seen anglers caress their lips with the hackle on the fly as a test of hackle quality. That method proves no more than the showcase bouncer. I've noted one experienced fly fisherman discard flies because they didn't feel just right to him and have another deliberately select the same flies because they passed his lip test. The flies could have been good ones or bad ones in either case. The only true test of dry flies is at the end of a leader and their subsequent performance on the water. As you tie flies and handle various grades of materials you will, in time, be able to ascertain, at a glance, whether or not the fly is a good one. Its outward, clean-cut appearance must, of course, be one criterion, next comes quality of the material used, lastly, and of great importance, comes the reputation of its maker, his experience, his tying procedure and his skill.

Obtaining factual criticism of your own flies in their tests on fishing waters, disregard the periodic occasions when trout will ruthlessly accept almost any pattern tied any way and every way. The true test time is when there are none or few fish working. Will your production stand the test of constant whipping, cracking it dry, floating satisfactorily after innumerable casts and, other things being equal, will it raise fish? After a fish is taken and the fly is thoroughly water soaked and slimy, can it be cleaned, dried and used again and again? If so, you have a fly, son, you have a fly.

Chapter *12*

Tools and Accessories

NOT TOO many years ago fly tiers used only their fingers in the building of flies. Some of these tiers developed, after many years, an almost unbelievable skill in the production of beautiful trout and salmon flies. But, as in most other arts which progressed, tools were designed that speeded up the operations and permitted less skillful hands to build flies at least as good, if not superior, to the hand-tied creations. (See Fig. A.)

The most important tool is the vise which holds the hook while materials, which make up the fly, are applied and tied in. Several good vises are manufactured, and like other tools some are better than others. The important thing is to get used to your own vise, regardless the type or kind. The writer prefers the Chase-Holbrook vise and the Thompson "A" vise, as being the best on the market at this writing, but that is a personal opinion only.

Hackle pliers are next in importance and if it is the desire of the reader to tie the small 16's to 22's the pliers must be really good. Again a personal opinion, but I like the Paul Young and the Thompson "midgit" hackle pliers best.

Scissors, and there should be two pairs, are of extreme import. I prefer the straight blades in both pairs, however that is incidental. One pair should have ultra-fine points and be of extra fine quality. Top grade cuticle or embroidery scissors

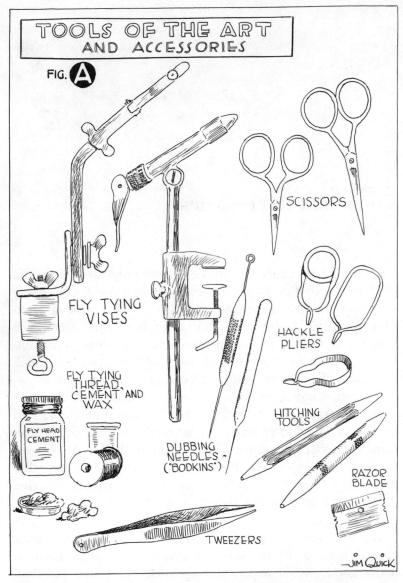

TOOLS OF THE ART
AND ACCESSORIES

FIG. A

SCISSORS

FLY TYING
VISES

HACKLE
PLIERS

FLY TYING
THREAD,
CEMENT, AND
WAX

FLY HEAD
CEMENT

HITCHING
TOOLS

DUBBING
NEEDLES
("BODKINS")

RAZOR
BLADE

TWEEZERS

—JIM QUICK

are superior to the generally marketed fly tying scissor. The second pair is for cutting coarse materials, tinsel and for trimming hair bodies. These should be small scissors but their quality is not so essential if they perform satisfactorily. Both pairs must be kept sharp.

A dubbing needle or bodkin is necessary but the fly tier can easily make one by inserting a medium or large sewing needle into a small wood billet or dowel about the size of a lead pencil and of whatever length is handy.

A hitching tool is not wholly necessary but it will save much time in finishing the fly off. The hitching tool should have the hole in one end that can be placed over the eyes of hooks sized from 14, 12, 10, etc., and the other end for inserting over the eyes on hooks from size 16 to the smallest. One distinct advantage of this tool is for holding back the hackle from the eye while putting in the finishing hitches—eliminating the necessity of having to pick out tied-in hackle barbs.

A pair of "eye-brow" tweezers are convenient to have for the purpose of picking up hooks, hackle, wings, etc., but they are not absolutely necessary.

Fly tying thread, an essential accessory, should be thread manufactured for the purpose. Sewing threads do not have the strength to do good work. Sizes range from "A" to 8/0 in general fly tying usage with the most popular beginner's size being 2/0. As the tier becomes more adept it is my suggestion that the size of the thread be decreased to the smallest size that can be handled without frequent breakage. Smaller sizes such as 4/0 to 6/0 permits more "securing" wraps without extensive build-up and they also allow the forming of smoother surfaces. Fly-tying thread should always be SILK. I had an unfortunate experience with the finer nylon thread which may explain my insistence on silk. A few years ago I tied several dozen size 16 and 18 flies for four of my customers. I used an extremely fine nylon thread (about 12/0 in size—I really thought I had found something). A few weeks later the first one of these customers came to me and told me that in using those flies the wings turned on the hook and after a short period of use the flies came apart. I immediately got hold of a few of the nylon thread tied flies and tried them. The customer was so right. Performing a careful autopsy on one of the "creations" I found that the fine nylon thread was, in spite of wax and varnish, slack—not at all tight as it had been originally tied. I then built a few more very slowly and discovered the fault. Nylon is quite elastic and stretches easily. I had used, in tying the flies, what I had estimated was the maximum pull on the thread short of breakage in securing the materials to the hook, but the thread still had more stretch in it. As soon as the fly was whipped for a short time the remaining stretch reacted, developing the slack that practically let the fly fall apart.

Color of thread is optional whether it be black, white or colored, as called for in many English patterns. I prefer white. I believe it is a bit stronger than the black threads in the identical sizes. After it is waxed and the head cemented on the fly the white has become a smoky gray anyway. Colored threads are of value as the background for dubbing. Yellow or primrose is the popular shade.

Flyhead cement or varnish is recommended as an accessory. It is used primarily in finishing off the head of the fly but it also is used to prevent tinsel tarnishing on tinsel bodies and for placing on the butts of hair, in tying hair wing flies and streamers—also for coating quill and raffia bodies.

A tin, a tube or a piece of good fly-tying wax is a necessary accessory. Most suppliers' waxes are suitable. Semi-dry varnish is a good substitute. Bee's wax or cobbler's wax is not quite tacky enough to perform satisfactorily. A few fly tier's material suppliers can sell you pre-waxed thread. If one ties flies in quantity this thread, only slightly more expensive, is a real luxurious economy. It saves much valuable time, and fingers do not gather the sticky coating which comes from waxing thread each time you prepare to tie a fly. If the pre-waxed thread is not used for long periods and appears to be dried out, a few drops of turpentine will bring it back at once to its desired freshness.

A razor blade to cut thread closely, for trimming butts of wet fly beard hackle, for stripping hooks of material when desired and for general close cutting is convenient to have.

There are other tools such as winging pliers, whip finishers, razor knives, magnifying lens and mirrors and gadgets of different kinds that come and go. I have a generous collection of these items, somewhere. Another tool I've tried and painfully watched others using is the bobbin. I'm going out on a limb regarding this so-called tool by pleading that if you're just starting to tie flies DON'T CONSIDER IT. If you're using one discard it right now. I have never seen or heard of one good fly tier or professional tier using a bobbin. I claim, with emphasis, that a GOOD fly, according to expert's standings, and my own conscience rating, cannot be tied using a bobbin.

Photo by Dean Vannice

HACKLE

Left to right:

Dark Grizzly, Medium Grizzly, Light Grizzly or Chinchilla, Badger, Cree Variant, Ginger and Honey Badger

Light Blue Dun, Medium Blue Dun, Dark Blue Dun, Bronze Dun, Andalusian, Honey, Ivory or Buff, Badger Saddle

Rhode Isl. Red (light), Rhode Isl. Red (medium), Rhode Isl. Red (Dark), Mahogany Red, Furnace, Coch-y-bondhu, Black

Chapter **13**

Materials and Hooks

A FLY is only as good as the material that goes into it. Mediocre or actually poor material will only result in an inferior product even when tied by the most skillful craftsman.

It is difficult in the extreme to verbally portray, in all aspects, just what is good and what is not so good in fly tying materials. Neither do photographs or drawings bring it out.

I can only urge that you observe studiously the materials you have in your possession as you use them. Does your finished fly resemble in a "material" way those you may have that were tied by a professional or an experienced tier? Determine in your own mind just what the difference is. Do not always blame yourself if your fly is a disappointment. It can be that hackles or the wings or the body material does not qualify as first grade "stuff." Experience in tying will bring you experience and knowledge in choosing materials—in knowing at a glance or a touch if the items are up to your standard.

Rather than just mention the various materials used in fly tying I have elaborated on those most in use deliberately because the subject ranks so high in importance.

HACKLE (*See Plate 1*)

The difference between good flies and the common or market variety is generally in their hackles. Hackles, without

181

question, form the most important ingredient in the material list. The ability of the fly to alight and ride properly on the water, in the case of dry flies, is dependent upon the quality of the hackle.

Regardless of the claims of fly tying material suppliers, top grade hackle and hackle necks are quite rare. Neither is the cost of the neck indicative of its use value but it is the only gauge one has unless from quite extensive experience in selecting hackle and tying many hundreds of flies.

The method of testing hackle for dry flies is first to observe whether or not it carries a glossy appearance on the outer surface. The second feature is its springiness and lack of web. Taking a medium or 12 size hackle hold it at its tip end and with the thumb and forefinger of the other hand stroke down the quill three or four times. If the fibers spring back to a right angle to the quill or tend to resume their former position it is considered good hackle. Sometimes the quill may be quite webby but the tip half has the correct stiffness. In cases such as this, using two or more of the tips on your fly will supply the right amount when wound as hackle.

Hackles, too, should have good color—that is, a definiteness of the shade you are selecting. In the reds and browns, look for color on both sides of the feather. Quills of this shade, particularly, tend to be brilliant on the outer surface while carrying a smoky faded-out appearance on the inner side. This is not a criterion of the quality of that hackle insofar as its use is concerned but it does give your fly an off color that may not be desirable.

There are many variations of the principal types of necks (capes) or hackle quills. For instance, the Grizzly or Plymouth Rock hackle ranges from a deeply marked pattern which overall looks dark gray, to an extremely sparse marking which is almost to the white range. This light hackle with the sparse markings is often called "Chinchilla" and is used primarily for mixing with other shades, used in place of white, or dyed any color desired. The Red (Rhode Island Red) hackle which is reddish brown extends from so-called dark ginger to a deep brown or reddish mahogany. Incidentally, when "red" is mentioned in descriptions relevant to fly tying this is the red which is meant and not the scarlet or crimson red with which we are most familiar. Ginger is definitely another shade which carries a lemon yellowish tinge. It ranges from buff cream to a deep tan mustard. True Brown is just that, flat without a red tinge.

Some white necks are available which, on their outer surfaces, carry an ivory or yellowish cream tint. This is a desirable hackle much used for hackle tip wings, and in place of pure white. The neck is usually of better quality than the regular stock white.

The blue dun shade which is used probably more often in dry flies than the other colors is, in its natural state, a freak cross between black and white birds. The Andalusian blues are almost unprocurable and this is no great loss because the coarseness and sparseness of the barbs make the hackles not too desirable. Unless you are fortunate enough to find a "freak" blue or are in a position to do your own cross breeding the next best is the dyed hackle. These hackles generally are from pure white necks or the light grizzly dyed light, medium or dark blue dun.

Furnace is a deep red to dark brown with a darker area following the quill from the butt to, or almost to, the tip. Some Furnace necks have this list sharply defined while others have but a vague suggestion of the coloration.

Coch-y-bondhu (or Cock-a-bondy) is a Furnace with the tip ends of the barbs a darker shade also, matching the center marking. Very rarely used.

Badger is a white, cream or light tan with a black marking following the quill of the feather as does the darker section on the Furnace hackle.

Blacks and whites are just that. Good natural blacks are rare and dyed black necks are preferable to the general run of market blacks. White necks, too, in top quality are scarce. The whites have, as a rule, an extremely long barb structure on the quills. Most of them are used as a base for dyed necks of various shades and colors.

Then comes the almost limitless range of regular "Freak" necks which include off-Badger, mixed color or Multi-color

Grizzly, Honey Dun, off-Furnace and off-Coch-y-bondhu, the latter two which extend to almost solid blacks. Customarily the "Freak" hackle is used for variant tied flies, for hackle tip wings, for mixing with other regular colors to create effective shades and for the amateur's experimentation.

Fly tiers, short of professionals, need have little concern with the acquisition of all types of hackle. The modern trend to mixed hackles has eliminated that worry. The necessary shades for tying over 90 per cent of the standard patterns are:

> Grizzly—Plymouth Rock
> Buff or Honey
> Light Red or Ginger
> Brown or Mahogany
> Blue Dun, medium
> Black

Try using a Grizzly hackle with each of the others as mixed hackle, then Buff with each of the other types, etc. The combinations cover nearly every possible shade.

In touching on the more commonly known and used hackle as listed to this point, the prime thought has been hackle for dry flies which must be more or less carefully chosen. Far be it from me to infer that one must not be careful in selecting hackles for wet flies, nymphs, and streamers however these flies do not require the high type springy hackle used for "drys." The softer hackle on regular necks is suitable for "wets" and regretfully many on the market of commercial quality, in their entirety, are fit only for wet flies. In picking out the hackle for the wet types one must look for the kind that will absorb water quickly and this is not too difficult. All hen necks are of this quality. Beyond the cock and hen hackles there is the plumage from land birds such as grouse or partridge, pheasant, guinea, etc., which make extremely effective legs or hackle on your wet flies and nymphs.

WINGING MATERIAL (See Plate II)

Perhaps I seem derisive when I touch on the old-fashioned cut wings from flight feathers of the duck, the starling, etc., but

Photo by Dean Vannice

PLUMAGE AND QUILLS

1—Amherst Pheasant Tippets. 2—Golden Pheasant Tippets. 3—Woodduck and Barred Mandarin. 4—Mallard Flank Plumage. 5—Pintail Flank Plumage. 6—Teal Flank Plumage. 7—Mallard Flight Quills. 8—Matched cut wings from flight quills. 9—Grouse or Partridge. 10—Golden Pheasant Plumage (Female). 11—Jungle Cock Eyes. 12 —Jungle Cock Plumage (small). 13—Hackle tips, ready for applying. 14—Guinea, or Galina, both gray and polka-dot.

I am convinced they're on their way out. They do look quite prepossessing when tied correctly even though they are opaque, which the wings they are supposed to imitate are not, but after one fish has clamped down on those wings they look more like the result of an all night session in a rough mixing bowl. Only a miracle technician could resurrect them to their original appearance. However if the fly tier insists on staying with this old English custom of cut wings from flight quills, follow this procedure. Secure your wings in matched pairs and use only the primary flight quills numbering two to six from each wing, mating the left and right pairs. One can also secure the matched duck quills in pairs from material supply houses. This applies also to the white or domestic duck wing quills. Before I leave this subject I want to strongly suggest that the fly tier try the hackle tip wings or the mallard and woodduck flank plumage wings in place of the above. First, they are more easily tied, secondly, they resemble the natural wings equally as well or better and they are not opaque—they permit light to filter through as does the real wing and they are much more rugged and lasting in use.

The finest winging material of all is the lemon woodduck. The American woodduck is protected in nearly all states so this plumage is quite rare. The mandarin from China is almost a perfect duplicate and this is procurable albeit somewhat expensive. The next in preference is well-dyed mallard in lemon woodduck tint. This wing is used on the popular Cahill flies, Gordon Quill, Hendrickson, Blue Honey Dun, Pale Mayflies and some Ginger Quill patterns among many others. Next in line is the regular undyed mallard, widgeon and teal flank feathers. The mallard, which is most desired, can be secured in natural, dyed woodduck, light blue dun, drake yellow and other colors or tints.

White breast feathers from both wild and domestic duck are used for the popular fan wing flies and for the "Wilson" tied patterns.

Hackle tips, a wing subject which I've managed to inject periodically throughout this treatise, is not new in practice but comparatively new in an almost over all winging method for dry flies. These are the tips of fine, generally light blue dun, ivory or buff and grizzly hackles, although many others are used.

There are other quills used for wings such as turkey, woodcock, pheasant, crow, grouse or partridge, coot and more, but the major wings and plumage covered above will serve admirably for the better known fly patterns.

An increasingly important wing material is hair. This can be bucktail, impali or calf tails, squirrel tails, capras or goat, woodchuck, monkey and baboon, mouse deer, polar bear, skunk, badger and many others. Hair is rugged and if securely fastened to your hook will stand much wear and abuse.

Maribou, or stork plumage, is much used in the building of pan fish flies and streamers, principally. It can be secured in natural white and in brilliant colors or tints.

BODY MATERIAL

Practically every fiber, animal and vegetable, has been tried and used in some way or other as a body on flies. New ones are discovered daily. Those that have been experimented with and found not wanting and have proven their value are primarily the dubbing furs such as fox, muskrat, opossum, seal, mole, badger, English hares, angora and others.

Then comes the spun fur which is generally angora or mohair spun into a soft yarn and dyed in popular shades.

Regular wool yarns, in the finer grades and in mending yarns, are used for many patterns.

Floss, of silk and rayon, is another material much called for. Raffia, a grassy palm fiber, makes an attractive body and a number of modern fly patterns call for it.

Quill bodies are formed from the stripped hackle stalks and from stripped peacock quills from the upper sides of the eye of the peacock tail feather. (See Fig. B.) Unstripped blue and yellow macaw and red macaw make very attractive bodies. Stripped ostrich, particularly in dyed colors, is a serviceable and appealing quill. Procupine quills' flattened, moose mane hairs, javalina or wild pig bristles are some others that are effective but little used.

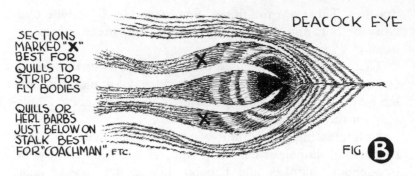

SECTIONS MARKED "**X**" BEST FOR QUILLS TO STRIP FOR FLY BODIES

QUILLS OR HERL BARBS JUST BELOW ON STALK BEST FOR "COACHMAN", ETC.

PEACOCK EYE

FIG. **B**

Chenille, a commonly used material, particularly on wet flies. Its use in building dry flies is limited because of its tendency to absorb water and hold it.

Other body materials include peacock herl, ostrich herl, condor quill, deer and caribou body hair clipped closely, horse hair, silk gut, burlap strands, straw—in fact almost any material that will wind and wrap well, looks well and is wearable, and at the same time fools the fish.

Plastics of some kinds for body building have been and still are creeping into the market but at this writing are not considered too seriously. The best way to determine their value to you is to try them yourself—that's the practical method of judging.

Plain and colored rubber from the common balloon and rubber bands have been utilized for a long time in constructing quite attractive bodies on wet flies, nymphs, ants, etc. It goes on well, looks excellent but is not as effective with the fish as with the fisherman. It has also the impractical quality of becoming sticky on exposure to a bit of mild sunshine or heat and from this point on thereafter is more or less useless.

Copper, brass and silver wire is an important factor in the construction of many steelhead and salmon flies. Fine brass, gold and silver wire is also a part of many popular patterns, used primarily for ribbing.

Tinsel, in both gold and silver, is a prominent body building item. It is used for solid bodies, for tips and for ribbing. Tinsel comes in many widths, also in thread form, in oval shape and in embossed patterns.

Kapok, as a body building filler on dry flies, is an excellent substance with which to form heavier looking bodies and giving the fly the utmost floatability. The kapok is usually covered with raffia, floss or other finishing material.

TAIL MATERIAL

On dry flies, the tail has an extremely important function, in that it assists greatly in floating the fly in a natural position. Also, inasmuch as the mayflies have this graceful appendage, it is a necessary part in simulating the appearance of the fly.

Tails are generally fashioned from stripped hackle fibers or barbs, hackle tips, golden, amherst and silver pheasant tippets, crests and some body plumage, natural and dyed segments from flight quills and larger tail feathers, wisps from pheasant tails, wisps of mallard and woodduck flank plumage, peacock plumage, turkey quills, hair and guard hairs from various furs and skins, etc. In the wet fly realm, all the above are used plus yarn segments and almost any fabric that will lend the appearance wanted by the tier.

HOOKS

Many authors have delved into this subject very thoroughly and have presented their findings in elaborate passages explaining the whys and wherefores of hooks for fly tying. I can only say I agree with most of 'em. To save your time this chapter will be brief and I hope will not leave you in a confused state of mind as to which hook to use.

Personally I like the Norwegian Mustad hooks in preference to English and French makes. In this I could be in error but I've tried a lot of them.

If tying wet flies or nymphs use a hook with "Regular" wire preferably with the ball eye but a tapered eye is not too much lighter in weight to serve satisfactorily if "Regular" wire is used. If tying dry flies use a hook with finer wire designated as "Fine," "2X Fine" or "3X Fine," with tapered eye. The use of either a turned down or turned up eye is an opinion matter. Both tie up equally well. A turned down eye is still preferred by many tiers but I'm sure this is only a habit complex. The trend is becoming stronger for turned up eye hooks in all sizes. The reason for this is that the fly is as easily tied, there is no difference in its action at the end of a leader (in dry fly fishing there's always an exasperating scrap or loop of leader sticking up anyway from the fly to the immersed section) and with the turned up eye there is a very visible "BETTER BITE" between the point where the eye turns (up or down) and the actual point of the hook.

HOOK RECOMMENDATIONS

In the description of hooks the "X" designations indicate sizes smaller or larger—for example "2X Fine" is the same wire diameter as the same make hook two sizes smaller—"3X Long" indicates that the length of the hook is the same as the identical make three sizes larger.

TUTE	means Turned Up Tapered Eye	
TDBE	means Turned Down Ball Eye	
"Viking"	means a model perfect bend	

MAKE	TYPE	NUMBER	USE	DESCRIPTION
Mustad	Sproat	3399	Wet Fly	TDBE
*Mustad	Sproat	3399A	Wet Fly	TDBE (Small)
Mustad	Limerick	3123	Wet Fly	TDBE
*Mustad	Sproat	3906	Wet Fly	TDTE
Mustad	Viking	94825	Dry Fly	TUTE—2X Fine—X Short
Mustad	Viking	94832	Dry Fly	TUTE—2X Fine—2X Long
Mustad	Viking	94840	Dry Fly	TDTE—Reg. X Fine
*Mustad	Viking	94842	Dry Fly	TUTE—Reg. X Fine
*Mustad	Viking	94843	Dry Fly	TUTE—3X Fine—4X Short
*Mustad	Viking	94844	Dry Fly	TUTE—3X Fine
Alcocks	Mod. Perf.	04991	Dry Fly	TUTE—1X Fine
*Mustad	Spec. Lim.	9579A	Dry Fly	TUTE—Slight Rev.
Mustad	Aberdeen	37265	Dry Fly	TUTE—Long Shank
Mustad	Sproat	3911E	Dry Fly	TUTE—2X Fine—3X Short
Mustad	Viking	9523	Dry Fly	TUTE—X Fine—5X Short
Mustad	Viking	9671	Streamer	TDTE—2X Long
*Mustad	Viking	9672	Streamer	TDTE—3X Long
Mustad	Limerick	3665A	Streamer	TDTE—½" Longer
Mustad	Sproat	9214	Streamer	TDTE—Spec. Long
*Mustad	Limerick	7970	Steelhead	TDBE—5X Strong
*Mustad	Limerick	3658B	Salmon	TULooped Eye

* My favorite in each bracket

There are, no doubt, many other numbers and makes that are as good as the above but I have found these listed to be completely satisfactory.

Chapter 14

Basic Operations

HOOK IN VISE

IN PLACING the hook in the vise some tiers grip it at the bend exposing the point and barb. Others completely bury the point in the lips of the vise with the part to be tied riding above and higher. There are advantages in both methods. Try both ways. (See Fig. C.) The "exposed point" offers a bit more space in wrapping the body if you can avoid the hook point every turn with your tying thread, floss, yarn, fragile quills, etc. It is exasperating when a part of your floss catches on the point or a nicely stripped peacock quill is severed or torn as it is wound. The "hidden point" eliminates this hazard but supplies a bit less room for wrapping materials. I use the hidden point method and have never had cause to change. The only time I place the hook in the exposed position is while fastening beard hackle on small wet flies.

THREAD MANEUVERS

Be sure always that your thread is waxed. The exact point on the shank of the hook where the thread is started varies somewhat with the type of fly to be tied. This factor is not as important as many other operations providing your "jam" of thread does not turn on the hook. This is important! The jam is formed by making two or three turns of thread around the hook away from you or clockwise, then crossing over the turns

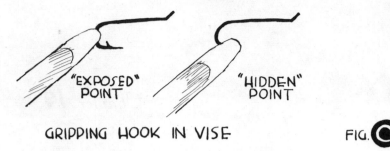

"EXPOSED" POINT   "HIDDEN" POINT

GRIPPING HOOK IN VISE   FIG. C

with one more turn then hitching the thread. (See Fig. D.)

The "Hitch" is formed by holding the thread taut with your right hand (providing you're right-handed) then placing tips of your left index and second fingers, palm down on the thread. (See Fig. E.) With the right hand carry thread over

1.   2.

THE "JAM"
(TO BE FOLLOWED BY THE "HITCH")

FIG. D

hook and down to meet the loop formed and place the single thread between the tips of the two left fingers at the base of the loop. Then with the index finger of right hand press lightly at the junction of the thread on the hook and hold. The two fingers of the left hand closes on the single thread strand and pulls it toward you through the loop and continues pulling until loop is closed at hook. Performing this operation a few times will make it almost automatic. Hitch each operation in turn as you build your fly. This eliminates the necessity of hanging a weight on the waxed tying thread and it makes your fly secure at every point hitched. It adds not one whit more of thread but instead of just loose thread binding down the material it is actually tied down.

In tying dry flies, particularly, no matter how fine the thread, eliminate every possible excess wind. Be sure the material is secure but from that point on every turn of thread adds a tiny bit of weight. Extra turns, within reason, on wet flies do not impair the structure and the little additional weight is desirable.

In finishing off "Heads" of flies the modern fly tier does not build up lumps of thread supposed to simulate a head then crowd the eye of the hook, making the fastening to the leader more difficult than not. When the last operation on your fly is complete and secure, QUIT except for hitching or whipping and this requires only a few turns for insurance. There is but one point to watch—that is where the up eye or down eye of your hook is formed. Where the metal end of the wire meets the shank there is usually a barely perceptible sharp edge or semi-sharp point or the junction of the two is not exactly complete, leaving an opening wide enough to allow fine nylon or gut leader to work into it. This gap or sharp point should be lightly covered with your tying thread to prevent cutting the leader.

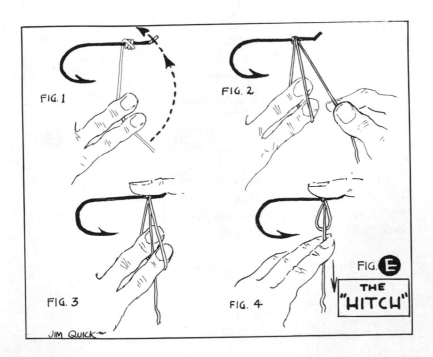

The "Whip Finish" is a smooth method of securing the thread following completion of the fly, but it is no more efficient and much slower than the multiple hitch. The "Whip" is merely three, four or five wraps of tying thread thrown over the thread end and pulled up tightly. When "Heads" were formed on flies, this was an essential operation to make a smooth looking job. It is still done to a great extent on steelhead and salmon flies. The "Whip" can be done by the "Scotch" method where the index and second finger of the right hand twists and wraps simultaneously or by the loop method the same as the wrappings on a rod is whipped in to secure it. (See Fig. F.)

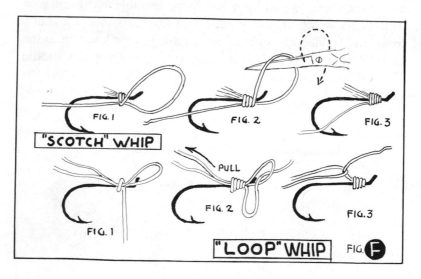

The multiple hitch is done generally with the hitching tool. It is first a single hitch then a double hitch or two wraps of thread around the point of the tool, sliding it off on to the hook, then another single hitch.

AT THIS POINT STUDY THE PARTS OF THE FLY AS
SHOWN IN FIG. G.

TIPS—TAILS—TAGS

The "Tip" is usually tied in before the tail is installed or

the quill from under a razor blade held at an angle lightly but firmly until all the herl has been removed. Another procedure is, with a pencil eraser, to erase the herl from the quill which is comparatively easy when stroked against the natural grain of the quill's herl. I have seen others remove the herl with the side of a fine sewing needle by holding the quill down with the needle against some hard cardboard while it is pulled from under. This is similar to the razor blade method. Others can remove the herl cleanly with the finger nails—I never could. The best method I've encountered is called wax stripping. The selected single herl strands are dipped in melted paraffin, the wax is permitted to harden, then the stalk is stripped with the finger nails. Naturally one doesn't do this each time a quill is needed. I usually perform this procedure preparing several dozen at one time. This system, too, has another advantageous feature in that the quill is completely waterproof and pliable months after the stripping, without water soaking.

Hackle quills, which are the larger quills usually of little value except for tail barbs, large wet flies, etc. Stripped of all the barbs, they are started at the same point on the hook as are the other quills mentioned above, with the tip of the quill being tied down up the hook toward the eye to the front part of the body. Then the quill is started carefully in a close wrap as far as you wish to go. Hackle quills must be thoroughly soaked in water for from eight to twelve hours, at least, to prevent their splitting or breaking. After the hackle quill is wound securely on the hook and fastened, it must receive one or two coats of lacquer or fly head cement.

Porcupine quills are flattened with the finger nail before tying in. Soaking sometimes helps them to become more pliable.

Moose mane is used in paired hairs for quill wrappings. One white and one dark.

Raffia is soaked well before using and is tied in the same as floss for a smooth job.

Herl, particularly peacock as used on Coachman bodies, for example, should be fastened towards the tip of the herl strips, approximately two-thirds of the way from the butt (the tip is

extremely fragile). For heavy bodies fasten in three or more
herl barbs or strips, determined from the size of the fly being
tied, then twist the herl and include the tying thread in the
twist, then wrap, continually twisting until the body is completed. The thread is separated from the butts for tying down.
Many fly tiers use the thread or a similar method when only
one strip of herl is used. A finer body can be wound with herl,
without the thread, however it is a body decidedly fragile.
Twisting just the herl strands together helps to keep each
strand wrapped under and more secure. Use of herl, as on the
Royal Coachman, on regular sized trout flies, usually but one
herl strip is used. Many wrap the red band material over the
remaining strip, following the completion of the butt clump,
then wrap the thorax clump with the same strip. A nicer,
neater fly can be produced by taking each section of the body
in turn and wrapping a fresh strip for each clump of herl.
Yarn and spun fur bodies can be started at the tail base if too
large a segment of yarn or fur is not used. It is much better
to use a smaller section of this material and if necessary go
over the body two or three times to build it in the proportions
desired. Neither yarn or spun fur should be wound too tightly
on the hook.

DUBBING

A dubbed body, although one of the oldest methods of
imitating a natural body, is a most attractive and effective
structure for bodies of flies. One of the simpler ways of building your dubbing is to clip or tear off small sections of the
fur spreading it on the knee in a line of about one or two
inches. Take a piece of well waxed tying thread six or eight
inches in length and holding it taut with the thumb and forefinger of each hand, spin or roll the thread as it touches the
patch of prepared fur. The wax will pick up the fur making
a "yarny" strip which is wound on the hook the same as would
be done with yarn. Some tiers roll the dubbed section between
their palms, one way only, to make the dubbing adhere better
and more compact but it would be advisable to avoid this
unless necessary. In preparing the thread of dubbing it makes
a more lifelike body if the "furring" is tapered somewhat so

that the section at the tail base is thinner than toward the thorax or upper end of the body. Another dubbing method is slightly more difficult but, with practice, results in finer, more secure dubbed bodies. Lay a ten- or twelve-inch piece of waxed thread lengthwise on the leg permitting the longer end to drop over the knee cap. Place the clipped or pulled fur on top of the thread a couple inches from the upper end and extending the fur approximately one and a half to three inches down toward the knee cap. When this is done place the second finger of the left hand on the thread firmly an inch or so below your dubbing. Then place the thumb of the same left hand above the dubbing holding down so that the thread is fairly tight. Pick up the loose end of thread that has been extended over the knee and carefully draw it over the left finger holding the thread so that the two sections of thread are together, one below and one on top of the dubbing. Holding the ends of the thread down with the right hand disengage the left finger while holding the two threads together with a free finger of the right hand. Grasp the two threads below the dubbing between thumb and index finger and start twisting gently. After the twisting is started grasp the two free ends of thread with the right thumb and index finger and continue the twisting. Drawn quite tightly you will find that the thread will hold much of the twist when released at either end. Secure the thinner dubbed end of your strip to the hook and wind the body. Continual twisting as the body is wound makes for better security. If one wishes he can prepare a number of these dubbed strips, storing them on a card between slits cut in the sides of the card to hold the ends.

CLIPPED HAIR BODIES

Deer or Caribou hair clipped bodies are developed by flaring the hollow body hair over the hook the distance you wish the body to cover. Then clip with scissors to form the shape. Cut a small clump (less than ⅛ inch in diameter) of the hollow body hair. Holding it against the hook at the base of the tail point throw two loose loops of thread over then tighten, winding as you do. The hair will flare up from the point where the thread cuts into it and tend to follow around the hook as you wind and pull. Clear the thread by pushing back the hair with the fingers. Hitch the thread and place the second clump close up and repeat the operation. Keep forcing back the flared hair on the hook shank as you build. This makes for a more closely packed body. When sufficient hair has been tied in to form the length of the body, secure thread with a couple of hitches. Remove hook from vise, if you wish, and trim the flared hair into shape. The flaring of body hair is done more easily over a bare hook than one that has a thread base.

WOVEN HAIR BODIES

Woven bodies of hair, raffia, straw, etc., make excellent appearing structures, however the time and effort involved in their construction is not warranted inasmuch as the more simply wound bodies appear to be just as efficient and wearable. One of the more common weaving operations is that of the bodies on the "Mite" series of flies or nymphs, originated by Wm. Potts. The material consists of a clump of mixed hairs, usually horse hair, cow hair, etc., to form a sandy appearance. This clump of hair should be approximately one sixteenth of an inch, or less, in diameter and long enough to handle comfortably with the fingers. The hook must first be wrapped with thread tightly and cemented. The material is secured at the lower end of body and the secured end wrapped tightly up the length of the body. A strip of orange, red or yellow floss, strong enough to withstand pulling, is tied in also at the lower end of the body. As the material is wrapped each turn is looped or encircled with the floss on the bottom of the body. When the body is complete the floss will have formed a straight belly line its whole length. When the body is wrapped and secured, the balance of the material is bent backward, adjusted around the hook and secured to form the stiff hackle of these flies. The hair hackle is cut off if longer than the length of the hook, where it should terminate.

RIBBING

Ribbing of bodies is just that. It is done generally with

"WINGS" is the first of the two major controversial aspects among fly tiers. The length of wings is a sub-controversial subject. Wings of the natural fly are as long, and in many cases slightly longer, than the body of the fly. Eastern tiers tend to exaggerate the length of the wings and the Western tiers do the reverse. The only advantages I can see are that the longer wings are more visible to both fish and fisherman. The shorter wings have less tendency to dip over on their side and the short wing flies are more skillfully placed on the water by the amateur or semi-amateur caster.

The remarks under "Winging Material" in the chapter on materials leaves little doubt, I trust, of my own convictions regarding certain types of wings. However here are the popular procedures for tying in flight quill cut wings. Some tiers prepare and tie in the wings before the body is wound. In this method the wings are fastened on with the tips out over the eye of the hook either right side up or upside down. Right side up means with the natural concave curve of the feather edge down. Upside down means the reverse, naturally, with the points of the feather pointing upward. When the wings are raised to a standing position in the first case the curve points forward and in the second they point backward. I could go on with this kind of description for a page or more but it would result probably in just more confusion. Note the illustrations picturing these wings. There are noted tiers in both schools. My suggestion is to try both ways. Pick the one you like best and you will not be alone in the method. Neither one holds up unless the wings are treated with cement or lacquer and this is an abominable practice. The other method is to tie the wings in after the body is formed and in this case the tips point backward with the butt of the segments toward the eye. They can be tied right side up or upside down this way also. On wet flies the majority of good fly tiers use the upside down wings.

In tying these wings, cut identical segments from a "Right" and a "Left" quill. Place the backs of the convex curve surfaces together so that the points are even. Grasp closely between thumb and forefinger of the left hand, determine the length of wing you want and the point at which your thread will grip the wing butts. Hold over the hook at the point you wish to tie. Pull or manipulate the thread in between your finger and thumb, with the thread looped over the selected tying point, hold tightly with the thumb and finger, actually squeeze the wings, then pull STRAIGHT DOWNWARD— loop again before you release your grip with the left hand. If the wings are tilted either way do them over. If wings ride correctly on top of hook and are not folded, start winding thread behind or in front of them to raise them to a vertical position. Then carefully wind a couple figure eight turns of the thread between the wings to separate them. Raising them to a vertical position and separating them applies, of course, to dry fly wings. Many of the old English patterns call for double wings. Why, I don't know!

The next type of wings are those formed of woodduck or mallard flank plumage and similar material including clumps of barbs from hackle quills. Again these wings can be tied in either before or after the body is constructed and they also can be tied forward or backward, whichever suits the convenience of the fly tier. This is the easiest type of wing to tie. Some tiers use the tip of the flank feather only—others use, if the feather is suitable, each side and the tip, getting three flies from one feather. This is possible in the smaller flies. Merely strip or cut the section you have prepared by spreading the barbs until the tips are even then holding tightly while cutting. Roll the clump lightly between thumb and index finger— determine length you wish wing to be—place on the hook and tie in so that it rests on top. Throw a loop or two of thread completely around the clump ON TOP SIDE OF HOOK (this holds the barbs together closely at their base)—wrap thread behind or in front of wings to raise them to a vertical position. Splitting the clump into two parts and spreading slightly with figure eight winds is done by some but is not particularly essential. The actual wings of the insect at rest or riding the water are perfectly vertical most of the time. Other than a few delicate partings of the wings during the drying stage when the wings are separated they're in use and the fly isn't on the water anyway. In tying this material for wet flies it is fastened in with the tips pointing to the rear. Some tiers leave the wing in this down position, some raise the wings to an approximate 45° angle with the body (more action in water). On wet flies the wings are applied generally after the hackle is wound.

The third type of wing is the "Hackle Tip" and the kind I am convinced is becoming more and more used to replace the antiquated flight quill cut wings. Although not the easiest set of wings to tie they are the most rugged and if correctly tied will last the full life of the flies' use. The smaller hackle quills are more suitable for hackle tips although the larger ones can be trimmed with scissors to a proper size. This does not mean the extremely large hackle feathers because the stalk would be out of proportion generally.

In fastening the tips to the fly under construction hold the two hackles at their extreme ends and judge as closely as you can the point where they will be secured to the hook. Carefully strip the hackle barbs for a distance below this point or better, trim with scissors. Still holding the tips between the left thumb and index finger place on top of hook and tie in, taking pains to see that they are secure ON TOP and not down the side of the hook. Wrap thread ⅛ inch over butts toward eye and return thread to first point of tying in. Clip the extruding butts closely. Now grasp the wings and raise them to an upright position, taking a few turns of the thread behind them to hold the tips in this position. If wings are to be divided or are to be tied spent, with needle or scissor points, separate the tips and wind between wings with thread to place them in the position you wish. Hackle tip wings, too, can be tied, as with the other wings, before body is wound or after. That's your choice.

The one other popular type wing is the down or flat style such as those of the stone flies, caddis, sedges, etc. These are built of most generally used wing materials and more. They usually consist of two segments of whatever material from which you are fashioning the wings. One hint to follow in getting the wings to lie flat is in building the body. At the point where the wings will be secured build to a larger dimension than the body proper with spun fur or yarn. This gives something to bite into without fastening the wings on a lower level thus raising them against the body.

Most tiers tie each of the segments in separately to get the proper "lay" of the wing which should follow the line of the body with only a slight spread at the rear end of the wings. Where tied in, the segments are an almost perfect overlap.

Tying "Hair" wings, which includes bucktail, badger, squirrel, capras, etc., the correct sized clump, usually ⅛ inch or less in diameter for the average fly, is cut from the hide. The butt ends are cleaned of fuzz or under fur, the right length of wing is determined and the clump is cut to fit. The butts then are touched or dipped in cement, placed on the hook and tied in carefully. Much of the hair for wings is hard and pains should be taken to see that they are really secure. A wrap of tying thread around the clump itself immediately behind the point where tied to the hook is advantageous in holding the hairs together. This also to raise the tips somewhat, which may or may not be desired. Again, hair wings can be tied in reverse or forward if one wishes, then the clump forced back into position and tied in. This procedure makes for security but also builds a sizable shoulder, which is not conducive to a pleasing appearance.

Imitating "Shell Wings," as on beetles (shrimp are tied the same way even though they haven't yet sprouted wings) is accomplished by securing the overlapping material or element, whether it be hair or plumage, by the finer ends at the base of the tail before the body is wrapped. After the body has been completed and secured, the overlapping material is brought forward over the top half of the body and tied down. Some materials require that the "shell" be treated with lacquer or fly head cement, after finishing, to give it a glossy appearance.

Jungle cock shoulders, hackles, etc., supplementing wings are usually tied in after the wings are complete. These additions are tied in one at a time so that perfect balance can be secured.

HACKLE *(See Fig. J)*

This part of the fly is the other major controversial feature among tiers and among users.

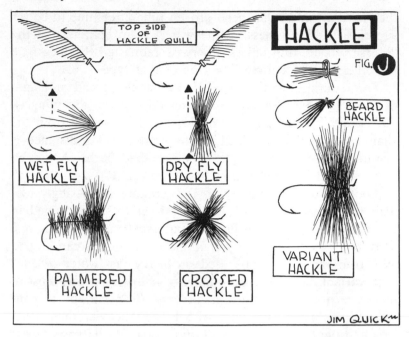

TOP SIDE OF HACKLE QUILL

HACKLE

FIG. J

WET FLY HACKLE

DRY FLY HACKLE

BEARD HACKLE

PALMERED HACKLE

CROSSED HACKLE

VARIANT HACKLE

JIM QUICK

Many expert fly fishermen incline in the direction of heavily hackled flies and an equal number insist upon sparsely hackled flies. The fact remains that the "bug" has six legs, seldom more than eight. With the hook and the weighty or absorbent materials used, a hackle spread consisting of six or eight barbs on the bottom of the fly and it would disappear under the surface of the water without hesitation. The old English tiers were strong for lots of hackle, and well greased. When one examines some of these flies, with the fragile soft hackle used, it's no wonder. The modern trend is towards sparse hackle but ENOUGH to float the fly. Here another condition arises. On what type of water will the fly be used and how skillful is the fisherman in dropping the lure lightly to the surface of the water? On heavy fast water the fly necessarily would require more hackle to stay afloat than on slow moving "chalk type" streams or smooth lake surfaces. Again there is the quality of the hackle. The better the hackle the sparser the fly can be tied to accomplish the same end. All things being equal, the sparser the hackle on the fly the better it represents the "natural" and it has been proven time after time to be far superior in effectiveness on the water. I am definitely of the "sparse" school and unless otherwise requested the flies I tie for others, and for myself, will be of that type.

The natural or normal size of the hackle spread or length of the legs which simulate those on the fly you are tying is, on the dry fly, one and one-half times the distance from the shank of the hook to the barb or point. If this distance is one-quarter inch, the length of the hackle barbs should be approximately three-eighth inches. (See Fig. K.)

Another strong trend which is becoming increasingly evident is that for "variants" and "semi-variants." Flies tied in this fashion are excellent floaters and excellent fish attractors. Most dry flies of the mayfly clan and many others can be tied as a true variant if to be used on heavy fast water or as a semi-variant on water a bit quieter in temper, such as most of the eastern and mid-western streams. The variant is constructed, generally speaking, with longer, heavier than usual tails and one of its two hackles up to two sizes larger or even longer. The second hackle is generally the normally correct size for the fly. Hackles, too, are usually of two different shades or kinds. It is strongly suggested that the fly tier include a few of the known patterns in his tying, such as Donnelly's Light and Dark Variants but we urge that also the same procedures be injected in fashioning variants of dry favorites such as Adams, Gordon Quill, Ginger Quill, Blue and Red Uprights, Mosquito, Black Gnats, etc.

On regular dry flies size 14 and smaller, and the hackle is top grade, one hackle should suffice. We will presume the hackle you have is average, so in preparing for this part of the fly two hackle quills of the same approximate size, and of a dimension to suit the fly being tied, are selected. Grasp the hackles at the extreme tips and fan out the barbs along the quill by running thumb and forefinger down the full length lightly. The point where the barbs do not spring back but stay lazily where your caress left them is the point from which you strip or scissor off the soft, webby section next to the stalk. Holding both tips together fasten the butt of the quills, close

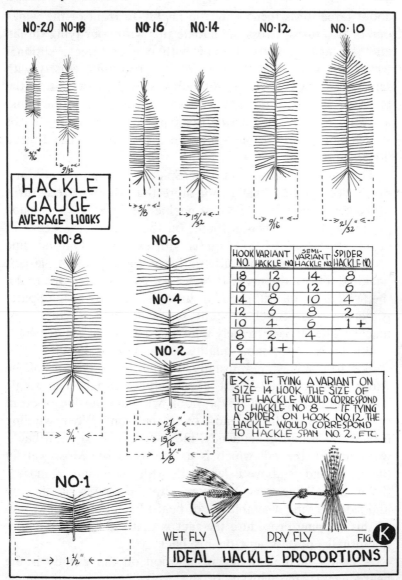

HACKLE GAUGE
AVERAGE HOOKS

NO·20 NO·18   NO·16   NO·14   NO·12   NO·10
NO·8   NO·6   NO·4   NO·2   NO·1

HOOK NO.	VARIANT HACKLE NO.	SEMI-VARIANT HACKLE NO.	SPIDER HACKLE NO.
18	12	14	8
16	10	12	6
14	8	10	4
12	6	8	2
10	4	6	1 +
8	2	4	
6	1 +		
4			

EX: IF TYING A VARIANT ON SIZE 14 HOOK THE SIZE OF THE HACKLE WOULD CORRESPOND TO HACKLE NO 8 — IF TYING A SPIDER ON HOOK NO.12 THE HACKLE WOULD CORRESPOND TO HACKLE SPAN NO. 2 , ETC.

WET FLY   DRY FLY   FIG. K
IDEAL HACKLE PROPORTIONS

to the barb section, securely behind the wings so that the natural curve of the feathers point slightly toward the front. This means, in other words, that the bright or outside surface of the hackle faces toward the rear. Grasp tips of hackle in pliers securely and start winding behind the wings. Make about three turns then bring the hackle in front of the wings one or two turns. Cross the hackle tips with your tying thread and jam against hook. Follow with two or three additional wraps and hitch. Cut the hackle tips protruding closely with scissors or razor blade. If difficulty is evident in getting the hackle to spread vertically try fastening the hackle to the hook, allowing a complete turn of the bare quill before the barbs start to spread. Adjustment is more easily accomplished using this method.

The hackle on American type Spider ties is extremely long but is tied sparsely, that is not more than three or four turns of hackle at the most. The best hackle for Spiders is the spade or throat hackle which is found on the sides of the necks or capes—those short hackle quills with extremely long but fine quality barbs. The other alternative is the tips of the largest hackle quills on the neck. It may take two of these tips to get the few barbs you will need on this fly. The body of the Spider is generally of tinsel or quill segment such as condor or macaw. The tail is extremely long and consists of ten or twelve hackle barbs of the same quality as mentioned above.

Wet hackle is wound, usually, preceding the tying in of the wings however this is not absolutely essential. The single hackle quill is secured to the hook with the outside or front of the hackle quill uppermost or to the front. When winding it in you will find its tendency, more or less, is to point backward toward the tail which is as it should be. Most wet fly hackle wound as above is left as is, with the wing tied in over the hackle. Some tiers, however, clip the hackle off the top and sides leaving a semblance of beard hackle. In justification of this clipping procedure the fact is that the natural fly does not usually possess legs on his back.

A neater method of leg installation on the wet fly is the beard hackle, the whisker or the "spike." The beard can be tied in either before or after the wing is placed and I find that tying it in after makes a cleaner job. Remove from the hackle quill a clump of barbs, cut to the correct length so that when tied in the tips of the barbs will reach just to the hook point. Hold in the right hand between thumb and forefinger, first, with butts of barbs to the right. (The hook should project from the vise in the "point exposed" manner as far to the right as practicable.) The left hand thumb and index finger or the second finger is looped over the vise and the hook, meeting below the point where the beard is to be fastened. Place the clump of barbs into the left fingers with the butts projecting beyond the point of tying far enough to get a grip with the tying thread. Raise to the hook and wrap thread around and tie in. If the barbs follow the line of the hook too closely a couple of wraps of thread behind and under the beard, close up, will help to project it outward so that the barbs aim approximately at the hook point. If you have extreme difficulty in following the above maneuver, take the hook out from the vise and turn it over, upside down, and tie in the whisker as you might a wing.

FINISHING THE FLY

Under the heading of "Thread Maneuvers," this part of the subject is covered. Each fly, following its completion, should be cemented at the head. Some do this while the fly is still in the vise and before the thread end is cut off. The cement should be thin enough so that when a drop is touched to the thread it immediately soaks in. Keep your cement thinned JUST ENOUGH so that it will do this. Too thin cement is little better than none at all and the too thick will only coat the surface and dry without sealing the thread thoroughly.

Many tiers finish off their fly with a touch of thin varnish. This is commendable—it certainly secures the thread. The chief objection to this is the hours it requires before the varnish is dry.

If the fly is finished with head cement or varnish be sure the fly is completely dry (at least eight or ten hours) before immersion in any floatant, if this is your practice, in the construction and completion of dry flies.

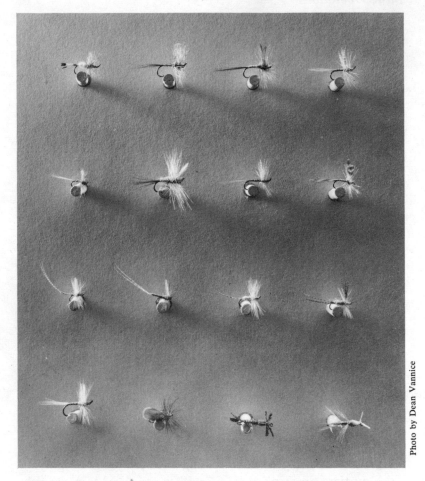

Photo by Dean Vannice

FLIES TIED BY THE AUTHOR

Left to right, top to bottom:

Blue wing Adams (Spent wing), Macaw Adams (Whit-craft), Bradley, Red Quill (Male Hendrickson), Blue Quill, Donnelly Variant (light), Gordon Quill, Mosquito

Little Marryat quill (detached body), Iron Blue Quill (detached body), Cahill (light), Hendrickson (light)

Ginger Quill, Black Gnat, Mayfly nymph, Stonefly nymph creeper

Chapter *15*

We Construct a Fly Or Two

IF CAREFUL study has been made of the previous chapter you should know how, and will develop the confidence to tie any trout fly, or flies, necessary for a successful fishing expedition any time and anywhere in this country.

Actually all you require now are the tools, the materials, the inclination, the time, and a brief description of the named fly, as to what colors or what material goes into making it. As you become more experienced in tying flies, just a glance at a fly will tell you the materials in its make-up and how it was tied.

Nearly all good fly tying books supply a "dictionary" listing of several patterns. Yes, there's one in this book, too, which was studiously prepared to supply you with a description of the most popular, most effective fly patterns. Included in this listing are the flies used, with few exceptions, by every expert and every fisherman's fisherman.

Let's tie a quartet of different kinds, now, that are listed in this book's dictionary, just for practice. Following these four flies is a series of instruction forms outlining the formulas for tying various types of trout flies.

One quite popular dry fly, good from coast to coast, is the Ginger Quill. There are many tied similarly.

GINGER QUILL (*size 12, for example*)

Fasten waxed thread ¼ inch from eye of hook with jam and hitch. Be sure thread does not turn or spiral on hook, or trouble will be encountered later. Wrap thread down hook to where the bend starts—hitch again. You are now ready for the tail. This will be of hackle barbs and the color should be a light ginger or buff ranging to as dark as light Rhode Island Red. If you have a neck or cape from which to select your hackle take one of the feathers from the edge of the neck about half way down. You will find that on most good necks these particular feathers or quills are short and wide also hard and stiff in the barbs. This hackle is called throat hackle and is the finest material for tail wisps. Spread the hackle from the tip down and select five or six barbs and cut from the stalk. Hold them on top of the hook so that the butt ends extend to the point where the first hitch was made, near the eye of the hook. If barbs are too long cut to correct length at the butt before tying in. The tail should be about one and one-half times the length of the body proper. Wrap thread carefully up the hook over these tail barbs with enough turns to make the surface comparatively smooth, then back to the "Base of Tail" point and hitch.

Prepare light-colored peacock quill by removing herl. If herl has been removed by other than the wax stripping method wet the quill and fasten in about one and one-quarter inches to one and one-half inches from the butt of the quill and wrap tip end under as thread is ribbed up to front end of body section. Carefully wrap quill with fingers or with hackle pliers so that contrasting dark and light sections of quill form segments simulating body of fly. On the completion of wrap and hitching the thread give quill body a light coating of fly head cement and let dry.

Prepare two hackle tips for wings. I suggest using light blue dun but they can be cream colored, badger tips or even white. The whole object is to try to imitate the wings of the May fly we are trying to simulate. On the natural fly the wings are transparent but they have an iridescent sheen prevailing toward a watery blue. On the size 14 fly, for instance, I would use two hackles near a small 16 or even 18 size. Prepare and fasten in as described in the section under wings in "Basic Operations." The hackle should be the same shade as is used for the tail. Select your two hackles, fasten in and wind. After hackle is wound to your satisfaction wrap with thread just enough to smooth the area between hackle and hook eye. The hitching tool can help you hold back the hackle as you wind. Finish off with multiple hitches or whip finish, cement the "head" and your fly is now complete.

MACAW ADAMS, BLUE WING, SPENT

This is a comparatively new tie that is effective throughout the entire country when the darker naturals are on the water. It has been found to raise fish when no other fly would do as well. The fly is good on both fast, rough water and on slower, smoother surfaces.

The tail consists of mixed brown and grizzly hackle barbs, or you can use just the brown, which are installed the same as those on the Ginger Quill. The tail also should consist of at least twelve to fourteen of the barbs for top floating efficiency.

The next step is to fasten in the macaw (blue and yellow), an unstripped barb or a few segments from the tail feather or larger flight quill. It is secured about one and one-quarter to one and one-half inches from the butts of the barbs and wound the same as the peacock quill. An alternative for the macaw is condor or large wild goose quill with an additional ribbing of fine yellow thread.

The wings are dark blue dun hackle tips tied spent and extending outward the same distance as the length of the body.

The hackle is "Adams," or one grizzly hackle and one brown hackle (dark Rhode Island red will do fine) wound on together, or singly, mixing the hackle as it is wrapped on.

BUCKTAIL STREAMER

This is one of the most popular streamer type patterns simulating the minnow, a tid-bit relished by all of the fish species. There are almost as many variations of the "bucktail" as there are colors of suitable hair and the materials for the bodies.

The tail, which is an optional appendage (some streamers have 'em and some don't) on this fly will be a scarlet segment from a goose cussette or inner wing feather, dyed. Secure it to the hook at the tail point so that it extends ½ to ¾ inches. Now run the thread up to the thorax and hitch. Tie in an 8- or 9-inch strip of fairly wide silver tinsel. Wrap down the hook closely to the bend of the hook and return to starting point covering all gaps left on the first run. Cement the tinsel thoroughly and let dry a few minutes. Prepare a clump of white bucktail by evening up the tip ends as much as possible —measure for length, cut the butts at that point and cement the ends, then tie to hook. Do the same with a clump of brownish colored bucktail. These clumps should not be too heavy, roughly ⅟₁₆ inch in diameter at butts. Now tie in a whisker of scarlet hackle barbs, pointing toward the hook point. A final touch before finishing the fly is to add 5 or 6 herl strands on top of the bucktail. Adding jungle cock eyes always makes the streamer more impressive and, I believe, more effective.

DETACHED BODY MAY FLY, SMALL

It would be advisable to use a fine white, waxed thread for this project. The basic body needs to be of a stable nature that will stand a bit of flexing and one which your tying thread will not cut through as it is secured to the hook. Stripped hackle quills in the larger dimensions are suitable but I prefer nylon, silk gut or a similar material. Do not use porcupine quills— they cut through or break off too easily in use.

Cut a section of the material and fasten it securely to the top of your hook with tying thread and cement, leaving an extension to the rear the length you wish the body to be. On a size 14 fly the extension should be about one-half inch or slightly less.

Select a pair or three barbs from a mallard or woodduck flank feather as stiff as you can find and, of course, they must be long enough to fasten the extreme butts to the hook and to wrap, with your thread, the full length of the body including the extended section and return, and the tail wisps extending beyond the body must be as long, at least, as the entire body itself. Cement the body lightly. If you will hold the tail segments parted a bit and the junction touched with a small drop of cement retaining them in the position you want while the cement hardens, the tail will tend to stay that way. With care the body can be ribbed with a stripped peacock quill, raffia, floss or fine colored thread, in fact any suitable material that will serve to simulate the natural. Invariably, it should be cemented when completed.

The procedure for finishing (wings and hackle) of the fly is the same as in the two previous dry fly patterns.

The following pages outline twelve different type flies and the procedure detailed for every operation. By a careful study of these steps and a deliberate follow-through in tying the flies and you will have learned all that is necessary to tie, at least, ninety per cent of the known standard patterns.

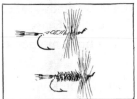

GRAY HACKLES (*Dry*)

Hackle flies were originated by the Macedonians over 1800 years ago.

Good all around pattern, throughout the year. Used more in the West than in the East.

Suggested sizes:—10 to 16

MATERIALS:

> Hooks—Mustad 94842—94840—3911E, Alcock's
> 04991
> Grizzly hackle
> Yellow floss
> Peacock herl
> Golden Pheasant tippets
> Gold tinsel, fine

PROCEDURE:

GRAY HACKLE, YELLOW
> Secure hook in vise—jam thread and hitch

Fasten in 3-inch strip of gold tinsel, wrap down bend of
hook approx. $\frac{3}{16}$ inch and back to bend of hook
point—secure—hitch. Leave tinsel that was left
over, this is for ribbing later.

Tie in 8 or 10 Golden pheasant tippet barbs for tail,
(extend so that both dark sections of the tippet
shows)—secure and hitch.

Wrap thread forward to end of body point—tie in strand
of yellow floss (7 or 8 inches of medium sized floss),
wrap down hook to base of tail, at bend of hook,
and return tapering body slightly as it is wound—
secure—hitch.

Rib tinsel, about 4 or 5 turns up hook to end of body
—secure—hitch.

Tie in grizzly hackle and wind, dry style, about 6 or 7
turns, more if wanted—secure—hitch.

Clip wild hackle barbs, if any.

Finish fly with multiple hitches or whip. Cement finish
thread.

GRAY HACKLE, PEACOCK

No tinsel ribbing on body.

At bend of hook point tie in 3 or 4 peacock herl wisps,
twist with tying thread, wrap up body to thorax.

Finish fly as above—hackle and thread finish.

Variations of the hackle flies consist of different colored
bodies and different colored hackles, various tail materials and various types of ribbing.

WOOLLY WORM (*Wet*)

The woolly worm is an old English pattern, originally, and
the originator is not known.

Primarily used in West, although is good anywhere.

Simulates, we think, the caterpillar or the helgramite.
Suggested sizes:—⅜ to 14, usually streamer hook.

MATERIALS:

Hook—Mustad 9672-3X long
Black chenille
Gold tinsel
Grizzly saddle hackle
Scarlet goose cussette

PROCEDURE:

Secure hook in vise—jam thread and hitch.
Tie in cut section wisp of scarlet cussette for tail approx.
  ¼ to ½ inch in length—secure hitch.
Fasten in 3-inch strip of tinsel.
Fasten in grizzly saddle hackle (butt end).
Fasten in 4-inch strip of chenille—hitch.
Wrap chenille closely up hook to ¾₁₆ inch from eye—
  secure—hitch.
Rib tinsel over chenille, about 5 or 6 turns to end of body
  —secure—hitch.
Wind grizzly hackle up body to end—secure—hitch.
Finish fly with multiple hitches or whip—cement thread.

The variations in this fly are unlimited. Color of hackle,
color of tail, color of body, length of body, etc. Some
tiers secure the tip of the hackle in at the tail base, instead
of the butt end and wrap the hackle simultaneously with
the chenille. The old method of making the woolly worm
was wrapping the hackle from the tip end. The change,
or reversing the hackle to the butt end, which is a definite
improvement, is credited to the late Don Martinez, an
outstanding fly tier in the West.

GORDON QUILL (*Dry*)

Originated by Theodore Gordon, Sullivan County, New York—circa 1890–1895.

Simulates Mayfly spinner, or dun.

An eastern fly but equally productive across the country. Extremely effective in early season and intermittently during season. Good daytime fly, at its best during hatches.

Suggested sizes:—12 to 20.

MATERIALS:

> Hooks—Mustad 94844–94842–94840
> Blue dun, medium, hackle
> Blue dun hackle, large, or spade, for tail barbs
> Peacock eye for quill
> Woodduck flank plumage (Chinese Mandarin duck excellent substitute, or correctly tinted mallard)

PROCEDURE:

> Secure hook in vise, jam thread and hitch.
> Tie in blue dun hackle wisps, for tail, one and one-half times length of body, at least.
> Tie in stripped peacock quill, wrap carefully to thorax, showing the simulated segmentation of the fly's body —secure—hitch. Cement body lightly.
> Prepare and fasten in clump of woodduck, secure—hitch —work into upright position, *do not divide,* secure thread behind wings—hitch.
> Tie in 2 blue dun hackles securely behind wings, hitch, clip butt ends of hackle stalks.
> Wrap hackles, together or separately, about 3 turns behind wings then a couple turns in front. Secure —hitch, clip wild barbs, if necessary.
> Finish fly with multiple hitches or whip—cement thread.

The original tail wisps, as tied by Theodore Gordon, were of woodduck. He also recommended a fine gold wire tied counter wind to the quill, primarily for securing the quill, rather than for color. Also, dun color used by him was light. If the body of the Gordon Quill were fashioned of dubbed, cream fox belly fur, tail of mallard flank plumage or Golden Pheasant crest barbs, you have a Hendrickson, which was originated by Roy Stenrod, New York, about 1916.

The Gordon Quill has few variations, it is just about the perfect fly. Some tiers like a tiny, light green egg sack, at base of tail. They claim more effectiveness. Many, many quill flies are tied very similarly to this fly, with just a change of color throughout, or a different wing. Examples: Ginger quill, Cahill Quill, Blue Quill, Blue Upright.

CAHILL (*Dry*)

Originated by Dan Cahill, New York, circa 1880.
Simulates the light colored Mayfly dun.
Effective dry fly during hatches of light colored Mayflies.
A hot weather, midsummer fly, but is known to appear up to late fall.
Good in nearly all trout streams across the country.
Suggested sizes:—10 to 18.

MATERIALS:

Hooks—Mustad 94842–94844–94840
Light red, or buff hackle
Light red, or buff, large, or spade hackle for tail
Fox belly fur, for dubbing body
Woodduck flank plumage, or suitable substitute

PROCEDURE:

Secure hook in vise—jam thread and hitch.
Tie in 8 or 10 long hackle barbs (from one and one-half to twice the length of the body) secure—hitch.
Prepare dubbing, light tan or buff fur from fox belly, mix in a very small amount of the grayish fur—tie in

and wrap fairly tightly, secure—hitch. Trim body
with scissors if too bunchy to make a comparatively
slender dubbed body.

Prepare and fasten in clump of woodduck, just slightly
longer than body, do not divide, raise to upright
position with thread and secure—hitch.

Tie in one or two buff or light red hackles behind wing,
secure, clip hackle stalk butts, hitch—wrap or wind
hackles, dry style, 3 turns behind wings, then two
or three in front. Secure—hitch. Clip wild hackle
barbs, if necessary.

Finish fly with multiple hitches or whip—cement.

The Cahill is dressed in many shades ranging from a light
buff, almost white, to medium or dark red. It also has a
variation in the Cahill Quill, where quill body is used
instead of dubbing. Bodies have been built of yarn, spun
fur, light condor quill, unstripped, ostrich herl, etc. A
recommended tail material is wisps of woodduck but is
difficult to float, in a dry fly. This was the original tail
material.

MOSQUITO (*Dry*)

Originator unknown, but fly probably has been tied, in
some fashion, since the popular inception of dry flies.

Good East and West, wherever there are mosquitoes.

Season from approx. June 1st to frost.

Sugested sizes:—12 to 18.

MATERIALS:

Hooks—Mustad 94842–94844–94840
Grizzly hackle, sized to fly size
Grizzly hackle, large, or spade, for tail
Moose mane
Grizzly hackle, small, for hackle tip wings

PROCEDURE:

Secure hook in vise—jam thread and hitch.

Tie in 6 or 8 grizzly hackle wisps for tail (long)—hitch.

Fasten in one white and one dark moose mane hair—hitch—wind thread back to thorax—hitch.

Wrap body so that contrasting moose hairs form segmented appearance, to thorax—secure—hitch.

Tie in 2 hackle tip wings, as long or longer than body—bring to upright position, separate—hitch.

Tie in grizzly hackle behind wings. Take three or four turns behind, then two or three in front of wings —tie in—hitch. Trim or clip wild hackle barbs, if any.

Finish fly with multiple hitches or whip—cement head threads.

Variations of the above mosquito tie could be the use of blue dun hackle tip wings—stripped peacock quill for body—mixed black and white hackle—mallard flank plumage wisps for tail, etc.

BEAVERKILL (*Dry*)

Originated by Harry Pritchard, New York, circa 1850.

Primarily, an Eastern fly.

High floating, as are palmered flies . . . . for rough water, for bank or windapping.

Suggested sizes:—10 to 16.

MATERIALS:

Hooks—Mustad 94842–94844

Brown hackle, sized to fly size

Brown hackle, neck or saddle, for palmering

Brown hackle, large, or spade, for tail

Gray mallard quills

White floss

Brown floss (fine)

PROCEDURE:

Secure hook in vise—jam thread and hitch.
Fasten in brown hackle wisps for tail (8 or 10) length
   of body—hitch.
Fasten in 3″ strip of brown floss.
Tie in, at tip, one palmering hackle—hitch.
Run tying thread to thorax—hitch.
Fasten in white floss, wrap down to tail base and return
   —secure and hitch thread.
Rib up body with brown floss—secure—hitch.
Palmer wrap hackle to thorax—secure—hitch, clip stalk
   butt.
Prepare, fasten in gray mallard cut wings, dry style—
   secure in upright position, separate wings—hitch.
Tie in one brown hackle, behind wings, secure and clip
   butt stalk. Take three turns behind wings then two
   or three in front of wings—secure hitch—trim.
Finish fly with multiple hitch or whip—cement head
   thread.

Beaverkill variations would be in color of body, a different hackle color, the use of hackle tip wings over the cut
wings, etc.

 ADAMS (*Dry*)

Originated by Len Halliday, Michigan, circa 1922.
Simulates the deer fly or a gnat.
Equally productive throughout America.
Good through day but better in the early evening and dusk.

Suggested sizes:—12 to 18.

MATERIALS:

> Hooks—Mustad 94842–94844
> Muskrat fur, for dubbing
> Grizzly hackle tips for wings
> Grizzly hackle
> Brown or dark red hackle
> Grizzly hackle, large, or spade for tail wisps
> Brown hackle, large, or spade for tail wisps

PROCEDURE:

> Secure hook in vise—jam thread and hitch.
> Fasten in mixed grizzly and red hackle tail and hitch.
> Prepare muskrat dubbing (gray blue, for body).
> Wrap body (about half way up to eye of hook), tie in and hitch. (Substitute for dubbed body would be spun fur or yarn in the correct color.)
> Tie in 2 grizzly hackle tip wings—secure—raise to upright position with thread, then to split wing stand. If "spent wing" is the type desired, work wings down with thread and secure—hitch.
> Tie in one grizzly and one brown hackle, together, behind wings. Wrap together, or separately, to mix hackle well, fasten—hitch.
> Finish with whip or multiple hitch—cement finish threads.

ADAMS VARIATIONS:

> Yellow body
> Female—(Yellow egg sack at base of tail)
> Blue-yellow macaw body, or condor quill
> Body ribbed scarlet or orange, with thread
> Full hackled without wings
> Wings, blue dun hackle tips
> Golden pheasant tippet tail, scarlet tail.

CHAPPIE (*wet—streamer*)

Originator unknown. The Chappie is a derivation of an old English wet fly.

Primarily used in West, but good in any water.

Can be tied small for stream trout or heavy for salmon and steelhead.

Suggested sizes:—4 to 14, 2X and 3X long hooks.

MATERIALS:

Hooks—Mustad 9671 or 9672
Grizzly hackle tips for tail
Grizzly hackle for wings (narrow—long) *not* saddle
Grizzly hackle, soft
Deep yellow yarn
Yellow thread, heavy (size A) on larger flies

PROCEDURE:

Secure hook in vise—jam thread and hitch (waxed, heavy yellow thread). Wind down to bend of hook and hitch allowing the free end to extend 4 or 5 inches (to be used later as ribbing).

Fasten in two hackle tips, convex faces together—extending ½ to ¾ inches for tail—secure—hitch.

Tie in yellow yarn—hitch—wrap body full and tapering slightly about ⅔ distance up hook—secure—hitch.

Rib yellow thread, about 5 or 6 turns up hook to end of body—secure—hitch.

Tie in soft grizzly hackle, wet style, wind about 2 or 3 turns only to leave sparse—secure—hitch.

Fasten in two long hackles for wings, streamer style, on top of hook, concave sides facing—secure—hitch.

Make head of yellow thread, full, whip finish—cement head.

Body variations of the Chappie are numerous. Body colors used are orange, scarlet, brown, white, light green, black. Some flies, in this order, are ribbed with tinsel, either flat or oval. Some have been tied with various colors of hackle, wings and tail. Some tiers weave the body producing a contrasting belly line on the fly.

BUCKTAIL COACHMAN (*wet*)

Originator, Tom Boswell, England, circa 1850.

One of the best known flies in the fly tier's dictionary has been converted to a semi-streamer. Good in all waters, any time.

What this fly simulates is anyone's guess, some say gnat, some say minnow.

Suggested sizes:—2 to 16 in either wet fly or streamer types.

MATERIALS:

> Hooks—Mustad 3906 (wet fly type)—9671 (semi-streamer type)
> White bucktail (Virginia white tail deer preferred)
> Peacock herl
> Scarlet hackle, large, for tail
> Gold tinsel
> Brown hackle
> Black tying thread

PROCEDURE:

> Secure hook in vise—jam thread and hitch.
> Fasten in gold tinsel piece (2 or 3 inch), wrap down bend of hook ⅛ to ¼ inch and return—secure—hitch.
> Prepare and tie in clump of scarlet hackle barbs, for tail, extend approx. ½ inch—secure—hitch.
> Tie in 8 or 9 suitable herl wisps—twist with black tying thread and while continuing the twisting, wrap the herl body up hook to thorax—secure—hitch.
> Prepare and tie in brown hackle whisker, under hook—secure—hitch.
> Fasten in ⅛ inch clump of white bucktail, slightly longer than body—secure well and hitch. (Be sure to

cement butt ends of hair clump before tying in.)
Finish fly with multiple hitches or whip—cement.

The Coachman, in any of its variations can be tied with,
or without tail (this is the way it originally appeared),
with or without the tinsel tip, with many types of winging hair or cut quill wings, as long as they are white.
Examples: Polar bear, capras, mountain goat, ox tail,
vampire bat, calf tail or impali, white turkey, goose, etc.
There are other variations of the Coachman with dark
wings such as the Cabin Coachman, Mallard Coachman,
etc. And to top it all, the Royal Coachman, a Coachman
variation, can and is tied with the same numerous
variations.

CINNAMON SEDGE (*Dry*)

Originator unknown. This pattern is just a pause in the
chain of caddis or sedge ties and variations.
Always good wherever there are caddis flies.
This is a small fly but when they are emerging and flying
in clusters over the water, the trout will have no other.
Suggested sizes:—14 to 18.

MATERIALS:

Hooks—Mustad 9579A—3911E, Alcock's 04991
Mouse deer, back, for wings (fine badger, ground
    squirrel, etc., substitute)
Peacock eye for quill
Light green, or insect green, goose quill dyed
Light blue dun hackle—(Light olive, ginger, buff, light
    red can be used)

PROCEDURE:

Secure hook in vise—jam thread and hitch.

Tie in and wrap small egg sack of green just down on bend of hook—hitch.

Fasten in light, stripped peacock quill and wind up hook to thorax—secure—hitch . . . . lightly cement quill (not the egg sack).

Build a small lump of the fly tying thread at this point to receive the wings. Hitch and cement.

Prepare and tie in a clump of mouse deer hair, a bit longer than the hook, on the prepared lump of thread. (This is done so that the wings will lay immediately on the body, not at an angle away from it.) Tie down securely and hitch. Cement the butts of the hair tied down.

Tie in hackle and wrap, dry style, over the butts of wing and towards eye of hook—secure—hitch.

Finish fly with multiple hitches or whip—cement.

There are almost as many variations, in the dressing of sedge and caddis flies, as there are materials available to simulate the different parts of the fly.

Some tiers like to palmer the bodies to make them better floaters. Some like to add tails, where the natural fly has none, for the same reason.

COCK-A-TUSH (*Wet*) (*Muddler minnow*)

Created by Don Gapin, Michigan and Ontario, Canada. . . . for squaretails, in the Nipigon River and elsewhere.

Underwater lure simulating the fresh water sculpin. Exceptionally effective for brook trout, in streams where this minnow is to be found.

Sometimes called the Miller's Thumb, or Miller Head.

Suggested sizes:—4 to 10 (2X & 3X long)

MATERIALS:

Hooks—Mustad 9671—9672

Mottled turkey quill
Brown bucktail
White bucktail
Gold tinsel
Gray-brown deer body hair

PROCEDURE:

Secure hook in vise—jam thread and hitch.

Tie in strip of tinsel (about 6 inches), ¼ inch from eye of hook, wrap down hook closely to just over bend of hook and return—secure—hitch—cement tinsel thoroughly and let dry a few minutes.

Tie in small clump of brown bucktail, with a few white hairs intermixed, on top of hook and not closer than ¼ inch from the eye—secure—hitch—cement where fastened. (The bucktail should extend to one and one-half to two times the length of the tinsel body on the hook).

Prepare 2 segments of mottled turkey, one from each side of the quill, ³⁄₁₆ to ¼ inch wide, place one on each side of hook, just short of total length of the bucktail. The natural curve of the turkey feather segment should point slightly upwards—secure and hitch.

Take ⅛ inch clump of deer body hair and flare just ahead of tied down bucktail and turkey quill segments—force rear hairs down to follow body, with thread. If necessary add second small clump of body hair which is to be clipped short to form a head on the fly. Secure—multiple hitch or whip—cement.

Although this is primarily a streamer type fly, many fishermen say that floated on the surface during grasshopper season, when they are around, it is pure dynamite.

Some tiers claim the body of this fly should be weighted somewhat near the thorax because the natural muddler clings to the bottom.

MAYFLY NYMPH (*Wet*) (*A general pattern*)

The writer will take credit, at this moment, for this particular "bug" tie.

The nymph fly, of any sort, is as good anyplace, in any water (where there are nymphs), as the fisherman handling the lure.

Eighty per cent, and more, of the trout menu is under water, where the nymphs live.

Suggested sizes:—10 to 16

MATERIALS:

> Hooks—Mustad 3906
> Peacock herl
> Peacock sword
> Tan floss
> Gray mallard quill
> Gold wire
> Grouse body plumage

PROCEDURE:

> Secure hook in vise—jam thread and hitch.
> Tie in 3 peacock sword wisp tips (¼ inch long)—hitch.
> Tie in 2 inch piece of gold wire.
> Tie in one wide peacock herl (from just below eye on peacock stalk)—hitch.
> Tie in and wind tan floss up the body to ¼ inch from eye—secure and hitch. Leave excess hang.
> Rib gold wire, counter wind, to end of floss body—hitch.
> Rib peacock herl wisp (5 or 6 turns) to same point—secure—hitch. Clip, with fine scissors, top side and belly side of body, leaving side wisps of herl sticking out.

Tie in 6 or 8 strands from a grouse feather, whisker
fashion, underneath hook, at this point . . . hitch.

Fasten in ⅛ inch segment, at its tip, of gray duck quill—
hitch.

Wrap the floss, which was left hanging, into a lump,
larger than body diameter—tie down and hitch.

Bring duck quill segment over top of the floss lump—tie
down—hitch.

Carefully clip remaining part of the above segment,
leaving the two outside wisps for "feelers"—hitch.
If these wisps are too short or inadvertently cut off,
feelers can be tied in of narrow herl strands off the
peacock sword stalk.

Finish fly with two or three hitches—cement.

Practically every fly tier, of nymphs, have their own
versions as to how to do it and there are probably as
many variations as there are tiers. There are no standard
nymph ties, as there are in the regular dry and wet flies,
but we're going through the trial phase now. Someday
the best concoctions will become popular, as they become
known, and standardization will come about. It won't be
here until more than the handful of anglers, in this
country, become really adept at fishing nymphs.

Chapter *16*

"Incidentally . . ."

IT WAS only a few years ago that a salmon fly fisherman "knew" that in order to create any action whatsoever with his top game fish he must fish with certain prescribed fly concoctions that contained all the colors of the rainbow, plus four—that it had a bit of every kind of plumage known to fly tiers. It was a sacrilege to make a cast with just a simple oversized "trout pattern," but a lot of misguided sportsmen sinners didn't know that. In spite of the jeers they fished with these unpretentious, modest flies and to the chagrin of the "deep-in-a-rut" die-hards the salmon cooperated shamefully. Now one rarely sees the old type salmon fly except in illustrations and antique collections. They were beautiful things to look at and a fly tier could produce one almost as fast as it took to tie a dozen or so trout flies.

The purely American steelhead fly is colorful but, more or less, simply tied, and they are productive. Whether or not, in the course of time, additions and more additions of tying materials and fancy touches will be added to the present patterns remains to be seen. A steelhead wet fly, according to many steelhead fishermen, generally, can be tied using any color as long as the color scarlet or orange is included someplace on the creation. There are steelhead patterns, however, that are almost totally black, or white, or yellow, or other colors than the traditional scarlet and orange.

No doubt you've read or heard of the steam method of renovating the hackle on flies by holding them, with tweezers, in a forced jet of steam from a tea kettle. It works wonders with hackle and some plumage, too, and the same procedure improves quills and feathers that have been closely packed in envelopes or containers. The steam, plus a little coaxing with the fingers, brings the material back almost to its original appearance.

I must add my bit to the increasing clamor against the promiscuous naming of flies. At the last count (I read this some place), there are well over 10,000 trout fly names and I'll wager it's really double that number, and more. Of course there are many duplications. For example, the Black Coachman was renamed, for some unknown reason, the Rio Grande King; one of the true Adams patterns is called the Whitcraft; the Algonquin, a deer body hair fly, used by Indians in Northern Michigan at least thirty-five years ago, is called the Goofer or Goofus bug in the West, and there are many, many others. If you create a NEW pattern (not just a change of tail color or a different body wrap or a slight change in wing or wing structure) name it by all means, with your name or that of a friend if you like, but let the name carry a bit of description of the fly itself. Wouldn't the "John Dough Special" sound better as the "John Dough Red Quill" or "Dough's Lavender Dun?" Heck, I'm as guilty as anybody, but it's wrong. At the rate new names are dubbed to concoctions on hooks, names that mean nothing, a few years from now it will take an army of researchers to develop a fly dictionary for you and for me.

Peacock quills, for quill bodies, can be stripped quite easily

with the sodium hypochlorite method. This product is a bleaching agent; trade names Chlorox, Roman Cleanser, Purex, etc. Some put the liquid, full strength, in a saucer or similar flat dish and immerse the whole peacock eye. (Caution: don't let the stuff spill or drip on your clothing, and keep it off your skin, if you can. In either case, get it washed off right away.) By carefully watching the action of the solution on the herl you can determine when to remove from the liquid. Sometimes a minute is long enough and it may take several minutes. When the herl has disappeared, been eaten off, remove and wash the peacock eye under running water until all traces of the bleaching agent is gone. A precaution that can be followed is to immerse the stripped eye in vinegar for a moment. Wash and put to soak in a glycerined water solution. Quill stripped by this method loses much of its life and becomes straw like in texture. The quill also bleaches, becoming somewhat buff or grass colored, and the sharp dark and light segment marking is much less pronounced. This quill should be soaked well in water before wrapping on a hook if it has become dry. Quill stripped this way, also, is in excellent condition to take dye, if one wishes colored quills.

Sometime, when you're perplexed as to what fly to tie, why not take a standard pattern and create your own "variant?" For instance, an Adams, Gordon Quill, Black Gnat, Hendrickson, Cahill, Pale Evening Dun, etc., would all make good, and probably effective, variants. If you want to do what every amateur does, vary the materials on the standard ties and, when the season opens, give your fly a workout. When you have finally developed a creation that is contrary to the accepted formulas and it's a real killer, do not be too disappointed when you discover that the same identical fly, your own brain child, was tied, back in Wisconsin by Joe Doakes in 1916, and is called, in Oshkosh, the "Joe's Marvel."

If the fly tier desires to make a collection of natural flies, to use as specimens or to study later, a satisfactory liquid in which to keep them temporarily is:

Grain Alcohol	70%
Acetic Acid	5%
Glycerin	5%
Benzol	5%
Distilled Water	15%

Any druggist can put together a small bottle of the stuff for you.

One noted, non-commercial fly tier with whom I am familiar, but do not know personally, ties most of his flies without the hard-to-tie wings. He states that it is his observation that there is no difference in effectiveness. (This writer does not believe that the so-called observation was carried out by alternating flies or for longer than a few minutes, if serious at all. We're inclined to believe that when he made the statement his fingers were crossed or else he doesn't know how to tie a fly with wings, and doesn't want the failing known or perhaps he's just a reluctant fly tier.) The creatures, which we are crudely imitating definitely HAVE wings and a fly without them is deformed or a cripple. With the same reasoning, why not eliminate the tails? Let's also cut out the body, too, then why not the hackle or legs? Why tie the fly at all in the first place? We can always use worms, salmon eggs, cheese, or cut meat.

IT IS MUCH, MUCH BETTER TO TIE ONE GOOD FLY, IN AN HOUR'S TIME, THAN A DOZEN THAT WOULD BE TAKEN ONLY BY TROUT WITH A SENSE OF HUMOR!

Chapter 17

Dictionary of Productive Fly Patterns

CODE:

CUT WING	Flight quill segment wings of mallard, teal, starling, duck, goose, etc.
GOL PH	Golden pheasant *tippet*
G	Gold tinsel
H	Hackle
J C	Jungle cock
MALLARD	Mallard drake flank or side plumage
PEACOCK QUILL . .	Means stripped of herl
RED	Rhode Island red (brownish auburn)
S	Silver tinsel
SW	Spent wing
UP W	Upright wing
WD	Woodduck
OP	Means optional

237

FLY	TYPE WET OR DRY	TIP	TAIL	BODY	RIB	WINGS	HACKLE	
Adams Male & female	Dry		Mixed grizzly and brown	Blue-gray muskrat, dubbed-spun fur or yarn		Grizzly H tips or Blue Dun H tips tied SW or UP W	Mixed brown and grizzly	Female Adams—yellow egg sack at tail base, no other change
Adams, yellow	Dry		Mixed grizzly and brown	Yellow spun fur or yarn		Grizzly H tips tied SW or UP W	Mixed brown and grizzly	
Adams, macaw	Dry		Mixed grizzly and brown	blue-yellow macaw tail or flight quill segment		Blue dun H tips tied SW or UP W	Mixed brown and grizzly	
Alexandria	Wet	OP S	Peacock sword strands (3 or 4)	S		Peacock sword strands (5 or 6)—just longer than hook	OP Scarlet—not generally used	
'All purpose'	Dry		Mixed grizzly and brown	Peacock quill		WD — UP W	Mixed brown and grizzly	
Beaverkill	Wet or Dry		WD wisps	White floss palmered brown		Blue dun H tips or gray cut wing	Red or brown	
Bee	Wet or Dry		OP Scarlet	Four joint, yellow, black, yellow, black chenille		Blue dun H tips or gray cut wing	Red or brown	
Bi-visible	Dry		Hackle wisps or hackle tips to match body	OP floss to match—tinsel ribbed or no under body			Full palmer—choice of color or mixed hackles	
Black gnat	Wet		Black H barbs	Black floss	OP Silver	Blue dun H tips, Black H tips or gray cut wing	Black, soft	
Black gnat	Dry		Small barely visible tag of scarlet	Black ostrich or emu herl		Small shoulder feather of duck tied flat down	Black	Wing can be trimmed rounding if wanted that way
Blue quill	Dry		Blue dun H barbs	Blue dun H quill stripped or peacock quill		Lt. blue dun H tips	Lt. blue dun	
Blue upright	Dry		Blue dun H barbs	Peacock quill		Mallard dyed blue dun	Blue dun	
Caddis	Dry		Insect green egg sack	Peacock quill		Pheasant flight quill cut wing—close to body	Lt. olive, ginger or buff	

Fly	Type Wet or Dry	Tip	Tail	Body	Rib	Wings	Hackle	
Cahill Lt., Dk., or Quill	Wet or Dry	OP G	WD, buff or ginger—lt. Red—dk.	Dubbed red fox belly fur—lt. Dubbed muskrat—dk.		WD W UP W	Lt. Ginger or buff—lt. Red—dk.	Peacock quill can be substituted for the softer body for the Cahill quill
Captain (black)	Wet		Gol Ph or yellow H barbs	Black floss	G	White cut wings or white hair	Red or brown	
Cathy B Spinner	Dry		Lt. blue dun H barbs	Delicate primrose spun fur—thin body	G wire	Cream or buff H tips	Lt. blue dun	
Cinnamon sedge	Dry		Red H barbs—short	Golden Pheasant tail segments wrapped as quill		Mottled turkey or Pheasant flight quill—tent style	Red or dk. ginger	
Coachman (Regular & cabin)	Wet or Dry	G	Gol Ph, scarlet or brown	Peacock herl, full		White cut wings or white hair	Red or brown	Gray wings on the Cabin Coachman-Mallard suitable
Coachman "Vampire"	Wet		Gol Ph dyed scarlet	Peacock herl, full		Cream vampire bat hair	Red or brown	
Cowdung	Wet or Dry	G		Olive floss or yarn—spun fur		Ginger or lt. brown cut wings	Red or brown	
Cross Special	Dry		Dk. blue dun H barbs	Dubbed Australian opposum, badger or other lt. cream (nearly white)		WD UP W or split	Dk. blue dun with bronze cast	
Cutthroat	Wet	G	Black H barbs	Claret, crimson or scarlet chenille		White cut wing or hair	Black	
Donnelly Variant (Dark)	Dry		Brown H barbs	Dubbed muskrat or dk. blue dun spun fur		Badger H tips	Brown and grizzly mixed	
Donnelly Variant (Light)	Dry		Brown H barbs	Dubbed fox fur belly or other lt. cream fur		Ivory or honey dun H tips	Brown and honey dun, or lt. ginger mixed	
Flight's Fancy	Dry		Ginger H barbs	Yellowish cream yarn or spun fur	G	Blue dun H tips	Ginger	
Flying Caddis	Dry			Deer hair flared loosely—rough clip	yellow floss	Four grizzly H tips	Brown and grizzly mixed	
Ginger quill	Dry		Lt. ginger H barbs	Peacock quill (light)		Lt. gray cut wings or Lt. blue dun H tips or WD	Ginger or Lt. ginger and olive mixed	

239

Fly	Type Wet or Dry	Tip	Tail	Body	Rib	Wings	Hackle	
Gordon quill	Wet or Dry		Blue dun H barbs or WD wisps	Peacock quill	OP gold wire	WD	Blue Dun (light)	
Gordon	Wet or Dry	G	Barred WD	Yellow yarn, spun fur or floss		WD	Grizzly or badger	
Gray Hackle (Yellow & peacock)	Wet or Dry	G	Gol ph, scarlet H barbs or grizzly H	Yellow floss or Peacock herl	G on yellow only		Grizzly	
Gray Wulff	Dry		Brown bucktail	Dubbed hare's ear (gray) or gray yarn		Brown bucktail tied UP W —split—	Blue dun	
Green drake	Dry		Pheasant tail wisps	Deer body hair shaped—tied extended over rear of hook	Heavy tan thread	Brown bucktail tied UP W —split—	Grizzly and brown mix	
Greenwell's glory	Wet or Dry		Gol ph	Dubbed olive fur or spun fur	G	WD	Red, brown or furnace	
Grizzly Wickhams	Dry		Grizzly H barbs	Silver tinsel palmered with grizzly H		Blue dun H tips	Grizzly and blue dun mix	
Hare's ear (Regular & G rib)	Wet or Dry		Hare's ear or mask guard hair (short)	Dubbed hare's ear or mask—rough—use guard hairs	OP G	Blue dun or grizzly H tips or gray cut wing	Hare's fur picked out—wet pattern Grizzly H on Dry	
Hendrickson (Dk. or Lt.)	Wet or Dry		Blue dun H barbs on Dry— WD on Wet	Red fox fur belly dubbed—mix in some gray fur	G	WD	Blue dun or blue dun and brown mix	
House and lot	Dry		Kip or Calf tail wisps	Peacock quill		Kip or calf tail (white)—tie semi-SW, wings slightly forward	Red or brown	(Dwight Eisenhower's favorite)
Irresistible	Dry		Brown bucktail wisps	Flared deer hair gray body hair—clipped to shape		Brown bucktail tied UP W	Grizzly or brown or both mixed	Gray caribou body hair an excellent substitute for deer hair on body
Iron blue dun	Wet or Dry		Dk. blue dun H barbs	Dubbed blue dun gray and brown mixed	OP scarlet or gold	Coot cut wing or Dark duck cut wing	Coch-y-bondhu or mixed black and red	Tiny scarlet tip is OP—and effective

240

FLY	TYPE WET OR DRY	TIP	TAIL	BODY	RIB	WINGS	HACKLE	
Joe's ('Michigan') Hopper	Dry		Scarlet H barbs (short)	Deep yellow wool palmered brown—(sides clipped)	OP gold wire	Mottled turkey—tie at sides of body	Grizzly and brown mix	In tying yarn body allow a segment of yarn to extend out at rear
Little Marryat quill	Dry		Cream or buff H barbs	Natural raffia		Blue dun H tips	Cream or buff	
March brown	Wet	OP G	Brown grouse wisps	Brown dubbing	G	Brown grouse or Woodcock cut wing	Gray grouse or soft grizzly	
McGinty (squirrel tail)	Dry		OP Scarlet H barbs	Four joint chenille—yellow, black, yellow, black		Gray squirrel tied semi-UP W—split	Red or brown	
Mormon girl	Wet or Dry	Scar. floss		Yellow floss palmered grizzly		Gray cut wing or mallard	Grizzly	
Mosquito	Dry		Grizzly H barbs	Moose mane quill—one white and one dark hair		Grizzly or blue dun H tips	Grizzly	
Olive quill	Dry		Olive H barbs	Peacock quill dyed yellow-olive		Gray cut wings or dun gray H tips	Olive or yellow and ginger mix	
Owen's sedge	Wet		Ginger H barbs (short)	Peacock quill		Segment of gray duck flight quill tied semi-tent fashion—close to body	Ginger or WD dyed grouse whisker	
Pale evening dun	Dry	G	Cream or buff H barbs	Pale yellow dubbing—or spun fur or yarn	OP gold wire	Lt. blue dun H tips	Lt. blue dun and cream mixed	
Pink lady	Dry		Ginger H barbs	Pink floss or spun fur		Blue dun H tips or gray cut wings	Ginger	
Professor	Wet		Scarlet H barbs	Yellow floss	G	Mallard	Red or brown	
Pot-o-gold caddis	Wet or Dry	*		Scarlet purple, green, brown or gold floss—thin body		Woodchuck, badger or gray squirrel—tied down wing—length of hook	Red or grizzly or both mixed	*Tie chenille egg sack at tip point on hook—yellow-black claret or green
Red ant	Wet	*		Peacock herl butt scarlet floss body		Grizzly H tips	Red or brown	*Tie scarlet floss tip down bend of hook
Red Macaw No. 1	Dry		Grizzly H barbs	Bright unstripped red macaw quill		Blue dun H tips or WD	Grizzly	

241

Fly	Type Wet or Dry	Tip	Tail	Body	Rib	Wings	Hackle	
Red Macaw No. 2	Dry		Lt. ginger	Bright unstripped red macaw quill		Blue dun H tips or WD	Lt. ginger and blue dun mixed	
Red quill (Art Flicks')	Dry		Dk. blue dun H barbs	Stripped red or mahogany H quill (soak well before winding body)		WD	Dk. blue dun	
Renegade	Dry			Peacock herl between red H at butt and white H at head			Red or brown at base of hook—White H at head	
Rio Grande king	Wet or Dry	OP G	Gol ph or Yellow H barbs	Black ostrich on dry fly—black chenille on wet—or black floss		White cut wing, polar bear, capras or bucktail	Yellow	
Royal Coachman	Wet or Dry		Gol ph, brown H barbs or scarlet H barbs	Scarlet floss between herl butt and herl thorax		White cut wing, polar bear, capras or bucktail	Red or brown	
Royal Coachman (fan wing)	Dry		Gol ph, brown H barbs or scarlet H barbs	Scarlet floss between herl butt and herl thorax		Duck breast, white tied fan wing	Red or brown	
Salmon fly	Dry		Woodchuck or gray squirrel— (short)	Raffia over thick kapok padding	OP gold wire	Gray squirrel— tied down wing	Mahogany red or black and ginger mixed	Wing should not extend beyond the length of the short tail
Sierra caddis	Dry		Insect green egg sack just over bend of hook	Peacock quill		Tan or brownish Mouse deer—tied down wing	Lt. blue dun or lt. olive	
Spider	Dry		Long H barbs to match the hackle	Small lump of floss to match color of hackle			Wide and sparse hackle of whatever color is chosen	Spiders come as: Black, brown, blue, dun, badger, buff and grizzly, etc.
Stone fly (dark)	Wet		Brown mallard	Muskrat dubbing, spun fur or wool	Yellow floss	Brown mallard, mottled turkey or goose quill segment tied flat	Brown	
Stone fly (light)	Wet		Grizzly H barbs	Yellow or orange floss		Gray duck quill segment tied flat	Grizzly	
Tobin's golden spinner	Dry		Buff or tan H barbs	Orange polar bear clump wound as body		Tan bucktail tied UP W-divided	Buff or light tan (full)	

Fly	Type Wet or Dry	Tip	Tail	Body	Rib	Wings	Hackle
Trout fly	Wet	OP G	Grizzly H barbs	Scarlet floss	S	Gray H tips, gray turkey cut wings or gray duck cut wings	Grizzly
Whirling blue dun	Wet or Dry		Brown H barbs	Blue-gray dun dubbing, spun fur or yarn		Dk. blue dun H tips or gray cut wings	Brown and ginger mixed
Wickham's fancy	Wet	G	Brown H barbs	Gold palmered brown or red		Blue dun H tips or gray cut wings	Brown
Willow special	Dry		Teal wisps	Dark condor or dark brown dubbing	OP gold wire	Blue dun H tips or mallard—tie down wing fashion	Grizzly and blue dun mixed

Streamer Fly	Tip	Tail	Body	Rib	Throat	Wing	Under Hook Other Than Throat	Shoulder	Eye
Baby Fario		Teal	Scarlet	G	Scarlet	Peacock herl / Yellow bucktail	Yellow bucktail / White bucktail— sparse	Teal	
Baby Fontinalis		Olive teal	Scarlet	G	Scarlet	Peacock herl / Olive bucktail / Scarlet bucktail— sparse	Lt. olive bucktail / Orange bucktail / White bucktail	Olive teal	
Baby Gairdnerii		Teal	Silver	Oval S	Scarlet	Peacock herl / Lt. olive bucktail / Scarlet bucktail— sparse	Lt. blue bucktail / White bucktail— sparse	Teal	
Bean special		Barred WD	White floss	S	Scarlet and yellow	Two white saddle hackles			
Black Dace			Silver			Brown bucktail / Lt. blue bucktail / White bucktail			
Black Demon	G		Gold	Oval G	Orange	Two black saddle hackles			
Black Ghost		Gol ph (full)	Black floss, chenille or yarn	S		Golden pheasant crest / Two white hackles			J C
Bucktail—Brown		Scarlet	Silver	Oval S		Brown bucktail			
Bucktail—Silver		Scarlet	Silver	S		Brown or black bucktail / White bucktail			J C
Bucktail—White			Silver			White bucktail			
Chappie		Two grizzly H tips— long	Yellow, orange, green or black yarn	silk color of body	Sparse grizzly collar	Two grizzly hackles— concave surfaces together			
Cock-a-tush (muddler minnow)			Gold		Deer body hair collar	Brown bucktail—mix in a few white and a few black hairs— Mottled turkey—side			clip rounded head
Cosseboom		Lt. green wool	Lt. green wool	S	Yellow collar	Gray squirrel			
Edson Tiger	S	Barred WD or guinea	Yellow chenille	S	Scarlet	Brown bucktail			J C

STREAMER FLY	TIP	TAIL	BODY	RIB	THROAT	WING	UNDER HOOK — OTHER THAN THROAT	SHOULDER	EYE
Gray Ghost	S		Orange floss	S		Golden pheasant crest / Four gray hackle quills		Silver pheasant	J C
Maribou—black		Scarlet	Silver	Oval S	Scarlet	Black Maribou, full			J C
Maribou—special		Gol ph	Silver	Oval S		Peacock herl / White Maribou, full	Golden pheasant tippet—long	Teal	
Maribou—white		Golden pheasant crest	Silver	Oval S		Peacock herl / White Maribou / Few scarlet hairs			
Mickey Finn			Silver or embossed silver	Oval S		Yellow bucktail (full) / Scarlet bucktail / Yellow bucktail (sparse)			J C
Nipigon Belle		Black H tips	Orange	Scarlet	Black collar	Peacock herl (4 or 5) / Two white hackle quills			OP / J C
Squirrel—fox		Scarlet	Yellow chenille	S	Scarlet	Fox squirrel			
Squirrel—gold			Gold		Scarlet	Two honey hackle quills—Fox squirrel			
Squirrel—silver No. 1		Scarlet	Silver	Oval S	Scarlet	Fox squirrel			
Squirrel—silver No. 2		Short scarlet maribou	Silver	Oval S	Scarlet	Two grizzly hackle quills—Fox squirrel			
Supervisor	Scarlet wool tag		Silver			Olive hackle quills (2) / Lt. blue hackle quills (2) / White bucktail			
Vampire Coachman	G	Gol ph dyed scarlet	Peacock herl (full)			Vampire bat hair (cream) or Vampire bat hair (gray)		OP / Scarlet	OP / J C

Nymph Fly	Tip	Tail	Body	Rib	Thorax	Wing or Wing Cover	Hackle or Legs
Black nymph		Short mallard	Black seal dubbed	Fine bronze or copper wire		Duck quill segment	Gray grouse—slip top and bottom
Cahill type		Two long wisps WD	Dubbed tan fox belly fur		Tan spun fur	Natural raffia	WD or tan dyed grouse whisker
Carrot and black		Brown grouse	Orange-carrot floss or yarn		Black chenille		Blue dun wisps—sides only
Coachman nymph	G	Short scarlet or pea. sword stubs	Peacock herl			Grizzly H tips or teal flank plumage tied flat—¼ inch	Gray grouse whiskers
Ginger nymph		Short mallard	Opossum (ginger) dubbed			Duck quill segment	Gray grouse—sides only
Hare's ear		Hare's guard hairs (short)	Hare's ear or hare's mask, dubbed (coarse)	Fine gold wire		Woodcock plumage segment	Pick out dubbing
Hendrickson nymph			Dark red hackle quill stripped		Dark tan dubbing or spun fur	Mottled turkey wing segment	Grouse dyed blue dun
Iron blue		Three short mallard	Dubbed muskrat (dark blue dun)		Dark blue dun spun fur	Coot or dark duck quill segment	Mallard or grouse—sides only
March brown		Brown grouse	Hare's mask or hare's ear dubbing	Gold wire		Brown mottled turkey segment	Brown grouse—sides only
May fly (general)		Three peacock sword tips	Tan or olive floss	Peacock herl (clip top and bottom, leave sides)	Tan or olive yarn	Coot or duck quill segment	Gray grouse—sides only
Mossback		Two goose quill segments	Woven raffia—Olive top, natural bottom		Olive floss or silk thread	Olive or brown dyed raffia	Single goose quill segments at rear sides and at front—tie in at thorax
Olive nymph		Short mallard	Dubbed olive fur or spun fur			Duck quill segment	Gray grouse—sides only
Partridge, yellow			Yellow floss	Gold wire			Gray grouse—sides only
Rock worm (short hook)			White chenille—Black or brown chenille head	OP S wire			Gray grouse—wrap collar fashion as hackle

Nymph Fly	Tip	Tail	Body	Rib	Thorax	Wing or Wing Cover	Hackle or Legs
Sandy mite			Woven sand color mixed hair—belly stripe yellow or orange				Portion of body hair turned back—clip, length of hook
Shrimp No. 1 (scud)		Short tan hairs	Otter dyed olive dubbed—Beaver will substitute				Grouse dyed WD
Shrimp No. 2 (scud)		Grouse wisps	Olive floss—wound down bend of hook	Lt. olive thread or gold wire			Grouse dyed olive
Stonefly creeper			Olive floss	Gold wire	Olive floss	Duck quill segment	Olive hackle slanted to rear—sides only
Strawman nymph			Deer body hair flared—rough clip	Yellow floss			
Vic Cramer nymph			Tan or olive floss	Gold wire		Dark bucktail tied in at tail point before body is wrapped—bring over and secure again above thorax —divide ends left	

Index